PISA IN THE EARLY

RENAISSANCE

DAVID HERLIHY

PISA IN THE EARLY

RENAISSANCE

A STUDY OF URBAN GROWTH

KENNIKAT PRESS
Port Washington, N. Y./London

PISA IN THE EARLY RENAISSANCE

CONTENTS

PREFACE

At the time of this Emperor Frederick II [d. 1250] . . . people with a little money thought themselves rich.

RICOBALDO OF FERRARA (CA. 1300)

IN THE LATE 13TH CENTURY, when cities had come so much to dominate the economic and cultural life of Italy, Pisa, in terms of size or economic or political importance, was neither the greatest nor the least among them. She was a seaport—indeed, the chief harbor of Tuscany—but the large land area she ruled lent her economy many of the characteristics of inland towns. Her moderate size and moderate importance, the division of her endeavors almost equally between enterprises on land and sea, would seem to make her a particularly good subject on which to center a study of urban development from the middle 13th to the early 14th century, in the period of the nascent Renaissance we may call the Age of Dante. Not that Pisa may be considered typical of Italian towns; she had, if anything, more than her share of catastrophes. The value of studying her comes rather from the fact that she presents an especially balanced pattern of growth, from which our understanding of the development of both larger and smaller towns, of towns more exclusively maritime or industrial, and of Italian urbanism generally, may hope to profit.

The history of the urban growth of Pisa from the middle 13th to the early 14th century is the story of a vigorous economic upsurge and of the men who led it. This upsurge is the local manifestation of a boom that all Italy seems to

have shared. Between 1214 and 1274 the value of the goods
moving through the port of Genoa doubled; between 1274
and 1293, it more than quadrupled. The number of notarial acts redacted at Genoa, about 56,000 in 1265, topped
80,000 in 1291. Florence's second circle of walls, begun in
1172, enclosed about 80 hectares of land; her new walls,
projected in 1284, completed by 1333, enclosed a staggering 630. And although we cannot measure the pace, in
these years, too, occurred the rise to international importance of Florence's wool industry and of her money and
banking interests.

For Pisa, this period has hitherto been considered one of
abject decline. And indeed, on August 6, 1284, near the
little island of Meloria south of the Arno's mouth, not fifteen miles from Pisa herself, the Genoese annihilated
Pisa's fleet and sent her permanently from the ranks of
Italy's maritime powers, among which, since the 11th century, she had stood so proudly. Pisa's losses at this Battle
of Meloria were huge. Seven galleys and thirty-three
smaller vessels were sunk; apart from the uncounted dead,
upward of nine thousand prisoners were carried off to
Genoa's jails. Many of them were never to see their native
city again. So disastrous a defeat could not help imparting
to historians the impression that Pisa, even for a century
before Meloria, was in full decline. During that period we
can scarcely note a stray Pisan ship fallen prey to the Genoese or a military band worsted in a border skirmish without finding that such events have been interpreted as indi-
cating both prevalent stagnation and approaching doom.

Unquestionably, Pisa in the late 13th century was out-
stripped by her maritime rival Genoa and her inland rival
Florence, and unquestionably, too, in this the Battle of
Meloria played a momentous though perhaps not decisive
role. Still, the widening gap between Pisa and these other

cities is no proof that Pisa was standing still. Actually, it
can be shown that the income of the Pisan commune was
in real value eight times larger in 1288 than it had averaged
over the six years 1227–32, and we shall adduce much
similar evidence that Pisa was enjoying a surprising rate
of growth. What looks like and was a decline in relation to
Genoa or Florence was actually an economic expansion of
no mean proportions. Why Pisa could not maintain the
pace of her rivals we must of course attempt to explain;
but attention will be given here mainly to the broader
aspects of Pisan economic history, to an analysis of the nature of the economic expansion which shows that Pisa,
though on a small scale, reflected the trend of the age.

This expansion of the late 13th century was, for Italy,
the brilliant culmination of the Commercial Revolution
of the Middle Ages, that upward trend which characterizes
Europe's economy for well over three hundred years, from
the late 10th to the early 14th centuries. Within this upward trend may be distinguished secondary cycles of especially rapid advance followed by relative pause. Because
the determination and measurement of these secondary
cycles, the clarification of the factors that influenced them,
are new fields for economic history, our present picture is
necessarily sketchy. Still, on the premise that certain types
of monetary disorders reflect growing economic activity,
we can now single out three periods in the history of the
medieval Italian town about which economic changes (and
social too) seem to be concentrated: the late 11th century,
ending with the stability achieved with the appearance of
the communes (which became established gradually and
not, at first, permanently from about 1080); the late 12th
century, achieving stability with the regime of the podesta
(from about 1190); and the late 13th and early 14th centuries, the period of this study, the Age of Dante.

For urban history, another aspect of this rhythmic advance is perhaps more meaningful, that of urbanization of production, the rebuilding within the city of productive processes shattered and ruralized during the violent centuries of the early Middle Ages. The 11th-century revival made the Italian city the center of trade, administration, and culture, and of course gathered within it many professional men, merchants, and some artisans. Not until a century later, however, does the spontaneous and widespread appearance of artisan guilds reveal the birth within cities of important industries. The period gave Pisa the industry which was for long her most important, to modern times her most characteristic: leather and furs. After about 1190 comes a half-century of slower growth. By 1250, however, the pace of urbanization has mounted again. At Pisa, and apparently too in other Tuscan towns, the processes of cloth manufacture—weaving, spinning, combing and washing of wool—are moved from their rural homes and concentrated, specialized, and professionalized within the city.

Urbanization, the fact and the factors that explain it—specifically for the period 1250 to 1300 but with some reference to the similar phenomenon of the century before —forms the underlying theme of this book, although in developing it we hope to present, too, a satisfactorily balanced picture of a medieval city's economic life. Or perhaps more specifically, the central theme is the vast immigration to the city from the countryside, which for Pisa and for other Tuscan towns is the most striking economic phenomenon of the late 13th century. To be sure, we are concentrating on the aspects of this immigration of greatest interest for urban history: its importance for the growth of the city, the ways that communal policies favored it, and the manner the urban economy was affected by it. We are not in a position to analyze as vigorously as their importance deserves the properly rural roots of this influx to the city, the demographic growth in the villages, the economic changes that in the late 13th century seem to have dislodged so many from the land. Not only do these rural movements remain especially shadowy and obscure in our sources, but also they have not attracted the secondary studies of scope and quality that have been dedicated to urban phenomena. While our treatment of rural matters is therefore limited to broad outlines, we must concede their importance, and recognize too that an urban history such as this deals with only one phase or aspect within the larger and more complex pattern of economic change.

Perhaps more precisely still, the central concern of this book is the cost of urban living: its fluctuations, its impact on agriculture, on both old and new industries, and on commerce, when approximately between the 1260's and the first decade of the 14th century it dropped between 50 and 66 per cent. Behind what amounted to a gigantic subsidy to city dwellers stood a political revolution, currency manipulations, extensive economic controls, and a radical recasting of the taxation structure. Behind the immigration to Pisa which this subsidy encouraged stood also an economic revolution by virtue of which it became possible to provide food and work for cities now swollen to unprecedented size—a revolution in communications.

The problem behind the subsidy—who paid and who profited?—provides a frame for the study of the important sectors of Pisa's economy, from grain production, which through pegged prices and restricted markets was brought to the verge of ruin, to the nascent wool industry, which gained a large and cheap labor supply essential to its growth. The problem provides, too, the frame for our discussion of Pisan society. We shall find that the old aristocratic houses found that one of the buttresses of their

economic status—namely their city rents—had been butch-
ered at the altar of this labor subsidy, and that new men
gained from it help invaluable to their economic enterprises, equally new.

These new men we shall call the bourgeoisie, the middle
class: the capitalists. These names are, of course, partially
labels of convenience; above all, they should not convey
the impression that these men were new types of businessmen supposedly unknown in the previous centuries. If the
bourgeois is one who lives by trade and industry or, perhaps more satisfactorily for urban history, one willing to
pursue a policy favoring trade and industry even to the
detriment of rents—in that sense our new man is not
unique. In medieval Italy during those years of economic
expansion, social differentiation, and political conflicts—
roughly about 1060, 1170, and 1270—there is discernible
a division of interests between a kind of "aristocracy" and
a kind of "bourgeoisie." But during the periods when economic torpor and political stability seems to have prevailed
—about 1130 and 1210—the bourgeoisie tended to fuse
with the old aristocracy to present a solid front, in fact a
new aristocracy, against the next upsurge of new men.

The culmination of the medieval Commercial Revolution, the economic boom of the late 13th and early 14th
centuries, is likewise its exhaustion. To be sure, out of
these years came that multiplied productivity, that marvelous outburst of material luxury, that we associate with
the Renaissance. Still, not long after 1300 Italy's economy
—as measured, for example, by the size of urban populations, the value of goods moving through the port of
Genoa, and the output of Florence's wool industry—stood
close to its medieval peak, and clear signs of economic
crisis are evident even before the shattering impact of the

Black Death (1348); not until after 1450 can we note a revival.

We must not of course exaggerate the depth of the plunge. By any comparison, the material standard of living in the 14th and 15th centuries stood at a level far higher than for any medieval period before 1250. The impression remains, however, that not long after 1300 Italy entered a new era, pitched at a higher material level, but in an economic sense poorer in potentiality and promise. In the 14th century in Italy we find a society which seems to have pushed along the old ways to their termination and which, to avoid stagnation, needed new technological and economic departures. None, of course, was in the offing. If over the years 1250 to 1300 the standard of living was raised to a new plane, there were nevertheless new social strains, and perhaps even a psychological malaise, which may have contributed to the later, long stagnation. The period we study stands as the pivot between two quite different epochs, the high and closing Middle Ages.

This book grew out of a dissertation written at Yale University. To Robert S. Lopez, who suggested the topic in the first instance and whose help has been indispensable at every stage in its growth to a book, the author owes a particular debt of gratitude. He is indebted likewise to numerous Italian scholars and friends, who made a year's study in Pisa as a Fulbright scholar fruitful and pleasant, and especially to Mario Luzzatto, director of the Archivio di Stato of Pisa, who familiarized the author with the resources of the Pisan archives. Special thanks go to Emilio Cristiani, a scholar whose short studies have made notable contributions to the history of medieval Pisa and whose general history of Pisa from 1250 to 1350, soon to be published, will represent a solid contribution to the history of medieval Italian urbanism. Unfortunately, Dr. Cristiani's work is appearing too late for this book to take full advantage of his research. I have, however, benefited from his close familiarity with the sources and history of medieval Pisa. The author is likewise grateful to the Carnegie Corporation of New York for a grant toward the cost of publication, and to the Ford Foundation, whose generous support has made publication possible.

DAVID HERLIHY

Bryn Mawr
June 1957

ABBREVIATIONS

ABBREVIATIONS have been used to shorten references both to unpublished documents and to some published works.

For unpublished materials, abbreviations are used to designate the archives in which they are found. However, all notarial chartularies cited are to be found in the Archivio di Stato di Pisa, Archivio degli Ospedali Riuniti di Santa Chiara, unless otherwise stated. In citing from them, only their catalogue numbers in that deposit are given, and "r" and "v" are used for recto and verso. All dates both for chartulary entries and for parchments have been adjusted to the modern calendar. To return them to the Pisan style, their original dating, one year should be added to all dates after March 25. The Latin forms of all proper names have been retained, except when such usage might cause confusion (thus, Pistoia for Pistoria, Florence for Florentia, etc.).

For published materials, abbreviations have been used to designate collections of sources, and journals several times cited. For single works, abbreviated titles are used for all works cited in more than one chapter. For works cited in only one chapter, the full title is given in the first reference, and an abbreviated title is used in any subsequent references.

ACA—Archivio della Curia Arcivescovile di Pisa. Pergamene.

ACC—Archivio della Certosa di Calci. Pergamene.

Amari, *Diplomi arabi*—M. Amari, *I diplomi arabi del r. Archivio fiorentino. Testo originale con la traduzione letterale.* Florence, 1901.

ASF—Archivio di Stato di Firenze.

ASI—Archivio Storico Italiano.

ASLSP—Atti della Società Ligure di Storia Patria.

ASP—Archivio di Stato di Pisa.

ASS—Acta Sanctorum . . . editio novissima curante Joanne Carnandet. Paris, 1863–1940.

Bonaini, *Famiglie—Delle famiglie pisane di Raffaello Roncioni,* ed. F. Bonaini. *ASI, 6,* Pt. II, Sec. 3 (1845), 813–980.

Borsari, "Rapporti"—S. Borsari, "I Rapporti tra Pisa e gli stati di Romania nel duecento," *Rivista Storica Italiana, 67* (1955), 477–92.

Breve antianorum—Breve vetus seu Chronica Antianorum civitatis Pisarum, ed. F. Bonaini. *ASI, 6,* Pt. II (1845), 647–807.

Brugaro, "Artigianato"—A. Brugaro, "L'Artigianato pisano nel medio evo," *SS, 16* (1907), 188–211, 271–316; *20* (1911–12), 377–453.

BSP—Bollettino Storico Pisano.

BSSP—Bollettino Senese di Storia Patria.

Caleffo—Il Caleffo vecchio del comune di Siena, ed. G. Cecchini. Florence, 1932–40.

Cancelleria Angioina—I Registri della Cancelleria Angioina, ed. R. Filangieri. Naples, 1953 ff.

Castellani, *Testi—Nuovi testi fiorentini del dugento,* ed. A. Castellani. Florence, 1952.

CEH—Cambridge Economic History.

Ciasca, *Medici*—R. Ciasca, *L'Arte dei medici e speziali nella storia e nel commercio fiorentino dal secolo XII al XV.* Biblioteca storica toscana, 4. Florence, 1927.

Consulte—*Le Consulte della Repubblica fiorentina dal MCCLXXV al MCXCVIII,* ed. A. Gerardi. Florence, 1898.

Cristiani, "Osservazioni"—E. Cristiani, "Osservazioni alla 'Raccolta di scelti diplomi pisani' di Flaminio Dal Borgo," *BSP, 20–21* (1951–52), 72–83.

Cronache senesi—*Cronache senesi,* ed. A. Lisini and F. Iacometti. RIS, n. ed., *15,* Pt. VI. Bologna, 1939.

Dal Borgo, *Raccolta*—F. Dal Borgo, *Raccolta di scelti diplomi pisani.* Pisa, 1765.

Davidsohn, *Forsch.*—R. Davidsohn, *Forschungen zur Geschichte von Florenz.* Berlin, 1896–1908.

Davidsohn, *Geschichte*—R. Davidsohn, *Geschichte von Florenz.* Berlin, 1896–1925.

DSSCDCI—Documenti e Studi per la Storia del Commercio e del Diritto Commerciale Italiano.

Herlihy, "Coinage"—D. Herlihy, "Pisan Coinage and the Monetary Development of Tuscany," *American Numismatic Society Museum Notes, 6* (1954), 143–68.

Heyd, *Commerce*—W. von Heyd, *Histoire du commerce du Levant au Moyen Age,* trans. F. Raynaud. Leipzig, 1885–86.

Leonardo, *Liber Abbaci*—Leonardo Pisano, *Liber Abbaci,* ed. B. Boncompagni. Rome, 1887.

Lopez, *Zaccaria*—R. Lopez, *Genova marinara nel duecento. Benedetto Zaccaria, ammiraglio e mercante.* Messina and Milan, 1933.

Lupi, "Casa pisana"—D. Lupi, "La Casa pisana e i suoi annessi," *ASI,* ser. 5, 27 (1901), 264–314; *28* (1901), 65–96; *29* (1902), 193–227; *31* (1903), 365–96; *32* (1903), 73–101.

Maragone, *Annales*—Maragone, *Annales pisani,* ed. M. L. Gentile. RIS, n. ed., *6,* Pt. II. Bologna, 1930.

MGH Ss.—Monumenta Germaniae Historica. Scriptores.

Müller, *Documenti*—G. Müller, *Documenti sulle relazioni delle città toscane coll'oriente cristiano e coi Turchi fin all' anno MDXXI*. Florence, 1879.

Pedreschi, "Geografia"—L. Pedreschi, "Pisa. Richerche di geografia urbana," *RGI, 58* (1951), 105–34, 217–51.

Pegolotti, *Pratica*—F. B. Pegolotti, *La Pratica della mercatura*, ed. A. Evans. Publications of the Mediaeval Academy of America, 24. Cambridge, Mass., 1936.

Piattoli, *Consigli*—R. Piattoli, *Consigli del comune di Prato, 15 Ottobre 1252–24 Febbraio 1285*. Bologna, 1940.

Pintor, "Elba"—F. Pintor, "Il Dominio pisano nell' isola d'Elba durante il secolo XIV," *SS,* 7 (1898), 353–97.

Plesner, *L'Emigration*—J. Plesner, *L'Emigration de la campagne à la ville libre de Florence au XIIIe siècle.* Copenhagen, 1934.

RCI—Regesta Chartarum Italiae.

Reg. pis.—*Regesto della chiesa di Pisa. Regestum pisanum*, ed. N. Caturegli. RCI, 24. Rome, 1938.

Relazioni—*Documenti delle relazioni tra Carlo I d'Angiò e la Toscana*, ed. S. Terlizzi. Documenti di storia italiana . . . per la Toscana, 12. Florence, 1950.

Repetti, *Dizionario*—E. Repetti, *Dizionario geografico fisico storico della Toscana*. Florence, 1841.

RGI—*Rivista Geografica Italiana.*

RIS—*Rerum Italicarum Scriptores*, ed. L. Muratori. Milan, 1723–51.

RIS, n. ed.—Rerum Italicarum Scriptores. Nuova edizione riveduta, ampliata, e corretta con la direzione di G. Carducci. Città di Castello, 1900 ff.

Roncioni, *Istorie*—R. Roncioni, *Delle istorie pisane libri XVI*, ed. F. Bonaini. *ASI, 6*, Pt. I (1844).

Rossi-Sabatini, *L'Espansione*—G. Rossi-Sabatini, *L'Espan-*

sione di Pisa nel Mediterraneo fino alla Meloria. Florence, 1935.

Salimbene, *Cronica*—Salimbene de Adam, *Cronica,* ed. F. Bernini. Scrittori d'Italia, 187. Bari, 1942.

Salvemini, *Magnati*—G. Salvemini, *Magnati e popolani in Firenze dal 1280 al 1295.* Florence, 1899.

Sardi, *Contrattazioni*—C. Sardi, *Le Contrattazioni agrarie del medio evo studiate nei documenti lucchesi.* Lucca, 1914.

Schaube, *Handelsg.*—A. Schaube, *Handelsgeschichte der romanischen Völker des Mittelmeergebiets bis zum Ende der Kreuzzüge.* Berlin, 1906.

Schaube, *Konsulat*—A. Schaube, *Das Konsulat des Meeres in Pisa.* Leipzig, 1888.

Sieveking, *Finanzwesen*—H. Sieveking, *Genueser Finanzwesen mit besonderer Berücksichtigung der Casa di S. Giorgio.* Freiburg im Breisgau, 1898–99. Also translated as *Studio sulle finanze genovesi e in particolare sulla Casa di S. Giorgio,* ASLSP, 25. Genoa, 1906.

Silva, *Gambacorta*—P. Silva, *Il Governo di Pietro Gambacorta.* Pisa, 1911.

SS—Studi Storici del Crivellucci.

Stat.—Statuti inediti della città di Pisa dal XII al XIV secolo, ed. F. Bonaini. Florence, 1854–70.

Stat. di Volterra—Statuti di Volterra. Vol 1: *1210–1224,* ed. E. Fiumi. Documenti di storia italiana . . . per la Toscana, ser. 2, no. 1. Florence, 1952.

Toscanelli, *Antichità*—N. Toscanelli, *Pisa nell'antichità dalle età preistoriche alla caduta dell'impero romano.* Pisa, 1934.

Toscanelli, *Donoratico*—N. Toscanelli, *I Conti di Donoratico della Gherardesca signori di Pisa.* Pisa, 1937.

Tuscia—Tuscia, ed. M. Giusti and P. Guidi, Studi e Testi, 58 and 98. Vatican City, 1932–42.

Villani, *Cronica*—*Cronica di Giovanni Villani*. Florence: Magheri, 1823.

Visconti—Federigo Visconti, Sermones. Manuscript in the Biblioteca Medicea Laurenziana at Florence, Cod. Laurent.–S. Crucis, XXXIII, Sin. 1. For description, see D. Lucciardi, "Federigo Visconti Arcivescovo di Pisa," *BSP*, *1* (1932), 7–48; 2 (1933), 7–37.

Volpe, *Istituzioni*—G. Volpe, *Studi sulle istituzioni comunali a Pisa*. Pisa, 1902.

Volpe, "Pisa"—G. Volpe, "Pisa, Firenze, Impero al principio del 1300 e gli inizi della signoria civile a Pisa," *SS, 11* (1902), 177–203.

1. THE NOTARIAL CHARTULARY

Lord! So many things are written of no purpose or use . . .
as do the notaries who with great pomp and caution summon
witnesses and write their words so that they will be remembered and held authentic.

FEDERIGO VISCONTI, ARCHBISHOP OF PISA (d. 1277)

IN THE COURSE of the 13th century, the sources for Italian urban history grow in volume and wealth with extraordinary rapidity. Not only do we have, by the closing
decades of that century, chroniclers, city and guild statutes,
and sermons in unprecedented numbers and quality, but
most especially, by that time we can take advantage of the
survival, in ever larger numbers, of a peculiar type of
source, of unique value in elucidating the private life of
the city: notarial acts. It would be hard to exaggerate the
importance for urban history of the notarial act and the
bundles of these acts known as chartularies. It has been
said, I think with fairness, that they are sources on private
life to which, before modern times, only the Egyptian
papyri may be considered comparable. Illustrations of their
breadth of application and wealth of content will come
profusely in the pages to follow. Here we must attempt to
analyze the nature of what is, for urban historians especially, a unique bounty.

The notarial act is a contract, will, or declaration drawn
up in the presence of and by a representative of the uni-

versal Christian society, a "public person," a notary.[1] The
notary received his commission to serve as a sort of consciousness of the Christian commonwealth from that commonwealth's leaders—the pope, the emperor, or their
authorized agents. By virtue of his commission, he could
lend to his acts the special quality of public faith: he could
render them valid means of establishing proof anywhere
at any time, even in the absence or after the death of himself or witnesses.

By the middle 13th century at Pisa, the redaction of a
notarial contract was a complicated affair involving as
many as three drafts.[2] Upon request the notary drew up
the contract in rough draft, usually on stray scraps of paper
(often found today inserted into the bindings of chartularies) or on the back pages of his chartulary. He wrote
such preliminary drafts with a hand scarcely legible, filled
the text with changes, and did not bother to include the
more standardized formulas of law. When all concerned
had agreed on the contract's provisions, the notary entered
the draft in his chartulary, this time with greater concern

1. On the early history of the notarial instrument in the Middle Ages,
see most recently the excellent treatment by Alain de Boüard, *L'Acte privé*,
Vol. 2 of his *Manuel de diplomatique française et pontificale* (Paris,
1929–48), where further references will be found to the many works on
diplomatics that deal with it.

2. The first draft is called frequently a *carta non firmata* or simply a
scriptum; the entry is physically a *scheda, schedula,* and technically a
rogatum. The complete chartulary is the *imbreviature* or *protocolla.* The
parchment is physically a *carta,* technically an *instrumentum.* For examples
of the terminology, "omnia mea acta et rogata et scripta per me et omnia
alia acta et rogata aliorum notariorum que penes me sunt rogata et scripta
ab eis . . . et potestatem instrumenta et cartas de ipsis conficiendi . . ."
(2544 19r 7 Nov. 1284); "instrumenta, contractus et scripturas alias, que et
quas in ipsis imbreviaturis invenerit non cancellatas, quotiens opus fuerit,
rite et fideliter exemplare et in publicam redigere formam . . ." (before
1285 from Florence, cited in A. Pannella, "Le Origini dell' archivio
notarile di Firenze," *ASI, 92,* 1934, 59).

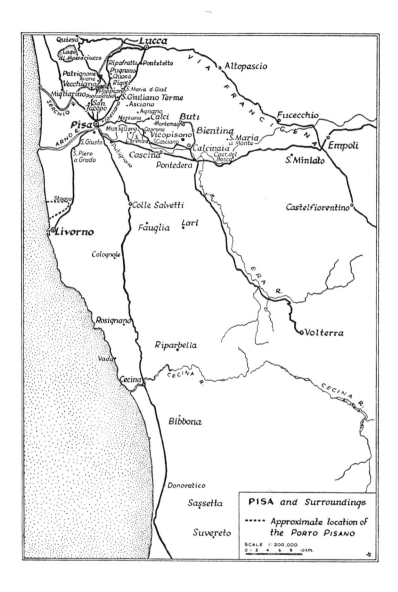

PISA and Surroundings

----- Approximate location of
the PORTO PISANO

SCALE 1:200,000
0 1 2 4 6 8 10km.

for legibility, though with liberal use of abbreviations and *et cetera*'s. The chartulary was thus technically the notary's own record or minutes of the contracts to which he had accorded public faith. Finally, to provide the contracting parties copies of the transaction, the notary redacted the contract formally on parchment, in his best handwriting, limiting his use of abbreviations to the standard and easily recognizable, and using *et cetera*'s roughly in proportion to the importance of the contract.

Historically, the *parchment* was the first of these drafts to appear. Up to the 11th century, however, it offered no independent proof, in the sense that the notary or witnesses still had to testify orally to its authenticity. Then, sometime about 1050, in a juridical development of far-reaching significance, parchments redacted by a notary were accorded full public faith. Because the written instrument now acquired unprecedented importance, substantial corrections or alterations of the text could not be tolerated. To be sure, even in the earlier period, probably rough drafts had been frequently used to assure the neat redaction of solemn testimonials. However, with the new importance of the parchment and the corresponding need to avoid substantial and suspicious changes in the text, the practice of first redacting parchments in rough draft seems to have become standardized in the late 11th century.

Apparently the earliest of these rough drafts took the form of dorsal notes on the parchments themselves.[3] The notary witnessed the transaction, scribbled the essential provisions on the back of the parchment, then at his convenience turned it over and formally redacted the contract. Even before 1100, however, certain considerations were leading notaries both to draw up those drafts on

3. Cf. A. Gaudenzi, "Sulla duplice redazione del documento italiano nel Medio Evo," *ASI, 41* (1908), 257–364.

separate material (soon, for reasons of economy, almost exclusively on *paper*) and to keep them permanently bound together as *chartularies*. Thus increasing demands for the notary's services were causing extensive delays in redaction. Sometimes notaries might die before they had formally redacted all their rough drafts, which had to be handed over to other notaries for transcription onto parchment.[4] For a not inconsiderable period, therefore, the rough drafts might be the sole evidence of the existence of the obligations; they had to be treated with care. Moreover, after a parchment had been redacted, the rough draft provided an excellent means of establishing its authenticity even many years later, after the death of the notary who had redacted it. By 1100, therefore, bundles of rough drafts (chartularies) were being permanently preserved. At the little town of Acqui, near Genoa, we hear of such *protocolla,* dating from 1101, being consulted eighty years later.[5]

By the early 12th century, therefore, the redaction of a notarial instrument involved two drafts: the entry in the chartulary, and the parchment. A central fact in determining the relationship between them was the apparently lengthening time lag between the two redactions; hard-pressed notaries were finding it difficult to keep abreast of the flood of business. We may well imagine that sometimes the contracting parties fulfilled their obligations and desired their contract canceled before the notary had redacted the original parchment. At any rate, at Pisa at least by the early 13th century the notaries had abandoned the pretense or hope of redacting all contracts on parchment.[6]

4. Cf. Boüard, *L'Acte privé,* p. 176, n. 2.

5. *Monumenta Aquensia,* ed. J. B. Moriondus (Turin, 1789), document of 1 Oct. 1101, copied in 1183 "ut in protocollo Ugonis notarii inveni."

6. ACC, 20 Dec. 1210, an obligation defined "in schedis" for which no parchment had been redacted. Cf. also 2544 7r 11 July 1284: "Et omnes

For the vast majority of transactions, the entry alone was
serving as evidence for the existence of the contract. Failure to redact the parchment meant, therefore, that the
entry had to be accorded a form of public faith. To be
sure, in a strict juridical sense, the entry did not replace
the parchment as a public instrument, for it never appeared in court. Whenever the contract contained in an
entry was involved in litigation, a parchment was "extracted" for presentation in court. For the majority of
transactions, however, which were created and canceled
without legal disputes, parchments became dispensable,
since to render them dispensable it was only necessary to
prevent the entry from ever serving in the future as an
exemplar and hence as the basis of legal action. By 1263,
to cancel an obligation contained in an entry, the notary
would write in the margin the fact, date, witnesses, and
circumstances of cancellation. The statutes of 1286 ruled
that even if a parchment had been redacted, if the entry
was canceled, the parchment had to be surrendered as
invalid.[7] Entries alone could therefore establish the existence or cancellation of obligations, and reliance on them
was such that even the terms *carta* (parchment) and *scheda*
(entry) tended toward confusion.[8]

But what if the entry creating the obligation was not
conveniently available for cancellation? The parties would
then draw up another entry, "ordering" the notary, "al-

cartas et sententias tenera et banna . . . rogata et rogatas . . . a quibus-
cumque notariis usque hodie cassa cassas et nullius valoris . . . vocavit
et per hanc cartam illa et illas cassari voluit . . . dando michi Bartholomeo et notariis *ea et eas habentibus* licet absentibus ea et eas cassandi parabolam et mandatum." Since these "cartas et sententias" were in the possession of the notaries, they were in fact entries. See also 2544 11r 1 Oct.
1284, where in a cession of six loans blank spaces are left for their respective dates, showing no parchments were surrendered.

7. *Stat., 1, 234.*
8. See above, n. 6.

though absent," who possessed the original entry, to cancel it.[9] Once the order was made, its actual execution was a matter of indifference, but by this fictional order any notary in the city of Pisa could modify in any way the entries of a Pisan confrère.

However, since parchments were extracted "when there might be need," and since the notary was paid for the service, the chartulary for years remained for him a potential source of income, probably his principal one. Like the valuable possession it was, it passed in wills from the notary to his heir.[10] This meant that the chartularies had to be left in the possession of the individual notary, and the guild kept only a list where they could be found. The unfortunate result has been that few have survived, and that in archival history deposits of chartularies are among the last to appear. Not until the 14th century did the city and guild interfere to ensure the chartularies' preservation, at a time when their function and interest were declining.[11]

One other circumstance made parchments necessary: when a contract was drawn up or meant to be canceled outside of Pisa. "And if with the debtor the instrument of debt is found canceled," say the statutes (1286), ". . . we shall force the creditor . . . to have the entry of that instrument canceled." [12] In 1299 when an obligation con-

9. For example, 2544 7r 11 July 1284.
10. 2544 19r 7 Nov. 1284.
11. For the history of the archival deposits of chartularies at Genoa, which city has far and away the earliest and richest collection in Italy, see M. Moresco and G. P. Bognetti, *Per l'edizione dei notai liguri del secolo XII*, DSSCDI, 10, Turin, 1938. For such deposits at Florence, see A. Pannella, "Le Origini dell'archivio notarile di Firenze," *ASI, 92* (1934), 57–92. For Lucca, A. D'Addario, "La Conservazione degli atti notarili negli ordinamenti della Repubblica lucchese," *ASI, 109* (1951), 193–226. For Siena, see G. Prunai, "I Notai senesi del XIII e XIV secolo e l'attuale riordinamento del loro Archivio," *BSSP, 12* (1953), 78–109.
12. *Stat. 1*, 234.

tracted at Pisa was canceled at Palermo, the creditor delivered the instrument "to be lacerated," and it was lacerated in the presence of a notary.[13] The debtor would then
keep the canceled parchment as a permanent proof of payment or send it back to Pisa so that the originating entry
might also be canceled. Whenever mobility was a factor,
parchments had to be executed. This meant that in the
sector of urban life where mobility was most a factor,
namely in commerce, they were particularly important.
At Pisa, therefore, archival deposits of parchments tended
to have a higher proportion of strictly commercial contracts than did a chartulary, although the number of parchments is not nearly so great as the number of entries.

This fact perhaps explains an interesting contrast between Pisa's chartularies and those of Genoa and her colonies of Bonifacio, Pera, and Caffa.[14] Obligations contained
in the 13th-century chartularies from those latter cities
seem not to have been canceled by marginal annotations.
But an entry which could not show the death of an obligation could not prove its existence; in those more exclusively maritime cities the need for mobility, and conse-
quently the parchment, so characterized transactions that
apparently the entry could not develop until quite late

13. Zeno, *Documenti*, no. 76. The laceration meant literally the slicing
of the parchment.
14. On Genoa's chartularies, see besides Moresco and Bognetti, *L'Edizione*, R. Doehaerd, *Les Relations commerciales entre Gênes, la Belgique
et l'outremont d'après les archives notariales génoises aux XIII et XIV
siècles*, Brussels and Rome, 1941; V. Vitale, *La Vita civile*, Pt. I of *Vita e
commercio nei notai genovesi dei secoli XII e XIII*, ASLSP, 72, Genoa,
1949. For Bonifacio, V. Vitale, *Documenti sul Castello di Bonifacio nel
secolo XIII*, ASLSP, new ser. 1, Genoa, 1936. For Pera and Caffa, G. Bratianu,
Actes des notaires génois de Péra et de Caffa de la fin du treizième siècle,
Académie roumaine, Etudes et recherches, 2, Bucharest, 1927. Cf. also
R. Lopez, "The Unexplored Wealth of the Notarial Archives in Pisa and
Lucca," *Mélanges Louis Halphen* (Paris, 1951), pp. 417–32.

into an independent means of proof. At the little half-Tuscan, half-Ligurian town of Portovenere, cancellation of obligations through marginal notes was known though not utilized as extensively as at Pisa.[15] In inland Tuscany, on the other hand, by the late 13th century the practice of canceling entries through marginal annotations apparently found wide application, as at Pisa.[16] The customs of Pisa show many such resemblances to those of the inland cities, and the mechanism of her chartularies, as indeed their content, seems to reveal the presence of a land economy of no slight importance.

So important was the entry and so busy the notary that by 1263 it, too, had first to be redacted in rough draft. The existence of this third document means that entries were not made on the date they bear. They are not always in chronological order, although the notary usually marked stray entries with the note "non dubitetur de datali quia verax est"—the equivalent of our editorial *sic*.[17] Notaries could nod, however. In 1299 Romanus de Musiliano, possibly because he couldn't read his own scribblings too well, possibly because he had not made the drafts he copied, for two months persisted in writing "April" and "May," which later had to be corrected to "August" and "September." [18] And that "August" could be misread as "April" empha-

15. See G. Falco and G. Pistarino, *Il Cartulario di Giovanni di Giona di Portovenere (sec. XIII)*, Deputazione subalpina di storia patria, séguito alla Biblioteca della società storica subalpina, 177, Turin, 1955.

16. Entries in Lucchese chartularies are canceled, and parchments from Siena refer to entries as offering independent proof at least by 1250. For Florence, see Pannella, "Archivio notarile," p. 59, "scripturas . . . que . . . in ipsis imbreviaturis invenerit non cancellatas, *quotiens opus fuerit*, rite et fideliter exemplare et in publicam redigere formam."

17. 2543 32r 31 May 1263. Sequence of contracts 29 May, 29 May, *31 May*, 30 May with the entry of 31 May bearing the note, "non dubitetur . . ."

18. 2527 34v–38r.

sizes how many months had passed before Romanus found time to enter the drafts.

By the 1270's this rough draft had such practical importance that like the entry before it, it forced its way into the juridical consciousness.[19] Notaries had to make their drafts on "good paper" or use the back pages of the chartulary; and on those back pages, or on "good paper" inserted into the chartulary's binding, those drafts may often be found today. Notaries were cautioned to include in the draft at least the date, witnesses and "tenor" of the contract. Certain contracts had to be entered in the chartularies within one month, though latitude in regard to others probably means that not all contracts were finding their way to the chartularies. Again a growing volume of transactions was breaking up the old patterns of traditional business practices, this time to the extent of undermining the notary's former importance in the city's business life.

From the late 1240's Pisa in company with the rest of Italy entered upon a period of vigorous business expansion. The boom demanded a volume of paper work that surpassed notarial abilities to keep up with it. Simultaneously, the ever more literate businessmen, themselves often trained in the notarial profession, were able successfully to dispense with those abilities. By 1263 the notary in the majority of instances witnessed not the actual transaction ("in my presence he received") but only a "confession" that the transaction had taken place ("in my presence he has confessed that he has received"). By then the businessman was frequently keeping his own records; he and other principals marched to the notary, "confessed" to the rec-

19. For what follows, *Breve collegii notariorum, Stat., 3, 797.* While the redaction of this Breve is from the early 14th century, the section cited almost certainly goes back to the 1270's at least, by which time the directives given were clearly being followed in redacting contracts.

ords' veracity, and left them, where, on analogy with the
notary's own rough draft, they were transferred to the
chartulary. In 1253, for instance, we hear of a mercantile
account book, a *quaternum,* from whose entries *"carte
have not been extracted by the notary Pace or any other
notary."* [20] But this burden of proof was becoming ever
more an anachronism for the literate businessman. By the
1270's investors are frequently made to declare in a notarized statement that in future accountings of their money,
no more notarized statements will be necessary.[21] By the
1270's, too, merchants could declare that their private records should be binding not only for what they owed, their
debita, but for what they could demand, their *credita.*[22]
The commune had evidently sanctioned this use of private
account books as a means of proof. Probably the fiction
was, however, that these private records were considered
rough drafts of notarial instruments as, in the earlier period, they were.

Thus, as business dispensed with the parchment, by the
late 13th century it was dispensing too with the entry, and
with it also the services of the notary. By the early 14th
century the chartulary's evidence on economy, while of
course still important, is largely indirect—that is, it must
be gleaned from wills, leases, marriages, in short from the
types of contracts for whose services today notaries are required.

In 1293, 232 Pisan notaries were paying taxes to the
Collegium notariorum—a figure that may be compared
with the 200 then practicing at Genoa and the 600 at
Florence.[23] A generation previously, in 1263, Iacobus de

20. ASP, Primaziale, 19 Oct. 1253. Will of Goctifredus quondam Petri
de Arborea.

21. ASP, Trovatelli, 12 Mar. 1277. 2544 3ʳ 30 June 1284.

22. 2515 119v 24 Aug. 1272. 2544 3ʳ 30 June 1284.

23. Matricula of Pisan notaries in *Stat. 3,* 841 ff. For Genoa, see ASL,
Capitoli 24, a fragment of the Genoese *Breve potestatis* of 1288 incorpo-

Carraria Gonnelle, whose practice was continued in 1293 by his son Bartholomeus, produced 240 entries in one year. To be sure, 1263 was a war year, the summer months were given to fighting, and Iacobus' output was hardly typical; we may say very roughly, however, that Pisa in the late 13th century was probably using considerably over 55,000 notarial entries each year. This figure may be compared with more accurate ones from Genoa: 56,000 entries in 1265, 80,000 in 1291.

Of this mass of material, little has survived.[24] The extant chartularies from 1263 to 1300 contain about 1500 entries, about one-tenth of the number in the archives of Lucca and barely comparable with those of Genoa, Italy's richest.

Yet even these scant survivals show extraordinary richness of content. All levels of Pisan society are there: the great counts of the house of Donoratico, one of whom, Ugolino, died to immortality in the pages of Dante; the rich merchant, the network of whose interests stretches from France to Alexandria; the hungry wool worker selling his tools for food; the impoverished peasant, the sum of whose property, fourteen pounds, has fallen under his creditor's grasp.[25] All parts of Pisa are there. Iacobus de Carraria Gonnelle worked mostly in his shop on the street "of the shirt" or on hot summer days in his garden. But he and other notaries roamed also from the city hall to

---

rated into a Genoese-Lucchese treaty of 1303, "per publicum notarium de numero ducentorum [collegii] notariorum ianuensium . . ." For Florence, Villani, *Cronica*, 6, 184, to which compare Plesner, *L'Emigration*, p. 148. For the number of Genoese redactions cited in the following paragraph, I am following I. Renouard, *Les Hommes d'affaires italiens du Moyen Age* (Paris, 1949), p. 96.

24. For a breakdown of Pisa's notarial archives, see "Note on the Sources," below, p. 215.

25. All examples from 2543, but similar ones could be taken from almost any chartulary.

the city jail to the city bridges and gates, from the towers of the aristocrats to the shops of the artisans to the lands of the bankrupt. In Pisa's churches they listened to solemn covenants; in the stables they inspected the corpse of a mule. All ages are there. A wife is pregnant; the husband crowds the pages of his will with speculations on the sex of the "stomach" and divides his goods accordingly. Tutors and guardians are appointed, boys apprenticed, girls given to household service, marriages contracted, wills made, and their provisions executed. Like the sacraments of the Church, notarial acts punctuated the Pisan's life from cradle to grave.

Overwhelmingly concerned with common life, these pages nevertheless afford odd glimpses of the antics of the world's great. Iohannes, called Sardus, a papal courier and son of a papal courier, accepts gratuities for conveying petitions to Rome.[26] His action gives voice to a frequently met problem in the erection of the papal bureaucracy. On papal business, perhaps the tangled issue of the imperial succession, Iohannes sets out for Spain in 1264.[27] In view of the dangers of the trip, he makes his will, dividing his goods between his two daughters. But in those parlous times, the quiet life of a Pisan girl could be as uncertain as the sea, and one year later Iohannes returns to find his younger daughter death's victim. Yet life moves on, and a few months later, his wife promises him another child.

Sometimes the program calls for tragicomedy. Actors: Guido, a pompous Florentine, probably a wool manufacturer, his daughter Bonaventura, and Master Iacobus the Little, whose nickname, "Astrologer," suggests activities

---

26. 2543 84r 8 Mar. 1264. On papal couriers, P. Baumgarten, *Aus Kanzlei und Kammer. Eröterungen zur Curialen, Hof- und Verwaltungsgeschichte,* Freiburg, 1907.

27. 2543 86v 15 Mar. 1264.

more romantic than working wool.[28] Iacobus has loved and
run away. In 1263 Guido marches four of his fellow Florentines to the notary's shop, where as witnesses they protest
that they indeed know the renegade astrologer and that
he was truly married to Guido's daughter. But the lack of
any written instrument of espousal suggests that Iacobus'
liaison with Bonaventura may have been less than licit.
Another Bonaventura, from Lucca, isolated in Pisa in the
war year of 1263, heard that her husband back home had
taken another wife, "by the name of Uguicionella," who
was even related to Bonaventura "in the third degree of
consanguinity." Cut off from Lucca, she appeals to Rome.[29]

But if the glamour of the contracts and most of their interest derives from their rich and varied content, the explanation of their importance in urban life lies more nearly
in another area: their form—in the mass of juridic formulas which constitute 90 per cent of every contract—which
are dull, monotonously repetitious, but which for the understanding of the function of the notarial instrument are
of basic significance.

From the middle 12th century and perhaps earlier, Pisa
set about codifying the elements of Roman and Lombard
law and the "good customs" under which she lived and
defining the functions of her communal officials.[30] The

28. 2543 48r 18 Aug. 1263.
29. 2543 84r 8 Mar. 1264.
30. For what follows, see especially A. Schaube, "Zur Entstehungsge-
schichte des pisanischen Constitutum Usus," *Zeitschrift für das gesammte
Handelsrecht, 46 (1897)*, 1–47, trans. and rep. in L. Ferretti, *Appunti sulla
genesi dei Costituti pisani*, Pisa, 1929; M. Luzzatto, "Le Più Antiche Glosse
ai Constituti pisani," *Archivi. Archivi d'Italia e Rassegna internazionale
degli archivi*, ser. 2, *21* (1954), 244–77. Besides the codex of the *Constituta*
in the Vatican Library (cod. vaticanus 6385) antedating the one on which
Bonaini's edition was based and discussed by Schaube, another codex has
come to light that appears to be the earliest surviving one, upon which a
needed new edition of the *Constituta* ought to be based. This codex,

resulting series of codes Adolf Schaube distinguished on the basis of public and private law. Regulating governmental structure are the two *Breve consulum* of 1162 and 1164 respectively, the fragmentary statutes of 1275, and a full redaction of the statutes in 1286 (the *Breve potestatis* or *Breve pisani communis,* and the *Breve pisani populi*). The kernel of these codifications is the oath taken by communal officials, about which were added communal enactments, *capitula.* The statutes are therefore an aggregate of such enactments with no external order or internal consistency. Concerned with the citizens' relations apart from the commune are the *Constitutum Usus,* which presents procedures and Pisa's customs on commercial organizations, and the *Constitutum Legis,* which besides procedures deals especially with family law. In contradistinction to the communal statutes, these are consciously ordered redactions, meant to assure uniformity in court decisions. Possibly the two Constituta formed originally one code which was later divided when Pisa established separate courts, *ad usum* and *ad legem.* At any rate, the Constitutum Usus was redacted from 1156 to 1160, although it was subject, of course, to numerous later revisions. Bonaini's edition is based on a codex of 1233; the discovery subsequent to publication of two older codices (both from the 12th century) has made a new edition a *desideratum* which for over fifty years has gone unfulfilled.

That these two series may be distinguished on the basis of different origins and content—inasmuch as the two Constituta contain nothing on government—is fair enough, but Schaube's application of the terms "public" and "private" law to them was not well thought out. The

---

formerly in the Phillipps collection in England and known to Bonaini but not utilized by him, has recently been acquired by Mr. Thomas E. Marston, Yale University Library, New Haven, Connecticut.

distinction leaves no room for the provisions regulating commercial societies contained in guild statutes, especially the *Breve curiae maris.* Moreover, the application of "private law" to the Constitutum Usus suggests that it was legislation meant to be universally followed by Pisa's citizens—a misconception of its nature. Further, the statutes themselves contain much on procedures, loans, leases, commercial societies, roads, and waterways—all of which came under Pisa's courts ad usum or ad legem. To this extent the 12th-century Constitutum Usus and the late 13th-century city and guild statutes are coordinate and comparable—not because their function was identical but because both are sources for the procedures and institutions of urban life. In this respect, too, the difference between them is the difference in Pisa in her "heroic age" and Pisa feeling the late 13th-century's manifold stresses.

The road between one and the other was blazed by the notarial contract. In comparison with the contracts, the most salient characteristic of both Constitutum Usus and the statutes is their incompleteness. The contracts unfold before our eyes a rich variety of cattle contracts—*soccita, societas ad medium proficuum, guardia ad melioramentum* —each subtly distinct from the others and none comprehended in Constituta or statutes.[31] Even a strictly commercial contract, the *societas terre et maris,* must be defined by the chartularies or parchments if it is to be defined at all.[32] All the numerous sophistications of which commercial societies were capable—sophistications so extreme as to change the societies' original nature—likewise find nothing but silence in the statutes. Even with the help of the statutes of 1286, who would find a full codification of Pisa's "private law" in our modern sense must look

31. Examples of all are given in the Appendix, nos. 24–7.
32. Example in the Appendix, no. 23.

rather to the aggregate of contracts gleaned from the chartularies. He must look to the notarial formulas.

For the notarial contract functioned as a juridical statute. To be sure, it regulated only particular persons within
a limited area, but within this narrower frame it had all
the characteristics of a statute: public recognition of its
provisions, sanctions, and the state's authority to enforce
it. This, comparison with the *Constitutum Usus* empha-
sizes. Not only is that code incomplete, but even when it
speaks it recognizes an authority greater than itself: in the
notarial contract. In all questions concerning the duration,
concerning profit-division—the parties' respective prerogatives in commercial societies—the provisions of the contract prevail over those of the code.[33] The Constitutum
Usus was a handbook intended for the guidance of judges
in the settlement of disputes where the contract creating
the obligation was silent. For its provisions regarding commercial societies no universal conformity was expected nor
sanctions imposed; to distill these customs into the stronger
vintage of the law required the contract. Little wonder,
therefore, that the *Liber consuetudinum* (1216) of Milan
calls the provisions of the notarial contract "lex." [34]

And like the law it was, within its limited sphere the
contract strives for completeness. Through "executive"
clauses it defines the procedures to be followed in the can-

---

33. Some examples from the *Constitutum Usus* (*Stat.*, 2), "si autem de
partibus nichil inter eos ordinaverit . . ." (p. 877); "si vero de partibus
inter se non convenerint . . ." (p. 876); "si vero tempus in societate
posuerit . . ." (p. 878); "si vero quando societatem fecerint, nominatim
hec verba adiunserint dicentes . . ." (p. 884); "si vero non aliud convenit . . ." (p. 884); "si proficuum nominatum non fuerit . . ." (p. 905).
In Chapter 25 of the *Constitutum* a table is presented giving the division
of profit in commenda contracts according to the voyage's destination, but
this too has force only when the contract is silent.

34. *Liber consuetudinum Mediolani anni MCCXVI*, ed. E. Besta and
G. Luigi (Milan, 1949), pp. 84-5.

cellation of the obligation or the enforcement of its terms.[35] It defines the rights of the parties *vis-à-vis* one another. Further, it tries to consider all contingencies that might affect the contract: if money should fall in value, if grain should rise, if others should have claims on goods exchanged or property sold, if property should be lost, if God should let ships sink or cattle die, if war should break out or Lucchesi invade, if transportation should be hampered.

Like a law, too, it dared "repeal" privileges and provisions of Roman, ecclesiastical, and even communal law which might interfere with the execution of the contract.[36] Roman law contained privileges which might prove obstructive: the *exceptio non numerate pecunie,* the *epistula divi Adriani,* for women the *senatus consultus Velleianus,* for persons under canon law the *privilegium fori,* for everyone every right "by which this agreement could be contravened." [37] Even the provisions of the Constitutum

35. See the contracts printed in Appendix V, giving the creditor the right to seize the debtor's property "sua auctoritate" if the debt defaults. For such a seizure "ex forma et tenore unius carte rogate a Nero notario," 2629 280v 15 Oct. 1285. Compare H. Brieglieb, *Geschichte des executiv-Prozesses. Ueber executorische Urkunden und executiv-Prozess,* Stuttgart, 1845.

36. Definitions with bibliography of the following terms in A. Berger, *Encyclopedic Dictionary of Roman Law,* Transactions of the American Philosophic Society, new ser., 43, Philadelphia, 1953. The "exceptio non numerate pecunie" was the claim that sums stipulated in the contract had not actually been received (for this at Pisa, see *Constitutum Usus, Stat.,* 2, 751). The "privilegium fori" was the right of special persons (especially clerics) to trial in special courts. The "senatus consultus Velleianus" forbad women to assume liability for other persons. On the significance of these renunciations, see P. Riesenberg, "Roman Law, Renunciations and Business in the Twelfth and Thirteenth Centuries," *Essays in Medieval Life and Thought . . . in Honor of Austin P. Evans* (New York, 1953), pp. 207–25.

37. For example, 2629 263v (1285), "renunciando omni iuri et legibus constitutionibus et auxiliis et desentionibus qua vel quibus se a predictis vel aliquo predictorum et nominatim a pena tueri vel iuvari possit."

Usus on juridical procedures, where the code looks most like legislation, the notarial contract changed, abrogated, and ignored, authorizing one of the parties to procede as if a court decision had been carried.[38]

The notarial contract is thus the most vociferous expression of the resounding theme of early urbanism, the challenge to directives of Empire, Church, and even commune. If the curia maris, Pisa's powerful guild of overseas merchants, could legislate by having its enactments inserted into the podesta's breve, the notarial contract legislated yet more sweepingly.[39] If the curia maris repealed law by declaring its own will valid "notwithstanding any chapter of the podesta's breve," the contract repealed more drastically.[40] If the curia maris used the commune's authority to enforce its wishes, the notarial contract applied it more widely. As society plowed into new fields, the notarial contract formed the cutting edge.

But let us not pretend that the notarial contract rendered communal legislation meaningless, any more than the curia maris made communal government powerless. The problem of the functioning and decline of the notarial contract—and indeed, of the curia maris—is not the ques-

38. Loc. cit. "Et sic precepit ei pro scripto capitali pena et expensis ingredi possessionem vel quasi bonorum suorum sua propria auctoritate sine decreto iudicum vel consulis iustitie aut nuntii communis seu curiarum presentia."

39. For example, *Breve potestatis* (1286), *Stat., 1,* 348, "Et operam dabimus . . . ut effectui demandentur prout in capitulis eorum [consulum maris] brevis et ordinamentorum continentur . . ." The subject is treated at length by Schaube, *Konsulat,* and A. D'Amia, "Appunti circa il diritto e l'ordinamento marittimo pisano dal Breve curiae maris," *Studi in onore di Arrigo Solmi,* Milan, 1940.

40. For example, ASP, Comune A, 81, 4v 16 Dec. 1245, "Et placet nobis consiliariis [consulum ordinis maris] quod scripti honores et gratie et scripte dationes sunt facti et facte . . . non obstante aliquo capitulo brevis [capitaneorum decathie] seu brevis potestatis."

tion of when the commune first felt the power to legislate. It is rather when the commune felt compelled fully to intrude into the realm of the "good customs," into its citizens' lives, and there completely to work its will. The birth of this concept of intervention, of the pursuit of definite policy with positive legislation, of the consequential stripping of the nobility, the archbishop, and the merchant guilds of their competitive powers and the notarial contract of its law-creating force—in short, the birth of what we may with justice call a modern state—did not come overnight. From about 1190 to after 1250 a kind of diarchy ruled urban affairs—a compromise in which for the moment the older elements—the archbishop, nobility, and merchant guilds—lay down in peace with that from which the new would come. A kind of diarchy too ruled urban legislation, in which contract and *capitulum,* notarial and statutory law, faced each other in balance.

In the later 13th century to periodic and finally permanent control of the Pisan commune came her *popolo,* her democracy. In the bitter and complicated conflicts over communal policies that marked its rise, the contending parties—the popolo especially, but the aristocratic factions too—seem to have brought to the old and still half-feudal world of archbishop, nobility, and merchant guilds a new concept of positive legislation. To favor or hamper, to twist or direct, the revolutionary currents then flowing through urban life, the factions enforced a level of discipline that left progressively less room for a feudal archbishop, an independent curia maris, or law-making contracts. First during this period we find the Breve pisani communis widely dictating procedures and expressing its superiority over customs and guild statutes, just as that new code, the Breve pisani populi (written probably in

1254 though perhaps older) was exerting its own superiority in communal government.[41] First, too, during this period, we find that the state has disciplined life so much that private account books could replace the notary's "pomp and caution" in the creation of obligations.[42] But in changing the notary's role, this new state absorbed his services. By 1324 in the fantastic bureaucracy it had erected, out of some 285 government officials (excluding ambassadors), 115 or about 40 per cent served as chancellors, notaries, or scribes.[43] By that time the government was probably absorbing almost 50 per cent of notarial services. Still, over the course of this revolution, notarial acts remain a unique source—the candid, intricately drawn vignettes of people unaware that their doings were the stuff of history.

41. An example of the statutes taking precedence over customs, 2545 41v 15 Mar. 1283, "Dummodo illa consuetudo non sit contra formam brevis et ordinamentorum pisani communis quod si fuerit forma brevis et ordinamentorum pisani communis conservetur et non consuetudo predicta." Over guilds, 2545 50r 10 May 1283, "exercere dictam artem corrigiariorum et observare et adimplere statuta dicte artis . . . dummodo non sint contra commune pisanum aut contra formam brevis pisani communis." Printed in full in appendix to Brugaro, "Artigianato."

42. Public faith was given to mercantile account books by the early 14th century at Florence. Cf. *Statuti della Repubblica fiorentina. Statuto del Capitano del Popolo (1322–25)*, ed. R. Caggese (Florence, 1910), p. 112.

43. As listed in the *Ordinamenta salariorum* (1324), *Stat.*, 2, 1135 ff.

2. GEOGRAPHY

> May God lead our merchants to the port of salvation and give
> us, in His time, the fruits of the earth.
>
> FEDERIGO VISCONTI

PISA'S peculiarity, the economic setting of her medieval years, is this: her geographical position left her free to direct her economic energies to land or sea, to either or both, as she might prefer.[1] For Pisa's geography struck a balance. A Tuscan town, she boasted a countryside subject to her control, a "contado," broad and fertile. A Mediterranean port, she offered outlet to the *partes marine* of her sources, the Italian merchant's world. In the interplay of these two environments, Pisa found first greatness then ruin. Here, too, a picture of Pisa must take its beginning.

A triangular plain, limited on the west by the Tyrrhenian shore, on the south by the low but unbroken Livorno hills, on the north by the stately Alpi Apuane and the northeast by the Monti Pisani's celebrated curtain, "for which the Pisans cannot see Lucca," Pisa's contado ties together four fertile areas.[2] Easily reached by sea or a broad seaside corridor, to the north lies Versilia, whose olive oil Pisan merchants made prized in overseas markets.[3] Beyond the Monti Pisani were the sheep-rich Garfagnana, the

1. Most recent of numerous works on Pisan geography, dealing with the city's contemporary situation but written with good historical perspective, is Pedreschi, "Geografia," where may be found a full bibliography of the older works on Pisan topography.

2. The citation on the Monti Pisani is *Inf.* XXXIII, 30.

3. Schaube, *Handelsg.*, p. 298.

Serchio valley, and Lucca, "of cities in Tuscany, none greater in wealth, in abundance of wine, of oil . . ."[4] Beyond Lucca lay Pistoia, "so lovely and useful a city, so abundant . . ."[5] From directly east came the Arno, that "imperial river of sweet water," the open highway to the hinterland, to the Valdarno and Florence, by the late 13th century famed "for the cunning of her masters and arts and beauty and ornament."[6] No similar highway ran southward to the Cecina valley and the Volterrana, but the sea tied Pisa to that valley's lower reaches, to the Maremma stretching from the Livorno hills almost to Grosseto, to the petty ports—Vada, Rosignano, Piombino, Castiglione della Pescaia—which channeled its riches.

Medieval Pisa stood close upon thick forests which covered the hills around her and parts of the plain between her and the sea, and which even in the late 13th century retained a primeval fierceness. Foolish the traveler who dared go to Lucca by night, when the mountain road was lined with outlaws and roamed by wolves. And if wild animals provided for noble sport, "chasing the wolf and little wolves on the mountain," we hear too of their attacking peasants in the fields, and the city's offering rewards for their capture.[7]

Even authors of antiquity comment on Tuscany's thick forests and the wealth they gave.[8] About 1050 a poet in

4. *Vita Anselmi lucensis episcopi auctore Rangerio*, ed. Sackur, Schwartz and Schmeidler. *MGH, Ss, XXX²*, vv. 4357–4358.

5. Dino Compagni, *Chronicon florentinum, lib. 1*. The best edition is I. Del Lungo, *Dino Compagni e la sua cronica*, Florence, 1879–87.

6. Loc. cit.

7. *Stat., 1*, 146. See the life of Lucca's St. Zita (d. 1272), *ASS*, 12, 513 C, 528 D, 530 D, 531 A, for examples of wolves attacking peasants in the fields. Even in the 16th century at Lucca, a bear could turn back a procession. See Sardi, *Contrattazioni*, p. 77.

8. For the descriptions of Strabo and Rutilius Namatianus concerning Pisa in antiquity, see Toscanelli, *Antichità*, 2, 237 ff. and 275 ff.

distant Germany speaks of "wood bought from Lucca." [9]
More realistic in her admiration, Genoa in 1142 exempted
from tariffs "opera silvatica et guarnimenta," the products
of Tuscan forests.[10] For Tuscany harbored woodlands in
two areas: the moist maritime plain which rims her coast,
and the parallel ridges which, starting from the Apennines
and dividing the populous valleys between, reach down to
the sea. Pisa, commanding the Tyrrhenian coastal waters,
the *mare pisanum* of her sources, guarding the Arno river
—the *nahr-bis,* river of Pisa, to the Arabs—had easy access
to both these wooded areas. North of the Arno to the
Serchio was the forest of San Rossore; to the south the
woods of Stagno were still thick enough in 1286 to shelter
thieves.[11] Further south, beyond Livorno, stretched

> Those fierce forests, which hold in hate,
> 'Twixt Cecina and Corneto, the cultivated fields.[12]

And beyond the limits of Pisa's contado there were other
"fierce forests." To the north, Viareggio, a town the suze-
rainty over which was hotly disputed with Lucca, was the
busy *entrepôt* for wood from the Alpi Apuane, and at
Motrone in the 12th century Pisans took their wood as
arrows from the outraged inhabitants.[13] Further north,
Lunigiana contributed to Pisa's Balearic fleet of 1115 its
"strength of forests." [14] From the Lucchesia wood could
easily be floated down the Serchio to the coast. From the

9. Cited in A. Mancini, *Storia di Lucca* (Florence, 1950), p. 109.

10. Schaube, *Handelsg.,* p. 623.

11. *Stat., 1,* 487.

12. *Inf.* XIII, 8.

13. For Viareggio, 2515 53r 22 May 1273, ten cart loads of wood sold,
"que ligna sunt in piagia de Viareggio et prope dictum castrum." Life of
St. Rainerius, *ASS, 24,* 359 D.

14. *Liber maiolichinus de gestis Pisanorum illustribus,* ed. M. Amari
and G. Calisse, Fonti per la storia d'Italia, 29, (Rome, 1904), v. 100.

Florentine, even in 1115, "celsae Mucellae," apparently Mugello, sent to Pisa its "strength of trees."[15] In Florence's extensive contado, the town of Legnaia, as the name suggests, was the center from where wood built into rafts was floated down the Arno.[16] In 1270 we hear of Pisans in Florence's forests, and the contracts point to a continuous commerce which even Pisa's defeat at the Battle of Meloria failed to dampen.[17]

Forests provided materials basic to three industries: wood for building; carbon, used in metallurgy; and wild animals and tannic acid, for leather. And if the area's most famous tree, the Roman pine, is more celebrated for beauty than for utility, other species were not lacking.[18] Four kinds of oak, *quercus, cerrus, leccus* (*quercus ilex*), and, most prized of all, *rovere* (*quercus robur*) provided wood durable enough for wine presses and strong enough for bridges. Among the oaks, too, must be listed cork (*sugherus*), whose fine hardwood made strong cartwheels and an excellent charcoal. However, chestnut (*castaneus*), abundant on Pisa's low plain, was the most widely used of the hardwoods for heavy construction. Fir (*abies*), favored for furniture and indispensable for ships' stores, was brought from Tuscany's hills. The staple of Pisan construction seems, however, to have been the alder (*ontane*) and, most common of all, the poplar, both white (*alberus*)

15. Ibid., v. 102.

16. 2515 118r and 136v 15 Aug. 1272. Lanbertus vinarius de Martiana qui moratur Pisis and his partner Lupus sell to Federicus quondam Ildebrandini Nasi "unam piattatam de bonis suvetis et lignis suvetorum sufficienter oneratam de partibus de Lignalia," to be delivered in fifteen days at Federico's caricatorium and furnace at Barbaricina. On the town of Legnaia, see Repetti, *Dizionario*, 2, 672.

17. In 1270 Pisans were given the right to export wood from the Florentine contado. *Relazioni*, no. 198; Davidsohn, *Forsch.*, 3, no. 70.

18. Lupi, "Casa pisana," *ASI*, ser. 5, 32 (1903), 90–100, discusses types of wood used in building.

and dark (*pluppus*). Not quality wood, they were fast growing in Pisa's wet terrain. Forest myrtle (*mortella*) yielded the tannic acid for Pisan leather. We hear of its use even before 1150.[19] Abundant on the Monti Pisani and in the Calci valley, the bush was cut every three years.

If forests were a factor in three industries—building, metallurgy, and leather—Tuscany's other wealth provided the complement. In building, the 13th century saw the age of timber give way to the age of mortar, stone, and brick.[20] To Pisa's furnaces to make needed lime was carted stone from the surrounding hills, and it was imported too from the Florentine, as the leather industry, using lime in cleaning skins, compounded the demand. Shale for roofs (*placte*) came from Buti, and stone or marble from Verruca in the Monti Pisani and from Elba. Perhaps more important was brick. *Tegularie*, clay "mines," dotted Pisa's contado, from the Livorno hills to the city walls, where the argillous and swampy land held both diggings (*cavata*) and furnaces.[21] From these furnaces came roof tile (*embrices*), shaped into

19. *Reg. pis.*, no. 421. For a sale of myrtle from the Monti Pisani, ASP, San Lorenzo alle Rivolte, 9 Jan. 1283. "Consules mortelle" in Calci, *Stat.*, *3*, 922 (1298). For an evaluation of the quality of myrtle taken from the Monti, ASP, Pia Casa di Misericordia, no. 460 (dated 1570), Libro di Girolamo Bertucci, "La mortella di terra fatta a Monti di Lucca . . . non e cosi buona come quella di marina perche . . . a monti la tagliano di tre anni et quella di marina n' anno 4 e 5 e 6 e anno piu possanza."

20. Lupi, "Casa pisana," is an excellently documented study of Pisan construction for our period.

21. A clay mine "extra muros civitatis pisane prope portam de lectiis in catallo," 2515 122v 7 July 1272. At Lari, 2515 46r 2 May 1273. In the Valdarno, *Stat.*, *1*, 489 and 522. A furnace for cooking "matones" and "quanta terra ei fuerit necessaria pro area pro dicto fornace," 2524 45r (1308). "Tegulas calcinam renam et lignam" sent on the Auser canal to Asciano, 2523 280r (ca. 1300). Sale of "duo miliaria de enbricibus sopranis et sottanis ad coperiendum videlicet de utroque pro medietate ut moris est," 2516 46r 2 May 1273. Earthenware in inventories, "quatuor cuppos de terra ab oleo," 2545 99r 16 Nov. 1283.

types upper (*soprane*) or lower (*sottane*) to ensure proper meshing; from them brick, too—in the 13th century at Pisa always *tegule*—was used for everything from street pavements to castle walls. And the presence of earthenware in Pisan inventories suggests that the city had already embarked on an industry she has maintained to the present.

Iron came from the Garfagnana in the Lucchesia, from Lunigiana to the north, from the Maremma hills to the south, and of course from Elba.[22] With carbon from Pisa's forests, iron products provided Pisan merchants with what was perhaps their most important exchange in the overseas trade. From the Maremma coast came another mineral, important for the hinterland and at times exported overseas: salt.[23] From these regions also—from Monte Argentario and the island of Ischia and the Lipari—Pisan leather drew a poor but usable alum.[24]

Pisa's extensive forests offered to her industries of leather and furs, which by 1200 were her most important, an abundant supply of skins: rabbit, hare, fox, wolf, buffalo, and boar. Forests, too, could support large herds of swine, the maintenance of which was characteristic of the primitive agriculture of the early Middle Ages. By 1200, however, the leather industry was coming to depend more importantly on other domesticated types: sheep, cattle, and horses. In animal husbandry, Pisa's well watered plain provided fodder in abundance, ever a precious commodity on the medieval farm. Then, too, the areas of still uncol-

22. See below, pp. 129 ff.

23. The age and extent of the exploitation of the Maremma's salt are illustrated by the *Reg. pis.*, no. 104 (1031), no. 129 (1052) and many following. For export to the Regno, see concession of Conradin to Pisa, 1268, Dal Borgo, *Raccolta*, p. 103, where Pisans are said to carry salt, pitch and iron. For export to the hinterland, Davidsohn, *Forsch.*, *3*, no. 120 and many following.

24. Lopez, *Zaccaria*, pp. 23 ff.

onized land afforded extensive pastures or sheep runs. By the late 13th century, under the impact of a growing wool industry, ever larger herds were coming to surround the cultivated land, and settled agriculture seems to have suffered considerably from the increasing demand for wool, and the growing herds that it favored.[25]

But before, Pisa had had in the Maremma one of Italy's bread baskets. Wine was less favored. Her flat and humid plain produces a bloated grape and a weak wine, although there were some good vintages—the white wine of Elba and the red of Castiglione della Pescaia. For vegetables the medieval taste cared little, but Pisan garden farms raised many onions, beans, and cabbages.[26] Pisa's mild climate, tempered further perhaps by the great forests then near her, was good for fruits: chestnuts (next to grain probably the most important food), olives, figs, pears, apples, cherries, later oranges and peaches. It was good too for apiculture.[27] To industries, Pisan agriculture gave important harvests of flax and hemp. Again for food, her rivers and swamps and the sea contributed a widely devoured eel and many varieties of fish.[28] This industry had the advantage of the Maremma's salt flats to permit export to the hinterland.

But of course, the chief importance of the sea to Pisa hardly needs expressing.

25. See below, pp. 118 ff.

26. See the list of fruits and vegetables contained in the *Breve potestatis* (1286), *Stat., I* 400–411.

27. 2545 70r 17 Oct. 1301, three hives given *in soccium*. For honey exported to Florence, see Ciasca, *Medici*, p. 521.

28. ASP, Roncioni, 5 Dec. 1297. A "pescheria" "que est a faucibus Arni ad Cotonem talliatum versus Portum Pisanum et ius piscandi" leased for five years for twenty pounds each year. Corsican waters seem especially important for fishing. ACC, 16 Aug. 1230, three pounds invested "in viadio de Cerlino . . . ad piscandum," for profit of six denarii per pound.

To be sure, as Chapter 6 will illustrate, Pisa's river harbor was miserable. However, not the Arno's depth but its location explains Pisa's importance. Guarding an easy road to the hinterland, playing the role Livorno has long since usurped, Pisa was the outlet for crowded Tuscany's people, wealth, and energy. When inland Tuscany's merchants first visited the Levantese marts, the men of the East reckoned them all as Pisans, and the inland traders thereby profited from the trade concessions and privileges the Pisans had earlier won.[29] Moreover, if Pisa was Tuscany's mouth, as a Florentine chronicler says, her importance transcended that single province.[30] Along Italy's straight-laced boot, she stood as the most important port from Genoa to Naples. The Constitutum Usus mentions merchants "from Tuscany, Lombardy, Romagna, or the March of Spoleto." [31] Giovanni Villani thought that Pisa earned her name by "weighing" Rome's tribute.[32] The papal couriers in the contracts, Pisan citizens and residents, apparently found quicker, surer contact with the world's corners from commercial Pisa than from pilgrim-flooded Rome. Their

29. Numerous examples in Davidsohn, *Geschichte, 1,* 383; *3,* 844; *4,* Pt. II, 256; *Forsch., 2,* nos. 2305, 2307, 2310; Villani, *Cronica, 2,* 78 (for Florentines); *Forsch., 2,* nos. 2302 and 2308 (for Sangemignanesi); Schaube, *Handelsg.,* pp. 356–7 (for Lucchesi).

30. Goro Dati, *Istoria di Firenze dal 1280 al 1405,* cited in Silva, *Gambacorta,* p. 3.

31. *Stat., 2,* 861; *vecturales* from Bologna members of guild of carters serving Pisa in 1218, *Stat., 3,* 1163 and Davidsohn, *Forsch., 3,* no. 996. Letter of exchange between Bologna and Pisa, ACC, 20 Jan. 1233. Bolognese merchant robbed on way to Pisa, 2629 274r 1 Sept. 1285. Letters of exchange between Cremona and Pisa, *Codice diplomatico cremonese,* ed. L. Astegiano, Monumenta historiae patriae, ser. 2, 21, (Turin, 1895), no. 676, 18 July 1256; no. 733, 18 Aug. 1260. See also 2521 175v 24 May 1306. Merchants from Parma at Pisa, 2543 35r 4 June 1263; from Rimini, 2543 38v 7 June 1263; from Milan 2629 274r 1 Sept. 1285. Papal *cursores* at Pisa, 2543 48r 18 Aug. 1263.

32. *Cronica, 1,* 69.

presence argues that if Pisa was Tuscany's mouth, she helped give Rome a tongue.

For Pisans themselves, their port made it possible to exploit a vast geographical and commercial frontier. Farthest removed from Pisa, on the north shore of the Sea of Azov, stood a Porto Pisano, though of its history almost nothing is known.[33] Federigo Visconti speaks of Tartar ambassadors at Pisa, but if this is not a dilettante's insult (*tartarus* equaling hell), he is confusing them with the Saracen rulers of the Holy Land—a mistake somewhat surprising, since Federigo had in his library a book on Tartar life and customs.[34] At Constantinople and at Salonica, Pisa's once flourishing colonies seem never fully to have recovered from the Fourth Crusade.[35] The south coast of Asia Minor also boasted a Porto Pisano, a pirates' haven and an *entrepôt* for trade with Armenia and central Asia.[36] By the middle 13th century the Pisan colonies once scattered through the Levant—Antioch, Tripoli, Tyre, Jaffa —had consolidated into one center, Acre.[37] After 1291, with Acre's loss, the colony retreated to Cyprus, there to

33. Lopez, *Zaccaria,* pp. 45 and 97. Borsari, "Rapporti," p. 491.

34. One of Federigo Visconti's sermons (41v) bears the title, given "respondendo nuntiis Tartarorum in clero pisano," in which Federigo demands that "terra sancta liberetur de manibus Tartarorum." Federigo also speaks (63r) of missionaries who had been "ad Tartaros" coming to Pope Innocent IV at the Council of Lyons "deferentes vitam et mores eorum scriptos in quodam libro quem idem dominus papa nobis dedit." This was almost certainly the account of the missionary John of Plano Carpini.

35. See Müller, *Documenti,* no. 46, where Pisa's colony at Constantinople in 1199 is shown to have consisted of thirty-two residents who owned or rented land in the city. For Salonica, ibid., p. 71. In 1223, the income of Pisa's two churches there was not sufficient to meet expenses (ibid., no. 72). Borsari, "Rapporti," traces the history of Pisa's colony at Constantinople in the 13th century.

36. Heyd, *Commerce, 1,* 235.

37. Ibid., *1,* 333.

have a long if undistinguished existence. In both Damietta and Alexandria, Islam's greatest port, Pisa had consuls, though by the late 13th century her headlong retreat from the Eastern trade had left her contracts without a trace of those cities. By then Pisa seems to have relied on Venetian *fondachi,* and the Venetian alliance permitted her considerable commerce in the Adriatic.[38] In North Africa, Pisa had churches and colonies in at least three cities: Tunis, Bugia, and Bona.[39] In Sicily, Messina, especially—but Palermo and Trapani as well—saw *universitates Pisanorum.*[40] At Naples stood another Porto Pisano, and at Salerno, too, Pisa had consuls.[41] In at least five Sardinian ports Pisa had "captains," and if Pisan hegemony in Corsica was crushed when the Genoese captured Bonifacio in 1195, trade was not.[42] In Genoa, Pisans had a church and loggia; in Southern France, Montpellier was the center of

38. Ibid., *1,* 412. The last privilege accorded to the Pisans by the Egyptian sultans dates from 1215. Although Pisa's statutes of the late 13th and early 14th centuries continue to mention consuls at Damietta and Alexandria (*Stat., 1,* 640; *3,* 426 and 528), the contracts have left no record of trade after the 1280's. For a contract drawn up at Alexandria in the "fondaco parvo Venetiquorum," ASP, Coletti, 6 Nov. 1252. For Pisans in the "gulfo Venetiarum," ASP, Comune A 82, 59v 16 Sept. 1299; at Ancona, 2523 40r 18 July 1308.

39. For a Pisan shop "posite in fundaco sive extra fundacum pisanum in Tunithi," and for the "consules mercatorum de Tunithi," ASP, Roncioni, 8 May 1240. For the "fundaco maiore pisano" and the Pisan church of Santa Maria at Bugia, ASP, Roncioni, 17 Oct. 1278. For the importance of the African consuls, ASP, Comune A 81 4r 4 Dec. 1245, "et ut consules maris et consules portuum Sardinee et consules de Tunithi et Bugea debeant securare eis naulum," in reference to ships requisitioned to fight the Genoese.

40. For several consuls at Messina by 1198, ACC 9 Oct. 1198, "apud Messanam in hospitio consulum Pisanorum Messane." Concession of Conradin in 1268 (Dal Borgo, *Raccolta,* p. 103) mentions colonies at Messina, Palermo, Trapani on Sicily and Naples and Brindisi on the mainland, and the *Breve curiae maris* (Schaube, *Konsulat,* pp. 159–60) at Salerno.

41. See above, n. 40.

42. For the Sardinian captains, Schaube, *Konsulat,* pp. 170–9.

Pisan trade.[43] With Catalonia, commerce in this early period seems largely limited to Majorca's alum, though even then Spain gave Pisa her famous leather, cordovan, which Pisa in turn imitated and sold.

In the middle 13th century Pisa's search for wealth in these overseas areas was, like every other phase of urban life, a compromise and a transition. The spice marts of the Levant had lost their pre-eminence and, for Pisa, much of their interest. For reasons later to be explored, Pisa was content to watch her Levant trade fall to a poor third behind Venice's and Genoa's. It was an age, too, before the Tuscan industrialization of wool carried all before it. Except for Flemish cloth, the wool trade slept. And if we ignore the Eastern luxuries so often and well described, Pisan trade before the peak of the wool traffic is found to be an effort to supplement the wealth her own contado had given her and for which, in incipient industries, her own contado had built the market.

Wood she carried from the Genoese riviera, from Salerno and the Kingdom of South Italy—the "Regno"—while Sardinia and especially Corsica still contributed "whatever she then had of forest timber." [44] For minerals, Cagliari in Sardinia and Provence provided salt. The uniqueness of Sardinia's contribution was, however, silver [45]

43. For Genoa, Schaube, *Konsulat,* p. 167. Merchants from Provence had a *fondaco* at Pisa by 1162 and Pisans a house at Montpellier by 1177, (Rossi-Sabatini, *L'Espansione,* p. 85).

44. For a Genoese selling wood at Pisa, 2530 168v 24 Jan. 1311. For Pisans taking wood from the South, *Relazioni,* no. 799 (1279), and concession of Conradin in 1268 (Dal Borgo, *Raccolta,* p. 103). From Salerno, ASP, Primaziale, 22 Oct. 1272; from Corsica, *Liber maiol.,* v. 98. For overseas imports in general, see the list of goods in the *Breve curiae mercatorum, Stat., 3,* 104–6 and 113–4; in the *Breve curiae maris, Stat., 3,* 589–93, copied partially by Pegolotti and included in his *Pratica,* pp. 204 ff.

45. On Sardinian mines, see R. Lopez, "Contributo alla storia delle miniere argentifere di Sardegna," offprint from *Studi economico-giuridici della r. università di Cagliari, 24* (1936), and Herlihy, "Coinage."

By 1131–32 Pisa had gained mining concessions on that island, and fifteen years later the Sicilian-Arab geographer Edrisi could comment that Sardinia exported silver to many lands of Christendom.[46] The 12th-century life of St. Rainerius relates how Germans traveling from Sardinia to Pisa during a storm hoisted, *in voto,* unminted silver on their mast.[47] The citation shows that Pisa exploited even then Sardinian silver and probably imported German miners for the task.

She took animals from the Regno, and horses from Provence.[48] On ships coming from Sardinia, Sicily, or the Regno, cheese seems never lacking, and salted meat is frequent too.[49] To supply Pisa's leather industry, Sardinia and Corsica both were the principal sources for wild animals, deer, and lamb. The squirrels of Sicily and Calabria, the goat and sheep skins of North Africa, the foxes of Provence, and the luxury furs from the North, from Hungary and Russia, added still more. Wine came from Corsica, and especially valued was the "Greek" wine of the Regno. Grain was sought in an ever-widening circle: first in Sardinia, then in Sicily and the Regno, Provence, Catalonia, Greece, and the Byzantine Empire.

Pisa, too, was conscious of spiritual wealth from this overseas world. According to Villani, the Pisans thought of the Florentines as "Arabs."[50] This term, used by cul-

46. The concession is in *Codex diplomaticus Sardinae,* ed. P. Tola, Historiae patriae monumenta, 10 (Turin, 1861), nos. 40 and 41. For Edrisi, *L'Italia descritta nel Libro del Re Ruggero compilato da Edrisi,* ed. and trans. M. Amari and C. Schiaparelli (Rome, 1888), p. 18.

47. *ASS, 24,* 374 C.

48. For horses from Provence taken by sea to Pisa, ASP, Comune A 86, 45r 22 Dec. 1316. For animals from the Regno, concession of Conradin in 1268 (Dal Borgo, *Raccolta,* p. 103).

49. For Sicilian cheese, 2544 23r 22 Nov., and especially the inventory of a cheese and meat shop, ASF, C 462 27r 11 Feb. 1302.

50. *Cronica, 2,* 78.

tured Tunisians in reference to inland nomads, the Pisans borrowed, we are told, for their own inland barbarians. Whatever the value of Villani's statement, Pisa could well lay claim to cosmopolitanism. When Federigo Visconti wished to illustrate for his flock the price of Christ's betrayal, he told them Judas received thirty silver "bezants," which as silver money came to Pisa mediated through the Arabs.[51] From Islam came, too, the geometric motifs so richly applied in Pisan-Lucchese architecture. From the Arabic are apparently derived the names of Pisa's most populous quarter, Kinsica, "enclosure," of two of her oldest gates, the Porta Samuel and the Porta Agazir, and perhaps some proper names.[52] Merchants came, too, enough even in the 11th century to dismay the pious; in the 12th century they still crowded Pisa, so that a woman possessed by the devil could without difficulty find infidel "friends," and we hear of intermarriage.[53] Most important, Leonardo Fibonacci, educated at Tunis, studying further at "Egypt, Syria, Greece, Sicily, and Provence"—probably the Middle Ages' greatest mathematician—popularized for Europe the Arabic numerals.[54] From Byzantium came customs; in 1218 a Pisan was sleeping in a "Greek" bed.[55] On her coins Pisa wrote Greek inscriptions.[56] At Constantinople, Burgundio Pisano learned his Greek, to play a leading role in the

51. 128v, "[Iudas] qui receptis xxx argenteis byzantiis arrengavit contra eum . . ."

52. Toscanelli, *Antichità*, 2, 436–7, and Amari, *Diplomi arabi*, pp. xxiv–xxvi.

53. P. Lonardo, "Gli Ebrei a Pisa sino alla fine del secolo XV," *SS*, 7 (1898), 174. *ASS, 24*, 360 E. For Arab merchants at Pisa in 1247, ASP, Alliata, 24 Nov. 1248.

54. G. Sarton, *Introduction to the History of Science* (Baltimore, 1931), 2, 611–13.

55. Among possessions of a Pisan, "unum ligneum grecescum," ASP, Primaziale, 27 April 1218.

56. See Herlihy, "Coinage."

12th-century's work of translation, so momentous for European thought.[57] With Catholic Europe, Pisa shares a hagiographical tradition with Messina.[58] Through her the art of Calabria and the thought of Islamic-Christian Spain irrigated the Renaissance.[59]

But the significance of Pisa's geographical position is not fully explored by describing the economic wealth and cultural cosmopolitanism it conveyed. The impact of Pisa's geography on the city's hygienic conditions, and through that on her population and demographic trends, is equally important, if distinctly less bright.

57. Sarton, *Science*, 2, 611–13.

58. See D. Puzzolo Sigillo, "Un'opera di pietà francescana dimenticata in Messina. La lanterna di S. Ranieri," *Archivio storico messinese*, 26–7 (1925–26), 235–80.

59. E. Cerulli, *Il "Libro della Scala" e la questione delle fonti arabo-spagnole della Divina Commedia*, Studi e Testi, 150 (Vatican City, 1949), discusses influences of Arabic-Spanish thought on Dante. An excellent introduction to Pisan art is B. Pace, A. Savelli, A. Niccolai and M. Salmi, *Pisa nella storia e nell'arte*, Milan and Rome, 1929.

3. DEMOGRAPHY

> There was much death at Pisa so that few or no one re-
> mained in the parish of San Cosma and San Cassiano and
> San Paolo a Ripa d'Arno.
>
> *Chronicon breve pisanum* (1257)

> I personally am a witness, since tertian fever did not in-
> fect me.
>
> FEDERIGO VISCONTI (1257)

ESTIMATING the population of a medieval town, always
a hazardous venture, involves two steps.[1] First, a suitable
base figure must be found, such as the size of a communal
army or fleet, the number of conjurors at a treaty, the
number of hearths in a tax list, and so forth. Second and
most difficult, a coefficient must be deduced which will
represent the relation of the base to the citizen core, that
is, the adult male members of the community who alone
figure in its public life and who constituted about one-

1. On the demographic history of Tuscany, see most especially K. J.
Beloch, *Die Bevölkerung des Kirchenstaates, Toskanas und der Herzog-
tümer am Po* (Berlin, 1940), Vol. 2 of his *Bevölkerungsgeschichte Italiens*.
It must be stated, however, that the figures for the areas enclosed by city
walls given by Beloch occasionally are at considerable variance with
estimates of other authors, and an effort should be made, where possible,
to check their accuracy. For the figures given in this chapter on the area
enclosed by Florence's walls I am following O. Marinelli, "La Carta topo-
grafica e lo sviluppo di Firenze," *RGI, 28* (1921), 18–38, (first circle, 23 ha.;
second circle, 80 ha.; third circle, 630 ha.) rather than Beloch (first circle,
32 ha.; second, 105 ha.; third 512 ha.), as Marinelli's are more in accordance
with my own calculations based on the map of Florence given by Davidsohn, *Geschichte, 1*, Pt. II. Beloch's figure of 114 ha. for Pisa's size is clearly
wrong, and I am rather following the estimate of 185 ha., excluding the
Arno, given by Pedreschi, "Geografia," p. 124. Beloch's figure is approxi-

35

third of the total population. The lack of an objectively based coefficient has rendered divergent the several attempts to calculate Pisa's medieval population. A hitherto unused base figure, however, offers a fresh approach. From the latter half of the 13th century, from 1293 but fortunately unaffected by Meloria's human loss, has come a matricula of the guild of notaries.[2] At that time exactly 232 notaries practiced at Pisa. Another source gives the coefficient. In 1228 over 4,200 Pisans, 4,271 by my count, swore to uphold a treaty.[3] Clearly a generous cross-section of urban society, the oath in giving the number of notaries (79) among the 4,271 gives, too, a ratio made secure by the numbers involved: 1 to 54. Estimating on both ratio and base, we arrive at a citizen core of 12,500 and a total population in 1293 of about 38,000. By 1293, Pisa had not yet ceased growing; but she was nearing her medieval peak.

More important than absolute figures are the dynamic and relative aspects of demography: dynamic in relation to trends of growth or decline, relative in relation to Pisa's principal rivals.

---

mately accurate for the area of Pisa north of the Arno, and may possibly have been intended by the author to represent the area actually enclosed by 1200, although he does not say so expressly. For further discussion of Pisan demography, see C. Barbagallo, *Medio Evo* (Turin, 1935), p. 948, Vol. *3* of his *Storia universale,* and especially A. Rossi, "Lo Sviluppo demografico di Pisa dal XII al XV secolo," BSP, *14–16* (1945–47), 5–62. Both estimates (40,000–50,000) are based on an oath of 4200 Pisans taken in 1228 (below, n. 3) and presumably are meant to express Pisa's population in that year. In 1228, Pisa's population was probably not half that number. Beloch's figure (p. 161) of upward of 15,000 is more prudent.

2. In *Stat., 3,* 841. The list is not strictly the guild's matricula, but an extract from the matricula made for tax-collecting purposes. It represents the number not of notaries physically present at Pisa but of those enrolled in the guild, as shown by the entry, *exbannitus,* after several of the names. Even a notary imprisoned at Genoa could be expected to be on it.

3. *Caleffo, 1,* 365 ff.

In 1164 against Lucca, Pisa fielded an army of 3,000 soldiers and 400 horsemen.[4] Since all citizens who could bear arms had to serve, since neither levies from the contado nor foreign mercenaries had importance in this early period, a coefficient of three and one-half to one is a fair one. In 1164 Pisa's population was no more than 11,000.

And though it can only be sketchily reconstructed, the demographic curve that joins these two figures demands a study. The closing decades of the 12th century saw rapid growth. The area of early medieval Pisa was about thirty hectares; her new walls, begun not long after 1150, enclosed about 114 hectares north of the Arno (the walls of Kinsica, the quarter south of the Arno, were not completed until shortly after 1300). In 1182, the men of the urban parish of San Cristofano could no longer fit into their old church.[5] Approximately between 1160 and 1190, the money of Pisa and of Lucca depreciated by 50 per cent, here as often in the history of medieval Italy evidence of profound economic changes.[6] Specifically at Pisa, for the first time commercially raised and processed fur—lamb pelts—cut the market from under foxes, rabbits, and squirrels—the products of the chase.[7] When the furriers in 1193 for the first time acquired themselves a church, their newborn brotherhood counted twenty-three.[8] In the oath of 1228 they were sixty-four and we cannot estimate absentees. The institutional changes were profound: the adoption of the commune's first proportionate direct tax on property, the *libra;* the appearance of the *curia maris;* the birth and recognition of Pisa's earliest artisan guilds (tan-

4. Maragone, *Annales,* p. 29, year 1164. Rossi, "Sviluppo," p. 26.
5. *Reg. pis.,* no. 560.
6. Herlihy, "Coinage," p. 149.
7. See below, p. 148.
8. Document in *Stat., 3,* 1092.

ners, iron workers, furriers and butchers); the agony of the communal consulate and the rise of the podesta. Then, too, Burgundio Pisano and Leonardo Fibonacci gave Pisa an intellectual stature she was never again to equal.

From roughly 1200 to 1250 the signs of growth and change subside in economy, guilds, and government. If a government notary could live on three to four pounds a year in 1227, in 1247 he still received that salary.[9] Then in the late 1240's and especially during the episcopacy of Federigo Visconti (1257–77), the demographic curve surges upward at what seems an almost incredible pace. In the six years of 1227–32 the communal treasurers averaged an income of less than 2400 pounds a year; in 1288 they counted near 40,000—an increase over sixteenfold (over eight in terms of the value in silver of the coins) in a city supposedly languishing.[10] If one could have lived on four pounds a year in 1247, by 1266 the cost was more like twelve to fifteen pounds.[11] Again we hear of a church so crowded that men within it could not breathe for room— this time San Piero a Grado at the Arno's ancient mouth, whose old church had sufficed since the time St. Peter him-

9. ASP, Roncioni, 4 June 1233, two notaries receive eighteen pounds each for six years of service, and ASP, Alliata, 24 Nov. 1248, a notary receives three pounds for a year's service.

10. The commune's income from 1227–32 was 14,091 pounds, eight solidi, one denarius (ASP, Roncioni, 4 June 1233). In 1288 for the months of January, February, and March, the income was 9968 pounds, eight solidi, and nine denarii (ASP, Alliata, 28 Dec. 1288).

11. In 1267 (ASP, Alliata, 27 Dec.) the year's salary for a tax official was twelve pounds; in 1282 the salary for a lighthouse keeper was fifteen (ASP, Coletti, 13 March 1282). Twelve to fifteen pounds is the average amount awarded by Pisan courts for the yearly support of dependents. See 2516 3v (1273), 2545 28r (1283), 2545 113r (1283), 2523 31v (1308), and ASP, Trovatelli, 24 Aug. 1284. Of the fifteen pounds, in one instance (2515 90r 8 Nov. 1272), two pounds went for rent, one for incidentals, and the remaining twelve pounds were spent for grain (five staia) and wine (five barrels) and clothing.

self, we are told, built it on coming from the Holy Land.[12] In 1262 when Federigo Visconti made his visitations, he remarked with pride and weariness that he must have confirmed 10,000 persons.[13] As the parish of San Cristofano heralded the first demographic upsurge by building a new church, so it marked the second by sinking a new well.[14] Of Pisan building—the Camposanto, the Baptistry, Santa Caterina, San Francesco, and the list goes on—this is the golden age. In size the two churches of Santa Caterina (Dominican) and San Francesco (Franciscan) rival the cathedral, and of course the art which this building brought is that of the dawning Renaissance. This is the age of brick, now widely applied in construction, of earthenware, of the peach and orange, of the use of vernacular in literature and spaghetti in the diet, in short, of a changing and advancing standard of living that argues an increase in population.[15] It is the period too of profound economic and social changes which this study must analyze.

Of all the evidence of demographic upsurge, most telling are the chartularies. They provide statistics from the unit where demographic history was written: an urban parish.

San Cristoforo, or, in its more vernacular spelling, San Cristofano, was a parish of Kinsica, Pisa's business quarter on the Arno's left bank. We have seen it building a new church in 1182 and a new well in 1273. And in 1273 when

12. Visconti, 49v. The old church was destroyed "propter pressuram hominum qui ibidem fere sufficabantur."

13. Ibid., 134r.

14. 2515 25v 3 April 1273. Cf. Lupi, "Casa pisana," *ASI*, ser. 5, *29* (1902), 217–18.

15. *Vermicelli*, apparently spaghetti, is mentioned at Pisa in 1284. 2545 118v 13 Feb. 1284, where a baker hires a helper "in faciendis et vendendis vermicellis." Oranges are common by the early 14th century, 2630 8v (1308). Peaches are found at Lucca by 1310, Sardi, *Contrattazioni*, p. 149.

the parish captains sounded the bells for the men to gather
to discuss the well, twenty-five persons responded. This
was a rump *parliamentum,* of course. The attendance in
1228—104 persons—was much better because the notary
came three times to the parish over several months to so-
licit conjurors. However, the meeting of 1273, recorded
by the notary Ugolinus, himself working in—if not a member of—the parish, may be used in reconstructing San
Cristofano's population, by means of which Pisa's demography can best be examined. For if San Cristofano came
collectively to Ugolinus to record its business, it came dis-
tributively as well, and in the years 1272 to 1274, the great,
the poor, the noble and the commoner, the exploiter, the
exploited, and the bystander are there to be counted.

From 1272 to 1274, 117 parishioners or residents appear
in Ugolinus' contracts as principals or witnesses.[16] That
the number is more than that of the conjurors of 1228 at
this one notary's is suggestive; however, our reconstructed
parish population permits a study of demography that pre-
scinds from the unknown and uncontrollable factor of absentees. It allows a study of the origins of the individual
parishioner, whether native or immigrant. Of course, chartularies do not tell all. Only if a man figures in many contracts will the chances approach certainty that Ugolinus
will let fall some hint of his background. A study of immigrants versus natives in San Cristofano will yield results
conservative in the extreme.

But if conservative, the results are the more remarkable.
Over 50 per cent of the parishioners (62 out of 117) are
new arrivals in San Cristofano.[17]

16. See Appendix I, Population.

17. The significance of the toponymic surname, "de N." has recently
come under considerable discussion. R. Emery, "The Use of the Surname
in the Study of Medieval Economic History," *Medievalia et Humanistica,*

The evidence of the chartularies is not isolated. With characteristic insight, G. Volpe noted that of the notaries from Kinsica in the matricula of 1293, 65 out of 98 appear to be recent immigrants from the contado.[18] Further, in the *Breve antianorum*, the list of citizens elected to Pisa's governing board after 1289, over two-thirds are rural in origin. Volpe, and P. Silva who followed him, interpreted this peculiarity as evidence of a marked influx from the contado specifically for the period after Meloria. The interpretation has validity, with the warning, however, that both notaries and anziani represent a relatively exalted economic status and their behavior cannot be too lightly generalized. The chartularies, besides illuminating all levels of Pisan society, place this immigration better in time than does the Breve antianorum. They show how much the 60's and 70's were years of growth and change.

This phenomenal urban growth in the late 13th century may well be considered the salient fact in the economic history not only of Pisa, but of Tuscany generally and indeed of Italy. Florence's new circle of walls, projected in 1284, completed in 1333, enclosed an area (630 hectares)

---

7 (1952), 43–50; R. S. Lopez, "Concerning Surnames and Places of Origin," ibid., *8* (1954), 6–16; R. Emery, "A Further Note on Medieval Surnames," ibid., *9* (1955), 104–6. Emery cautions that a toponymic surname is no sure proof that its bearer came from the place in question. While his point is well taken, there can be no doubt that the use of "de N." in Pisa in the 13th century indicates recent immigration and that the toponym is not yet standardized as a family name (with the exception of noble houses, which possessed surnames considerably earlier than the *popolani*). Cf. 2515 82r, "Nuccius de Singna filius quondam Puliensis de sancto Miniato." Evidence of this is the fact that the name "de N." is consistently used in conjunction with the formula "qui moratur Pisis, in cappella N.," which, in contradistinction to the formula "de cappella N.," describes new arrivals in, rather than the natives of, a parish. Cf. 2543 32r 30 May 1263, "Lazarius quondam Talliapanis qui fuit de scripto burgo sancti Genesii et nunc moratur Pisis in cappella sancti Cristofori . . ."

18. Volpe, "Pisa," p. 295, and Silva, *Gambacorta*, p. 13.

over seven times greater than the area (80 ha.) enclosed
by the older walls, begun in 1172, which had girded her
in the early 13th century. Moreover, this growth of cities
seems to have represented much more than the result of
natural increase, and the draining of unneeded younger
sons from the rural farms and estates. From the one area
in Tuscany where full statistics of population trends in
the countryside have survived—from the contado of Pistoia
—we can conclude that the density of rural population
was falling considerably in the latter half of the 13th century, undoubtedly as a result primarily of this influx to
the city.[19] From Pisa too we have evidence, albeit much
scantier, of a similar, sharp decline in the density of rural
settlement in the later 13th century.[20] Some of the factors
behind this mass exodus from the countryside we shall be
dealing with extensively in the chapters to follow; here,
however, let us draw a tighter comparison between the
demographic history of Pisa and that of her inland rivals.

In comparison with Lucca, Pisa's bitterest Tuscan enemy, Pisa was both clearly more precocious in her growth
and probably remained, even in the fourteenth century,
a slightly larger city. Lucca began her second circle of walls
about 1200, and completed them in 1265, about a half
century after Pisa had begun her comparable circle. The
75 ha. of land they embraced were less than, though not
significantly less than, the 114 ha. enclosed by Pisa's walls
north of the Arno. Though Pisa in the late 13th and early
14th centuries was to bring her area to about 185 ha. by
enclosing her quarter of Kinsica, south of the Arno, Lucca

19. Cf. *Liber focorum districtus Pistorii (a. 1226)*. *Liber finium districtus Pistorii (a. 1255)*, ed. Q. Santoli, Fonti per la storia d'Italia, 93,
Rome, 1956. The comparison (p. 22) of these two surveys shows a "progressive depopulation of the countryside." L. Zdekauer believed that by 1294
the population of the contado of Pistoia had fallen by as much as 50
per cent, (ibid., p. 24).

20. See below, pp. 124 ff.

was not to add further to her walls until the 16th century. Moreover, in 1334 Lucca drank 168,300 barrels of wine every year.[21] On the objective coefficient of the medieval Tuscan's considerable thirst—five to six barrels per year— she had a wine-drinking residency of from 28,000 to 30,000 and a population of about 40,000. The figures would seem to show that for all their ruinous wars, neither of the enemies had secured a decisive advantage. The critical comparison is rather with Tuscany's miracle: Florence.

Florence's second circle of walls, begun in 1172 and carried rapidly to completion, enclosed about 80 ha., less than the area of 114 ha. of contemporary Pisa. Almost certainly, throughout the 12th century Pisa remained Tuscany's largest town. Giovanni Villani states that in 1252 Pisa had not half the population of Florence.[22] This is the boast of a Florentine and a noncontemporary. It does, however, set the trend, as with the trend if not the pace the evidence of city walls is in agreement. When shortly after 1300 Pisa had extended her walls to enclose the quarter of Kinsica on the Arno's left bank, her area was about 185 ha. Florence, on the other hand, in 1284 projected a completely new third circle of walls, which when completed, by 1333, enclosed 630 ha.—extremely high for a medieval city. The comparison would show that Florence secured her own demographic advantage the same generation that Pisa, too, was growing most rapidly.

But by 1300, that advantage was decisive. According to the figures given by Giovanni Villani, Florence's population was then about 95,000.[23] We can reach a comparable figure (96,000) by applying our coefficient of notaries to the

21. Cited in Sardi, *Contrattazioni*, p. 138.
22. *Cronica*, 2, 78. Villani does not of course here have the authority of a contemporary witness.
23. For the latest and best reconstruction of Florence's population on the basis of the statistics given by Villani, see E. Fiumi, "La Demografia fiorentina nelle pagine di Giovanni Villani," *ASI, 108* (1950), 78–158.

600 Villani later says served the city. By the end of the 13th century Pisa was indeed not half Florence's size. To explain this differential growth is to search for diversity in likeness.

Of course, for Pisa's people, the sea had its lure. To give instances of Pisans found or even settled from Catalonia to Kiev, from Tunis to Provence, of numerous half-colonists, half-conquerors in Sardinia, is easy. Did not even the father of St. Bona leave wife and babe and settle permanently in the Levant, to marry again (and from the adulterous union were born, we are told, the Patriarch of Jerusalem, the Master of the Templars, and the Master of the Hospitalers)? [24] Yet of mass colonization in these overseas areas there was nothing. From this flux of population —ever the mark of the maritime—Pisa might have gained as much as she lost: we don't know.

More serious a check was war, for war in the late 13th century was serious business. When Lucca's gentle maiden St. Zita thought of visiting a favorite shrine in Pisan territory, she was told that if the Pisans found her, she was apt not to escape alive.[25] A Lucchese agricultural contract speculates on losses "from the hail or the Pisans." [26] In the generation before 1305, the frontier town of Quosa dropped from thirty to ten men, as her people sought a safer home.[27] Pisa's heavy losses at Meloria were of course basic in slowing her population growth, especially since the Genoese decided not to kill their Pisan prisoners, thereby to prevent their wives back home from remarrying, and thereby to cut the Pisan birth rate. Still, even Pisa's

24. *ASS, 20, 146* A.
25. *ASS, 12, 509* C.
26. "Pisanorum vel glandine" in contract of 1224 in Sardi, *Contrattazioni*, p. 54.
27. ASP, Comune A 83 7or 31 Oct. 1305.

ill fortune at Meloria and Genoese ingenuity cannot sufficiently explain Pisa's slower population growth, since
they come too late—in 1284, when Florence, as shown by
her newly projected walls, had already secured her predominance.[28] In Pisan demography the critical element is
neither the lure of the sea nor the losses of war but the
lay of the land.

Pisa's plain is low.[29] Pisa herself, some seven miles from
the sea, stands above sea level only twelve feet; Cascina,
ten miles above Pisa, only twenty-four. Falling at the rate
of less than 0.3 per 1,000, the Arno cannot drain the high
waters of the Tuscan autumn and winter. Of a great flood
in 1332 a Pisan chronicler has left an awesome description,
telling how the whole Pisan plain was submerged and that
only by boat or horse could one travel in Kinsica, Pisa's
largest quarter.[30] The picture is not unique. In the late
13th century the river seems yearly to have passed its
banks; in 1167, it flooded nine times in one autumn.[31]
Even in the Constitutum Usus, Pisa was desperately fighting this problem. In times of flood the Valdarno's numerous communes north of the city were ordered to cut their
dikes, to let the Arno drown their lands, so that the city
at least might preserve its "pulcherrimus aspectus." [32]

Pisa's plain while low is not flat. Water collects in la-
goon-like *tomboli* along the shore and in extensive swamps
inland. The area northeast of the city stretching to the
Monti Pisani was a swamp throughout the 13th century.
Pisa herself was surrounded by water: the Arno and a half-
canal, half-river called the Auser, which, coming down

28. *Stradario storico e amministrativo della città e del comune di
Firenze* (Florence, 1913), p. xv.

29. Statistics on the Arno in Pedreschi, "Geografia," p. 108.

30. *RIS, 24,* 668 D.

31. Maragone, *Annales,* p. 44, year 1168 (Pisan style).

32. *Constitutum Usus, Stat., 2,* 955.

from the Monti Pisani, formed a moat for the city walls and created, even within those walls, a swamp.

Drinking water was a problem.[33] Although wealthy houses might possess an elaborately engraved plumbing system, drawing well water, or perhaps rain water, pure and precious, from private cisterns, the bulk of the people depended on wells. From Pisa's inability to build an aqueduct, a key in the Medici revival, undoubtedly the health of her people suffered much. Some houses had wells in the narrow courtyards into which they opened, and such private wells could serve whole neighborhoods. Or else, with booming populations, parishes like San Cristofano sank the wells from which the people drew water with buckets (*caldarias a puteo*), or even helmets turned, like swords into ploughshares, to peaceful purposes.[34]

In spite of these dubious health conditions, Pisa's republican years have been viewed as something of a golden age in the spotty history of Pisan hygiene.[35] The interpretation is based on a double argument: Pisa's undeniable status, maintained at least up to 1200, as the largest and commercially most advanced city in Tuscany—a status enhanced further by her marvelous overseas expansion; and the provisions of her statutes which legislated valiantly against her rampaging waterways. Indeed, to the latter argument the chartularies can make a contribution, since if mention of a project does not prove its execution, the

33. For a well, placed between a house and stable and serving "illi qui habitant in aliis suis domibus scripti Mathei de terris circumstantibus," 2543 49r 24 Aug. 1263. For a well in a "claustrum" or courtyard, 2523 213v 7 Feb. 1309. For engraved metal drain pipes, see Lupi, "Casa pisana," *ASI*, ser. 5, 29 (1902), 222.

34. 2521 58v (1306), "caldariam unam a puteo que fuit una cervelleria."

35. Cf. A. Feroci, *Le Condizioni igieniche di Pisa e del suo circondario*, Pisa, 1875; R. Fiaschi, *Le Magistrature pisane delle acque* (Pisa, 1938), pp. 18–19.

chartularies point up the actual expenditures of energy
and wealth to meet the problem.[36] The argument performs
a service in emphasizing that the health conditions of Pisa
suffered a marked deterioration paralleling her political
collapse; indeed, other sources can spell out the cost of
Pisa's exhaustion in terms of floods, ruined crops, disease,
and flight.[37]

However, this view has had the unfortunate result of
tying hygiene too closely to public works and hence to
political factors, so that the deterioration is looked upon
entirely as the result and not as a cause of Pisa's decline.
In Volpe's rich studies on 13th-century Pisa, hygienic conditions are never considered. But of course, the expendi-
ture of much wealth and energy on public works does not
prove that conditions are salubrious but only that the problem is great. To evaluate those conditions we must look
elsewhere.

Of course, there are plagues. In the year of Meloria,
Salimbene describes a pestilence which decimated the
city.[38] "And the city that went out a thousand there shall
remain a hundred; and the city that went out a hundred
there shall remain ten." In 1257, another plague reduced
to "few or no one" three urban parishes.[39] Significantly,
all three parishes are in Kinsica, near neighbors of San

36. The chartulary of Cherlus, 2629, mentions eight separate public-
works projects on which Pisans were working in 1285. See below, p. 96,
n. 27.

37. For example, ASP, Comune A 88 6or (1322), a broken dike on the
Arno caused a flood so that "quamplures familie vallis Arni . . . vix
modo etiam possunt exire de domibus." ASP, Comune A 88 93r (1322),
since the Crespina river had not been dredged for over ten years, the
valley was flooded with every rain and the water ruined "quasi totam
bladam vallis communis."

38. Cronica, p. 770.

39. Chronicon breve pisanum, ed. in appendix to Maragone, Annales,
p. 108. The year should be 1257. See Davidsohn, Forsch., 4, 123.

Cristofano, and in the oath of 1228 were among Pisa's most populous.

Plagues, however, are common to all medieval towns; they may even be signs of growth. And without statistics to evaluate mortality, history must rather consider the types of diseases to see if Pisa had a cross greater than her neighbors.

And for such a diagnosis of Pisa's endemic diseases, we have suitable sources. In the lives of Pisa's saints, in the miracles they wrought, is a thorough catalogue of medieval ills, and the ghastliness of the description is only slightly mitigated by the unfailing happy ending. Most rich are the almost one hundred miracles of St. Rainerius, most of which were performed after his death (1160) and are described by a contemporary. Thus a left-handed compliment to Pisan cattle-raising is the prevalence of lockjaw, ranging from swollen jaws to cases where the patient had to be fed with a knife.[40] Dysentery and stomach pains confirm what could have been imagined from our knowledge of Pisa's water.[41] Most significant, however, is the number of fever cases, of all diseases the most numerous.[42] Fever, common to so many diseases, is likewise the most difficult to identify. The one clue is periodic occurrence: *febris quotidiana, semi-tertiana, tertiana, quaterna,* and so forth. Periodic occurrence is characteristic of malaria, and when reference to such a periodic fever comes from an area (such as the coastal regions of Tuscany) with a long history of malaria infestation, the identification seems certain.[43]

And the ominous rhythm appears in the miracles of St.

40. *ASS, 24,* 367 F, 369 A, 377 F.

41. "Fluxium disenterie," ibid., 364 D, 368 F.

42. Ibid., 362 E, 368 A, 369 A, 369 B, 370 A, 372 D, 373 D, 375 C, 377 A 377 B, 377 F, 380 C. And from the life of St. Bona, *ASS, 20,* 146 E, 151 A, 157 A, 157 F.

43. For the identification, see E. Kind, "Malaria," *Realencyclopedia der classischen Altertumswissenschaft, 14* (1928), 830–46.

Rainerius: *hemitritaeum,* Greek for semi-tertiana, and again febris quotidiana.[44] In the life of St. Bona (d. 1207), we find among her miracles the curing of a *febris quaterna,* and the saint herself suffered from fever all her life.[45] Indeed, with all reverence to Pisa's saints, we may wonder how many of these miracles were permanent cures and how many the tricks of a malaria infection. Even before 1200 Pisa faced a lingering endemic malaria she could not stamp out.

But only with the population increase after 1250 does malaria work its full havoc. In 1257 when Federigo Visconti remarked that tertian fever had not infected him, he tells us what was behind the plague that leveled the three parishes. Another time he told his flock: "The weather is having a tremendous effect contrary to nature and if it doesn't change for a while we must fear some pestilence."[46] And we know what pestilence he means. In 1285 when exuberant Lucca sent an army down the Serchio to Pisa's plain, her soldiers met an enemy more lethal than the prostrate Pisans.[47] That year at Lucca a plague "de terzianis," of malaria, broke out, and Lucca's chronicler Tolomeo tells us that its chief victims were the valorous veterans of the Serchio campaign. From this too we can identify the plague which Salimbene describes at Pisa after Meloria.

By the end of the century, Pisa of a summer was always half infested. For the year 1299, a year undistinguished in the crowded annals of plagues, the *Provvisioni* of Pisa's anziani tells us what Federigo Visconti's bad-weather pestilence could do. On July 19, Franciscus Bellomus had to be

44. *ASS, 24,* 371 D, 380 C.
45. *ASS, 20,* 146 F, 157 A.
46. 123v. "Quia contra naturam temporis maximus est effectus propter quod [*read:* quem ?] multum timendum quem [*read:* quod ?] si tempora temporaliter se non recludent de aliqua pestilentia dubitatur."
47. *Die Annalen des Ptolomeus von Lucca in doppelter Verfassung,* ed. B. Schmeidler, MGH, Ss, new ser., *8,* (Berlin, 1930), p. 207, 7-20.

relieved from service in the *planus portus* because of
"fever." [48] His successor lasted less than two months before
declaring he could serve no more "since he is sick." On
August 10, Bacciameus Tadi had to be relieved of service
in Elba; at that post his successor could take no more than
one month. Ganus Del Ponte sent to Castiglione della
Pescaia in the Maremma was good only "for a few days"
before fleeing back to Pisa. At the same time, so many
government notaries became sick "some in the city and
some in the contado" that rural administration in "certain
captaincies" was paralyzed so that the captains could not
perform their services. Little willing, however, were the
captains to remain at such posts, and of them we are told
"many . . . are away from Pisa." All business had to be
prorogued until autumn from San Piero a Grado to the
lower Livorno hills and into the Maremma.

The wonder may seem not that Pisa declined but that
she was ever great. However, Pisa had controlled her endemic malaria, partially through public works. Federigo
Visconti was well aware that stagnant water was "rotten,"
and the standard theme of Pisa's river policy was to keep
the water flowing. [49] However, the most effective means of
holding the disease in check seem to have been a rarified
population coupled with a flight from the city one step
ahead of the hot weather. For the cycle of malaria is built
as much on men as on mosquitoes, and the more numerous
the infected, in geometric ratio the greater the chances
of new infections. This flight is most evident where the
problem was severest: Elba and the Maremma. Up to the
late 13th century, Pisa worked her iron mines intensively
only in winter, and the year-round, intensive operation of

48. For what follows, ASP, Comune A 82 6or–64r.

49. 122r "Quod prout in aquis que si in aliqua fovea vel alio loco
fuerint sine motu et non labantur super terram corrupte sunt et infime
. . . si vero moveantur et labantur sane efficiuntur et meliorantur."

the mines after that time, which seems to have reduced
the miners to physical ruin, may be considered as much as
mosquitoes the cause of the upsurge of malaria.[50]

From the city, too, an exodus in the summer is evident.
Recent immigrants were reluctant to break ties with the
contado. To become a citizen and attain the privileges
thereof, the immigrant had to live in the city nine
months.[51] Even to serve as a notary, the required residency
was nine months per year.[52] In the earlier period, we hear
of cityfolk returning to the countryside to help with the
harvests; by 1286, however, to prevent peasants from en-
listing in a city parish, securing the tax concessions thereof,
but continuing to work their farms, the commune had
come to forbid such agricultural labors on the part of its
citizens.[53] Cityfolk were still allowed, however, to live in
the countryside for a three-months' period. Those who
could might still flee the city during the mosquito-infested
months of July, August and September—those whom economic advantage had forced to the city but whom reasons
of health drove back to the countryside during the summer whose dangers they knew.

It remains to place these hygienic conditions in the over-
all picture of Pisa's 13th-century history.

That in Pisa's fall from expanding Europe's forefront
to a sleepy provincial town hygiene played a role needs no
argument. "You who were once as the stars in the heaven
in multitude," said Salimbene to the Pisans, "shall be few
in number." [54] Indeed, few in numbers, malaria-smitten
Pisa was weak in moral energies as well. Federigo Visconti

50. Pintor, "Elba," has much on Elba's hygienic conditions in the 14th
century.
51. *Stat., 1,* 204–5.
52. *Stat., 3,* 776.
53. *Stat., 2,* 1000 and *Stat., 1,* 205.
54. *Cronica,* p. 770.

compliments Pisa's merchants on profiting the world through intelligence (*per sapientiam*) rather than through violence (*per potentiam*).[55] In Tuscan lyric poetry the theme appears again, but with a significant twist.[56] The Pisans are the wolves who get nothing through energy (*forza*) but only through cheating. By the 14th century the city's cultural contribution is almost nil. She has not even a chronicler, and three men from the contado—Corvaria, Vico, and Sardinia—write of her ruin. From the contado, too, comes her single important heretic. For the 14th century G. Volpe has again well noted the remarkable cultural status of the contado *vis-à-vis* the city, but he interprets it as evidence of the contado's growing importance rather than the city's progressive decadence.[57]

By the middle 14th century Pisa was no place to reside. Boccaccio describes the women of Kinsica as "wormy lizards." [58] In 1345 when a Milanese army camped ten miles south of Pisa at Colle Salvetti, the soldiers complained that "because of flies and mosquitoes which were there and because the land was rotten, many got sick and died and almost everyone became yellow with swollen bodies because of the bad state there." [59] By 1550 Pisa had a population of 8,600.[60]

55. 80v. "Cristus filius dei dicitur negotiator sive mercator per excellentiam qui vollens negotiando humanum genus lucrari per sapientiam . . . fecerat . . . non per potentiam." 81v "Patet quanto filius dei fuit negotiator sive mercator et lucratus est . . . genus humanum per sapientiam et non per violentiam."

56. Cf. Volpe, "Pisa," p. 193.

57. Ibid., p. 298.

58. *Il Decameron*, ed. G. Petronio (Turin, 1950), 1, 287, second day, story ten.

59. Cited by Fiaschi, *Acqua*, p. 19. Other examples of Pisa's hygienic conditions in the later Middle Ages may be found in Palmieri, "De Captivitate Pisarum," *RIS, 19*, 12.

60. Repetti, *Dizionario, 4*, 374.

Pisa's utter collapse in the later Middle Ages is the appearance of the familiar pattern of a malaria-infected community: high mortality particularly among the young, exhaustion of physical and moral energies, and the loss of the population's stronger elements to better homes. In part it is the history of her military crisis which crippled efforts to control her environment. As such it forms part of a cycle of military defeat, financial exhaustion, ruinous taxation, breakdown of public works, worse hygiene, worse military defeats, and so forth. In part it is the history of a mounting level of social control and social obligations which prevented the physical freedom of former years. In 1286 Pisa had to screen her sewers to prevent debtors from slipping out at night, away from the city and their obligations.[61] But the prosperous artisan found in his economic interests as effective a screen. More nearly, Pisa's catastrophe was the cost of growth: the booming population, urbanization, industrialization, and integrated living that growth brought. In this sense Pisa was foredoomed to ruin in the same way all urban Europe was foredoomed to the later ravages of the Black Death. The difference is that for Pisa, her swamps imposed on her a sort of Malthusian limitation which she had neither the medicine nor the technology to break. But before she had pushed toward that limitation, she had made a history which paralleled and at times anticipated the profound economic and social changes witnessed by towns more fortunate than she.

61. *Stat., 1,* 475.

4. POLITICS

[St. Francis] after he had grown rich from trade wanted to become a noble as do the Lucchesi and the Genoese. The Pisans don't follow this custom but do things in another manner as you are seeing.

FEDERIGO VISCONTI (CA. 1275)

FROM 1250 TO 1300 the political development of overriding significance was the rise, in Pisa and in all Tuscany's principal cities, of the *popolo*.[1]

The popolo was a commune, in the sense of a society created by a sworn pledge. It was, more accurately, a commune of communes, a union of from twenty to thirty *societates armorum*, armed companies, geographically based but unevenly distributed among the city's four quarters. Appearing in the first decades of the 13th century, apparently as in other Italian cities taking their juridical model from Bologna, these military companies recruited and provisioned the units of the communal army. Because

1. The political history of Pisa from 1250 to 1350 is the subject of a book, soon to be published, by E. Cristiani. Until its appearance, see, for constitutional development, Volpe, *Istituzioni* (which does not, however, go much beyond 1250), and U. Congedo, *Il Capitano del popolo in Pisa nel secolo XIV*, Pisa, 1908. Of works dealing with the popolo in other Tuscan cities, Salvemini, *Magnati*, is old but still highly stimulating, and U. G. Mondolfo, *Il Populus a Siena* (Genoa, 1911), is short but good. For the foreign relations of the Pisan commune, see D. Winter, *Die Politik Pisas während der Jahre 1268–82* (Halle, 1906) and, out of many general studies that touch upon Pisan history, E. Jordan, *Les Origines de la domination angevine en Italie* (Paris, 1909), G. Caro, *Genua und die Mächte am Mittelmeer 1257–1311* (Halle, 1895–99), Davidsohn, *Geschichte*, and C. Manfroni, *Storia della marina italiana*, Livorno, 1902.

of pressing military needs, the armed companies were of
all urban societies the most accessible to the immigrant;
they therefore gave the newcomer his principal institutional expression. During the 1230's the companies seem
to have had some sort of union, a *societas concordie,* and
some sort of chief, a *rector.* But by neither union nor chief
was the city's constitutional system permanently impressed.

The popolo has been called with reason a "state within
a state." The term, however, could as well be applied to
any number of urban societies, noble consorteries (which
collected taxes), for example, or guilds (as the *curia maris,*
which fought wars). More accurately, the popolo was that
one of many "states within a state" which eventually reduced the others to subservience, seized the *signoria,* the
sovereign power, and became the State.

In Tuscany, the emergence of the popolo is intimately
connected with the momentous struggle between the imperial house of Hohenstaufen, then trying to weld the
South and North of Italy into a unified state, and the
papacy, which saw in the success of the Hohenstaufen am-
bitions Rome's encirclement and the compromise of its
own political independence. Of course, the parties in the
Italian cities that took their names from the contending
giants, the Guelfs (papalists) and Ghibellines (imperial-
ists), can hardly be thought of as zealous, unfagging, and
faithful supporters of their great allies, and still less as the
representatives, within the city, of fixed social groupings.
To be sure, aristocratic parties are traditionally thought
of as Ghibelline, popular parties as Guelf, and to this we
may still concede a grain of justification. However, excep-
tions are so many as to make even this suggestion of a
categorization appear perhaps overly bold. At Pisa approximately between 1250 and 1270 the aristocrats tended to
change from Ghibelline to Guelf without ceasing to be

aristocrats. By the 1270's, too, the popular parties of Florence and Lucca were strongly Guelf; at Pisa the popular party was as strongly Ghibelline. More stable an element in Italian politics was rather the hostility of neighboring cities, which tended to drive the traditional enemies into hostile camps with relatively little attention paid to the broader implications of the Guelf or Ghibelline names they adopted. Within the commune, too, the natural repulsion of the parties contending for power led to Guelf-Ghibelline divisions that bear only a remote connection with the papal-imperial struggle.

Still, so delicately balanced was the power structure in Tuscan intra- and intercity politics that it reacted immediately and decisively to any shifts in papal or imperial fortunes. We must leave it to historians of politics to clarify how these shifts carried themselves down to the local level. Suffice to state that it seems almost a premise of Tuscan politics that Hohenstaufen hegemony in the province meant aristocratic supremacy in the communes. Of this the most dramatic illustration is the reaction that follows upon the death of Emperor Frederick II (1250) and the temporary collapse of Hohenstaufen strength. A torrent of popular uprisings breaks out, and numerous popular regimes are established: Florence (1250), Lucca (1250), Orvieto (1250), Volterra (by 1253), Siena (by 1253), or outside of Tuscany, Bologna (1255), Faenza (1256), and Genoa (1257).

The origins of the popular regime at Pisa are likewise to be placed during this great popular upsurge following the death of Frederick. In 1254 a chronicler relates that the popolo at Pisa had seized the signoria.[2] In that year, too, appear the "captain of the people" as the democracy's leader, a council of elders (anziani) as its governing board

2. Fragmenta historiae pisanae auctore anonymo, *RIS, 24,* 645 A. Cf. Schaube, *Konsulat,* p. 43.

and representative in the commune's own great council,
and a *Breve pisani populi* (by 1259) as the popolo's constitution; about the same time the Pisan denarius seems to
have begun wavering in value, apparently reflecting popular policies.[3]

At Pisa, however, it is difficult to assess either the amount
of power this *Primo Popolo* in fact exercised or the duration of its regime. Our best indication of who controlled
the commune is finances, the right to authorize expenditures and demand accountings. Before 1254 the Pisan senate, the old assembly of her aristocrats, authorized such
expenditures. In 1257 it either was still doing so or had
reasserted its briefly lost prerogative.[4] The popolo, while
its own constitution was recognized and it had been accorded a voice in the commune's great council, was still
no dictator.

Restoration of Hohenstaufen power in Tuscany brought
sharp aristocratic reactions in the communes. Hohenstaufen restoration came in the person of Manfred, Frederick
II's illegitimate son. After victories in South Italy and
Sicily, in 1260 he interfered decisively in Tuscany; at the
battle of Montaperti, the Tuscan Ghibellines, with Manfred's help, crushed the Guelfs. Florence's own Primo
Popolo was abolished along with other Guelf-popular regimes, and a new period of aristocratic supremacy begins
for Tuscany.

3. ASP Pia Casa di Misericordia, 2 Dec. 1254, for the first appearance
of the captain of the people; ACC 6 May 1259 for mention of the Breve
pisani populi. For changes in the commune's great council, compare
Regestum volaterranum, ed. F. Schneider, RCI, 1 (Rome, 1907), nos. 629
(17 Dec. 1250) and 686 (25 July 1257). On the denarius, see Appendix II,
no. 2.

4. Cf. ASP Roncioni, 4 June 1233, for expenditures authorized "sena-
torum consilio," and for the report of the tax accountants given to the
senate. In ASP Alliata, 24 Nov. 1248, a tax is sold "ex forma consilii
senatus inde data." In ACC, 29 Dec. 1257, the report of the tax accountants
is still being given to the senate.

But again, when the Hohenstaufens fell, this time for good, they dragged down the city aristocrats, though not so permanently. The instrument of their destruction was Charles of Anjou, younger brother of St. Louis of France, champion of the papacy and Guelfs, who on papal invitation marched into Italy and at the battles of Benevento (1266) and Tagliacozzo (1268) defeated the last of the Hohenstaufens and extirpated their line. In 1266 Guelf-popular parties took command of numerous inland communes (Florence, Lucca, Pistoia, Volterra, Prato, San Gimignano, Colle), Ghibelline Siena was crushed militarily, and Pisa barely escaped a similar fate by buying peace with the victorious Charles. But with the establishment of popular regimes in inland Tuscany, at Pisa too, in a less clear-cut shift, a Ghibelline popular party came to the helm.

Thus at Pisa, in the decade after 1266, a whole series of changes betrays the presence of a new hand on urban government. In 1266 or 1267 the Pisan denarius, wavering since the popular upsurge of the 1250's, crashed in value, falling in ten years by 50 per cent.[5] Simultaneously, in 1267–68 Pisa's guild system was overturned and four new guilds won recognition.[6] In 1270 outright civil war broke out in the city and members of prominent aristocratic families—Donoratico, Upezzinghi, Visconti, Gualandi, Lanfranchi, Gismondi, Orlandi, and so forth—were exiled to join the Guelf hinterland in war against their native city.[7] Pisa's traditionally Ghibelline aristocracy, cooling rapidly to the imperial cause after the death of Frederick II (1250), had turned Guelf with the victory of Charles of Anjou,

5. See Appendix II, especially nos. 2 and 3.
6. See below, n. 13.
7. Historiae pisanae fragmenta auctore Guido de Corvaria, *RIS, 24,* 674 C–675 B. Cf. Roncioni, *Istorie,* p. 574.

perhaps in the interest of salvaging its southern trade by conciliating Charles. During these years too the commune stripped both the archbishop and cathedral chapter of their feudal jurisdictions.[8] By 1278 a parchment tells us what we might have expected. Control over communal finances had passed out of the hands of the aristocratic senate and under the control of the popolo's council of elders.[9]

In 1276 Tuscany's Guelf League carried the nobility back from exile, and a new moderation in communal policies reflects their return. In 1278 Pisa returned to the archbishop and cathedral chapter their expropriated jurisdictions.[10] The pendulum swings farthest in the direction of aristocratic reaction immediately after Meloria, with the tyranny of Ugolino della Gherardesca (commander of Pisa's fleet at Meloria, 1284; ruler of Pisa to his imprisonment in 1288). The reaction is best typified by the money. From about 1280 the Pisan denarius was kept stable for about the following fifteen years. We even possess in the statutes of 1286 the provision by which this stability seems to have been achieved. That provision (itself dating, we

8. See the chapter *De Citationibus* in *Stat. 1*, 252, where the commune offers to "defend" any layman cited by any ecclesiastic. The upshot of this seems to have been that the Church could not force laymen to pay tithes, whether "sacred" from all the faithful or "dominical" from her own lands. On types of tithes, see C. Boyd, *Tithes and Parishes in Medieval Italy* (Ithaca, New York, 1952), p. 2. Cf. the compromise between the bishop and commune at Reggio in Emilia in 1281 (Salimbene, *Cronica*, p. 209), where no one could be forced to pay tithes unless "according to his conscience." At Pisa the chapter *De Citationibus* was revoked in 1278; see the document published in *Stat., 1*, 691 ff.

9. ASP Olivetani, 27 May 1279. The "small council of anziani of the Pisan people" gives the income from the gate of San Martino in Guassalungo as security for a loan, "non obstantibus aliquibus capitulis brevium communis et populi statutis consiliis vel ordinamentis lege vel contrarietate aliqua."

10. Cf. *Stat., 1*, 691.

may presume, from 1280), forbade any further issues of the *denarius nigrus,* limited thereby the volume of that coin in circulation, and pegging its value, prevented further inflation.[11]

The overthrow of Ugolino (1288) and the summoning of Guido da Montefeltro to direct the commune's fortunes represent a swing in the direction of popular government. In a sudden exertion of power, however, the dissatisfied "rich," the aristocrats, drove Guido from power and at the Peace of Fucecchio (1293) exempted from tariffs the "proud" Florentines and gave Lucca land "almost to the city walls." [12] In reaction, two years later (1295) a revolution set up another popular regime. In 1296 or 1297, the Pisan denarius began wavering in value again, becoming stabilized in the opening years of the 14th century at about two-thirds its former worth.

A word about two changes we have attributed to the popolo: the guilds and the money. In the early 13th century and up to 1267–68, Pisa had "recognized" two major or merchant guilds *(ordines),* that is, granted them a seat in the commune's great council and granted them juridical powers; these two were the "order of merchants" *(ordo mercatorum)*—the inland merchants, organized by 1162— and the "order of the sea" *(ordo maris)*—the overseas merchants, themselves organized by 1201. She had chartered four minor or artisan guilds *(artes):* tanners, iron

---

11. *Stat., 1,* 292. "Et teneamur nos Potestates et Capitanei, quod non patiemur . . . cudi usque ad kalendas ianuarii . . . aliquam monetam minutam nigram . . . Si videbitur Potestatibus et Capitaneis et Antianis faciemus fieri consilium senatus . . . in quo faciemus poni et formari titulum: si dicta moneta minuta nigra debeat cudi . . . in civitate pisana ab inde in antea, vel non . . ."

12. Ranieri Sardo, *Cronica pisana,* ed. F. Bonaini, *ASI, 6,* Pt. II, Sec. 2 (1845), 91. For the disturbance at Pisa in 1295, cf. Roncioni, *Istorie, sub anno.*

workers (*fabri*), butchers, and furriers, all of which were
granted privileges before 1234.[13] The popular upsurge that
overturned this system was born of elements outside these
two orders and four guilds. Indeed, the tanners seem to
have suffered nearly as much as the aristocrats. Two formerly subservient professions (the shoemakers and the hot-
water tanners) won independence, and a component guild
(the *pellarii*) was fractured into three. The iron workers
were reduced to relative insignificance in economic life.
The victors included the three guilds which by 1267 had
won recognition alongside the artes: the vintners, the shoemakers, and the notaries. The statutes of the vintners dating from this decade claim control over the inland waterways to the detriment of the curia maris—Pisa's maritime
court, the bastion of her commercial aristocracy—and

13. The guilds recognized by 1277 are the three ordines (the ordo
mercatorum, the ordo maris, and the ars lane) and the seven artes (tanners,
fabri or iron workers, butchers, furriers, vintners, shoemakers, and notaries). Before 1267–68 the two recognized ordines were the ordo mercatorum and the ordo maris. The problem is what were the four artisan
guilds which had secured the commune's recognition before 1267–68.
Schaube, *Konsulat*, p. 44, followed by Brugaro, *SS, 20* (1911), 291, thought
they were the lanarii, notaries, fabri, and tanners. Both reconstructions,
however, were based on the appearance of consuls of the ars lane in an oath
taken by 1,000 Pisans in 1188. Recently the oath of 1188 has been shown a
later fabrication (cf. Cristiani, "Osservazioni"), and the way is clear for a
reconsideration of the problem of Pisa's earliest artisan guilds. Of the
four guilds, the statutes identify only one, the tanners (*Stat., 1, 347*). We
know further, however, that in 1235 the ars fabrorum was exercising
juridical authority (Volpe, *Istituzioni*, p. 243)—conclusive evidence that the
fabri were also one of the recognized guilds. In a document of 1250
(*Stat., 1, 311*), the butchers of Genoa petitioned to the "viris providis
et discretis consulibus macellariorum ac universis macellariis pisane civitatis" to use their influence to free a Genoese captured by Pisan pirates.
That the butchers had both consuls and influence in communal councils
shows that they too were a recognized guild. Of the remaining guilds, the
only one for which an independent organization can be shown is that of
the furriers. In 1193 (*Stat., 2, 1092*) they had already three captains, as, in
their later statutes they are described as having three consuls.

claim the right to trade overseas independently of the latter's supervision.[14] Over the carters of the Arno valley, the
homines vie Arni, the guild seized the jurisdiction once
exercised by the aristocratic Gaitani family.[15] The shoemakers broke free from the tanners' guild and the notaries
from the college of judges, to which they had formerly
been subject. Most remarkable, however, is the rise of the
guild of wool workers (*ars lane*). Subject to the "court of
the merchants" before 1267, wool by 1268 not only won
independent status but also recognition as an ordo, a major
guild.

The relation of the popolo to the plunging denarius is
more difficult to define. Of course it is related to the commune's financial needs, and of course, too, in the later
13th century those needs were desperate. In 1279 the commune had not even 300 pounds to pay some importunate
Anconese creditors, and a private individual, Rossus Buz-
zaccarinus, volunteered to advance the money.[16] Still, financial need constituted a continuous pressure and itself
cannot explain this staircase debasement which brought

14. Cf. Breve curiae maris, *Stat., 3,* 433, "quod plactaioli non habent
consulem vel capitaneum, preter consules Maris," and the Breve hominum
viae Arni, *Stat., 3,* 1147 ff., where the plactaioli of the Arno have become
subject to the wine guild. See also *Stat., 1,* 353, for the privilege given the
vintners to import or export wine. The statutes of the vintners seem to
have been composed during the episcopacy of Federigo Visconti (d. 1277),
as they refer to "statutis conpositis ab olim domino Frederigo pisano
archiepiscopo," (*Stat., 3,* 1118).

15. Cf. the Breve hominum viae Arni, *Stat., 3,* 1147, and the parchments
published by Bonaini, *Stat., 3,* 1163 (year 1218) and by Brugaro, *SS, 20*
(1911), 449, respectively, in which nobles of the Gaitani served as the
"capitaneus et rector vecturalium de Tuscia."

16. ASP Olivetani, 27 May 1279. Rossus did this "ut nulla novitas vel
represallia fieret mercatoribus pisanis apud Anconam" and received the
income from the gate at Guathalungo until repaid. Cf. Davidsohn, *Forsch.,
4,* 111, where the Sienese state that Pisa's enemies Florence and Lucca
"funditus pecuniam exhauserunt" and that Pisa is near ruin.

the Pisan denarius by the opening years of the 14th century
to one-third the value it had maintained virtually up to
1250. The decision to debase, however great the financial
need, reflects more immediately the directing hand in communal affairs. Thus Meloria (1284), a battle whose prelude
entailed a huge economic effort and whose results were a
huge economic loss, had no impact on the money. Indeed,
the statutes (1286), redacted at the height of the aristocratic
reaction, look for a limitation on the minting of the
denarius nigrus and hence for a virtual reinforcement of
the coinage.[17] Behind the denarius' contortions were local
politics, primarily.

Primarily but not exclusively. The money of each of
Tuscany's five principal mints circulated so freely in the
territory of the others that what one mint did with its
money was of acute interest to its neighbors. When in 1280
both Lucca and Pisa issued coins slightly below the proper
weight, Florence considered sending ambassadors to warn
those cities that such practices "the Florentine commune
. . . cannot tolerate." [18] The convulsions of the denarius
were born of a double root: in local politics, the control
of the commune by a group which wanted debasement,
and in Tuscan intercity relations, a situation that permitted its pursuit with impunity—either because of a state
of war or, more likely, because in the other communes
groups were in power which likewise favored debasement.
As a result, the denarii of all Tuscany's mints seem to have
fallen almost as one coin. They seem to have begun wavering in value in the 1250's, during the period of the Florentine Primo Popolo, and all had their silver content cut in

17. See above, n. 11, and Appendix II, no. 2.
18. *Consulte, 1,* 24. On the devaluation of the Florentine denarius,
which parallels very closely the Pisan, see especially the table of coin
values in Castellani, *Testi,* p. 940.

half with the restoration of popular regimes after the victory of Charles of Anjou (1266). All too seem to have been virtually stabilized from the late 1270's to the 1290's, when again, after a period of wavering value, their silver content was by the early 1300's cut by a third. Tuscan coinage and its debasement deserve to be studied as a unit. Unfortunately, present research is years from that goal; but even if all the factors involved in this debasement cannot be grasped from a single city's money, debasement itself emerges as an integral part of the democracy's revolution.

And in examining the roots of that revolution, let us emphasize the complex reality beneath these terms "aristocracy" and "democracy" which we must wield so freely. Even the phrase "commercial aristocracy," so frequently applied to Pisa's rulers, is dangerous. If the foreign policy of the Pisan commune was colored heavily by commercial interests, her aristocracy was never exclusively mercantile. Who would search the contracts for commercial interests whether as investors or entrepreneurs of the greatest Pisan houses—Donoratico, Visconti, Upezzinghi—searches in vain. Around these were grouped other nobles of less prominent rank—Gaitani, Gualandi, Sismondi, Seccamerenda, Roncioni, Laggius, Assopardi, Lanfranchi, and so forth—who figure prominently in the contracts and were the real bearers of Pisa's maritime tradition. Let us not say with the great German student of the history of capitalism, Werner Sombart, that the latter were subservient to the former, that commerce grew as the rather anemic servant of agricultural surpluses and the men who controlled them. But neither let us see in the commune an organ of embattled merchants bent on conquering and defeudalizing the contado. The city, the aristocracy, was bred from complex social groupings.

The democracy was, too. Volpe's characterization of the

military companies and hence of the popolo as the "artisans grouped around their churches" is one of those half-truths which when pressed too far become a distortion. Pisa's great democratic houses are never found in surviving records as artisan, and the connection we cannot presume. Indeed, some of these houses seem to have enjoyed considerable affluence even before settling permanently in the city. Conversely, the aristocracy counted in its ranks the older artisans as well.

The statutes of the leather workers contain a provision, almost certainly the result of democratic policies, which rules that one-half "at least" of the guild's council had to be foreign born.[19] The line of democracy versus aristocracy was, primarily, that of the newcomer versus the native.

On this basis, too, the demographic history of the parish of San Cristofano, in which in the 1270's over 50 per cent of the residents are recent immigrants, illustrates perhaps better than anything the force behind the popolo's seemingly irresistible march to power. We cannot sound out here all the frictions—economic, social and especially psychological—between newcomer and native, democracy and aristocracy. Suffice to examine only the economic aspects of this larger conflict—aspects which will be of basic importance in understanding the economic changes during the age of the popolo.

What was the economic basis of the aristocracy's strength? The family of Porcellinus quondam Talenti was not one of Pisa's greatest.[20] Of the eighteen pieces of land Porcellinus owned, only four were in the city, and on one of these Porcellinus himself lived. Still the pattern of his life is

19. Breve coriariorum aque irigide, *Stat.*, 3, 932. For date of the Breve, see below, p. 137.
20. What follows is based on ASP Primaziale, 9 Jan. 1269, an inventory of Porcellinus' possessions made after his death.

similar to that of Pisa's great aristocrats. We hear he was in Messina; when he died shortly before 1269, he had 299 pounds invested in five enterprises, which, expressly for two and implicitly for the others (his partners in them were prominent shippers), were all maritime ventures. From his land, Porcellinus received yearly seventy-three staia of grain and fifty-six pounds in money, since, as a rule, city rents were paid in money and agricultural in grain. In monetary values, the three pieces of city land were giving him as much wealth as his extensive rural holdings; indeed, the profits from his 299 pounds in overseas investments could not have been much more, and income from rents ran no risks.

If Porcellinus' economic base was pivoted on city rents, what of a Guido Seccamerenda, whom we meet in the curia maris in 1245 and who owned eight pieces of urban property, one of which alone had five houses upon it and which probably made up most of the parish of San Silvestro? [21] And even with the Seccamerenda, we are not among the greatest of Pisa's aristocratic families.

By the 1260's, the contrast between urban and rural property had reached fantastic heights. In 1263 for four pounds Iohannes Falcone purchased from a noble of the Gualandi a third part of sixteen pieces of land in Colognole in the Livorno hills, a sixth of three others, all the pieces of land the noble expected to receive from his mother's inheritance, and all his claims to the feudal jurisdictions of Colognole.[22] And four pounds was the average year's rent for a city house.

---

21. ASP Primaziale, 22 Oct. 1273, an inventory of the possessions of Donatus Seccamerenda, son of Guido, who owned this property undivided with his brothers. Guido himself took part in the discussion in the curia maris in 1245 regarding the Genoese war, ASP Comune A 81, 2r.

22. ASP Cappelli, 20 Dec. 1262.

The stranglehold that aristocratic families, as the first arrivals in the city, maintained over urban property provided a central issue in the political battles, and had profound repercussions on the economy, of 13th-century Pisa. It permitted the old families to capitalize on immigration to the city and the resultant demand for urban housing or shops, to exploit through rents the newcomers to a degree that by 1263 was horrendous. In 1263 the lady Sigalguida rented a shop for three pounds a year; this was more than her tenant would pay for grain that year, and he had yet to find a house.[23] Another tenant paid to Periciolus Alsalaganba fourteen pounds eight solidi to rent a house; this was the cost of enough grain to feed five men for one year.[24] You might buy with it seventy barrels of wine, enough for fourteen men to drink in a year.

Economically, the rent structure under the aristocratic commune, and the inflated cost of urban living that resulted from it, discouraged a sizable immigration to the city, a differential growth of the urban and rural populations, and urbanization generally. It discouraged, too, the concentration of a large labor force within the city. Moreover, by keeping the cost of living within the city high, it kept high the cost of labor, to the dampening especially of new industries which needed cheap labor. Industries such as textiles therefore fared better when they were distributed in the countryside, but in turn suffered from the inefficiencies of decentralization and could not introduce extensive specializations into the various productive processes.

It was, of course, the theory of Sombart that the rising income from city rents through immigration led to the first significant capital accumulations and the birth of cap-

23. 2514 13v.
24. 2543 42v, 21 July 1263.

italism.[25] In Tuscany, however, the situation is quite the reverse. In the building of important urban industries, city rents were the deadliest of enemies, and only with the reversal of their deleterious effect upon production was the way cleared for the coming of Tuscany's Renaissance capitalism.

And that deleterious effect was reversed simultaneously as the popolo was seizing power in the communes. As L. Zdekauer said of another Tuscan city, Siena, "the question of the popolo . . . presents itself above all as a question of taxes." [26]

25. Cf. W. Sombart, *Il Capitalismo moderno*, trans. G. Luzzatto (Florence, 1925), p. 187.
26. Cited by Mondolfo, *Populus*, p. 33, n. 6.

5. DIRECT TAXES

> And at that time the first direct tax was imposed by the
> commune of Parma according to the above mentioned assess-
> ment, two *imperiales* per pound, so that the calves should
> learn to plow.
>
> *Chronica parmensia* (1302)

IN THE LATE 13th century, the democratic commune
made of debasement and direct taxes the two blades of a
scissors that squeezed down city rents and with them the
cost of urban living. Between 1250 and 1300 the Pisan
denarius was cut in value by two-thirds. The natural result
of this debasement should have been a sweeping inflation
in all sectors of the economy. In two sectors that were basic
in determining the cost of urban living, however, in grain
prices and rents, the commune interfered to prevent prices
from rising in response to this debasement. The effort was
successful, since—at least between the 1260's and 1300—
the cost of urban living, as measured by salaries, by the
decisions of Pisa's courts regarding support of dependents,
and especially by the cost of grain was effectively held.[1]
The market controls that succeeded in pegging grain
prices, their impact in turn on agriculture, will be discussed in Chapter 8. Here our interest is in the structure
of direct taxation that bore the brunt of the democracy's
campaign against city rents.

The commune's system of direct taxation was the *libra*
(pound), so called because it was imposed on property

1. See Appendix II, nos. 6 and 7, and above, p. 38, n. 11.

proportionate to that property's assessed value in pounds (librae) of denarii rather than on the basis of its size or the number of families living on it.[2] When fully matured by the early 14th century, the system functioned as follows. An assessment was made of all property, real or movable, of the city and contado (in some communes, certain necessities of life or incidental possessions—a house if unrented, furniture, slaves—were exempt, or liabilities and debts could be deducted). This assessment, called the *extimum*, was a permanent record irregularly revised, usually at lengthy intervals. In making the assessment, to ensure equality between city and contado, a portion of the city (quarter, sixth, etc.) was subjoined to a like portion of the contado to form a single assessment and tax unit. At Pisa, fourths of the city were so joined to fourths of the contado.

When the commune needed money, it would divide the sum it hoped to collect into the extimum, and the resulting figure was the tax rate, the *datum*, expressed in so many denarii per pound or per hundred. To be sure, the libra probably never functioned as a paradigm of administrative efficiency. In the early 14th century the Pisan commune seems to have entertained little expectation of collecting the full declared amount. It would set the tax rate at astronomical levels and proceed to confiscate what it could. As a result, a tax could be extended over years, and while one

2. On the commune's system of taxation, see the excellent bibliography gathered by A. Sapori, *Le Marchand italien au Moyen Age* (Paris, 1952), p. 110. Much of importance can be found in the standard histories of Italian public law, E. Mayer, *Italienische Verfassungsgeschichte* (Leipzig, 1909); P. S. Leicht, *Storia del diritto pubblico italiano* (Milan, 1938); E. Besta, *Il Diritto pubblico italiano* (Padua, 1930). Of special studies, G. Biscaro, "Gli Estimi di Milano nel secolo XIII," *Archivio Storico Lombardo*, 55 (1928), 343–495, is excellent. B. Barbadoro, *Le Finanze della Repubblica fiorentina*, Biblioteca storica toscana, 5 (Florence, 1929), is somewhat sketchy for the earlier period.

was being collected another could be imposed.[3] In 1319 one unhappy rural commune was paying to six such independent imposts.[4] Nonetheless, this tax system had certain characteristics of basic importance for economic and social history: theoretical equality between city and contado (assured by the subjoining of a section of the city to one of the contado in a single tax unit) and among social classes; in fact, however, a disproportionately heavy weight borne by real property (which could not be hidden) in contradistinction to easily concealed liquid capital.

The origins of this system antedate the appearance of the commune, and are lost in the shadows of the early Middle Ages. They seem to go back to the principle, whether Germanic or feudal or simply primitive, that subjects owed their lord or "chief" aid when he needed it.[5] We can say with certainty that this aid, this first direct tax, was in origin an extraordinary impost and remained so pretty well up to 1300. While the chief beneficiary of this system of aid tended to change in the 11th and 12th centuries from emperor to bishop and great feudatories to commune, the system itself remained relatively stable until the last decades of the 12th century.

During the first period of communal history, that of the "consular" commune (late 11th to late 12th centuries), the city demanded aid pre-eminently, though never exclusively, for military campaigns. In distributing the tax

3. Cf. ASP Comune A 88, 85r, 17 March 1322, "Data denariorum xviii per libram presentialiter in civitate pisana et comitatu." Ibid., 69v, 7 Feb., "imposita pro defensione terrarum pisani comunis de Sardinia data soldorum quinque."

4. Abbathia de Fango in the Maremma, ASP Comune A 87, 91r (1319).

5. On the nature of this "aid" and its relation to medieval taxes, see most recently O. Brunner, *Land und Wirtschaft, Grundfragen der territorialen Verfassungsgeschichte S. O. Deutschlands im Mittelalter* (Vienna, 1942), pp. 312–47.

burden, it had therefore to recognize that a portion of the population, the *milites,* knights or horsemen, were already contributing to the campaign by coming with those costly war machines, horses.[6] The knights were therefore exempted from further taxes. Their lands, too, were exempt, since to support themselves in the campaign the knights were already claiming aid from their dependents, and for the commune to do likewise would mean for them a double tax.

Under the consular commune Church lands, too, were exempt. From the 8th to 11th centuries, Church lands had pretty much supported the imperial or royal armies, were handed out as fiefs for the direct support of soldiers, or were forced to pay the *fodrum* or fodder tax to provision the army. Even the many immunities granted by the Ottonian emperors to bishops were not strictly tax exemptions for the episcopal lands but only authorizations for the bishops themselves to supervise the collection of the imperial taxes.[7] However, as a result of the 11th-century reform movement, the Church had pretty well gained exemption for her lands, on the argument that income from them was needed for the support of the clergy and the poor. The lands from which the commune could demand aid were its own property, which had not been alienated by the granting of military benefices, and the lands of freemen too poor to provide horses.

The unit by which the tax burden was distributed over these lands was the yoke of oxen or cows, or more frequently, the hearth, both in fact measures of the land's agricultural productivity.

The crisis of the commune in the late 12th century, lead-

6. Cf. Mayer, *Verfassungsgeschichte,* p. 7; Salvemini, *Magnati,* p. 52.

7. On the status of the city under episcopal rule, see F. Niccolai, *Città e signori,* Bologna, 1941.

ing to the appearance of the podesta, and, as Lombard historians phrase it, "the first coming of the people," brought important modifications into this tax system. The commune of the podesta (late 12th to late 13th centuries) still relied primarily on services for the support of its army. However, it now distributed those services, most important of which was the maintenance of horses for the communal army, according to the relative assessed wealth of its citizens as determined in an extimum. Rural communes, too, were at Pisa assessed in horses.[8] Distribution of services remains the most common use of an extimum at Pisa up to the appearance of the popolo.[9]

However, money was becoming ever more a factor in maintaining a strong army, especially because the commune had taken to enlarging its vital cavalry by subsidizing anyone willing to maintain a horse.[10] The commune

8. The earliest record of an extimum is found in the Pisan Breve consulum (ed. in *Stat. 1*); Siena used one by about 1178, Lucca before the close of the 12th century. Cf. for Faenza, *Statuta Faventinae*, ed. G. Rossini, RIS, n. ed., *28*, Pt. V (Bologna, 1929), p. 70. In 1168, the consuls determine "que arma, quod pondus pro posse et statu persone singulis conveniatur civibus." For the extimum as a means of distributing horses at Pisa, cf. 2543 78v, 6 Feb. 1264, "unum medium equum noviter impositum," on the nobleman Curtevecchia Roncioni. 2543 85v, 12 March 1264, the consul of the commune of San Sisto borrows forty-five pounds "occasione solvendi datam equi hoc anno imposti scripto communi a commune pisano." ASP Pia Casa di Misericordia, 27 March 1269, "denarios equorum de cavallatis a communibus comitatus de equis impositis." The commune, however, compensated knights who lost horses in war. Cf. for Volterra, *Stat. di Volterra*, p. 12.

9. Cf. ASP Comune A 81, 2r, 7 April 1245, reference to a "partimentum pisane civitatis intus et extra," originally made for the siege of Genoa in 1243, now to be applied for the equipping of vessels against the Genoese. At Pisa, the sole surviving records of monetary sums collected on the basis of an extimum (except for commutation payments for horses) show that the sums were collected from churches.

10. Cf. *Stat. di Volterra*, p. 67, "De solvenda pecunia militibus." Ibid., p. 77, whoever kept a horse for the commune worth more than twenty-five pounds, should receive "adiutorium."

found itself accumulating debts which in turn forced it
to cast about for new sources of income. It sought to modify or sweep away the broad tax exemptions of the consular
commune. While Church lands remained theoretically
exempt, the clergy, through more or less fictional "charitable subsidies," was made to assume part of the commune's
new financial burdens.[11] Moreover, as money assumed a
greater importance in the support of military campaigns,
the full tax exemption of the milites on the basis of their
service in those campaigns lost much of its former justification. The knights like the clergy were forced to assume a
share of the financial burden.[12] We hear of their lands being taxed.[13] In the early 13th century, the commune of
Pistoia divided its public debt into two parts, one of which
was imposed upon the corporation of knights, the other
upon the corporation of the people.[14] This distribution
of the debt on the basis of social status shows that the
knights still enjoyed preferential treatment, but their full
exemption had been swept away.

Most interesting for our purposes is, however, the new
role of city property. The growth of the city made the
older tax system, based on assessments made according to
yokes of oxen or hearths and hence on the basis of agricultural productivity, unrealistic, unfair and, for the commune, productive of only meager returns. Immigration to
the city had forced up rents and given city property a value

11. See the provisions regulating the charitable subsidy, and the protests
against excessive taxing of Church lands, at the Eleventh Ecumenical
Council (1179), C. Hefele, *Histoire des conciles*, ed. and trans. H. Leclercq,
(Paris, 1913), 5, Pt. II, 1101.

12. Cf. Biscaro, "Estimi," p. 352.

13. Cf. *Stat. Fav.*, p. 90. Taxes were imposed for the first time on the
nobility's property at Faenza in 1184.

14. *Statutum Pistorii anni MCCLXXXVIIII*, ed. L. Zdekauer (Milan,
1888), p. xxx, year 1237.

that was left untapped by an assessment according to
hearths. To force city property owners to pay their share
(and, at the height of this crisis, probably more than their
share), the commune began to assess urban property on a
new basis, according to its value in money. This was the
first libra, which appears over much of urban Italy in the
closing decades of the 12th century.[15] Moreover, as city
statutes occasionally state, the capital value of rented urban
property was best assessed proportionately to its rental income. Being pegged to rents, the libra tended to depress
those rents (how precisely we shall soon clarify). Simultaneously, the value of the denarius was being cut, in Tuscany between 1160 and 1190 by 50 per cent.[16] Already in
the closing decades of the 12th century, debasement and a
new tax system were apparently combining to cut urban
rents; the immigration to the city, and the first important
growth of urban industries, which the period witnessed,
undoubtedly owed something to them.

However, this new tax system was still flexible enough
so that, in subsequent reactions, it could be bent once
more to favor high-valued urban property and the aristocratic landowners. The libra was as yet imposed only on
the city, not on rural property, since a full assessment of
the contado lands was quite beyond the meager administrative resources of the 12th-century commune. At about
1200, the libra functioned roughly as follows. The commune decided how much money it needed. It then arbi-
trarily divided the sum between the city and the contado.
In the city, the impost was further divided according to an
extimum. In the contado, on the other hand, it was divided

15. Cf. Biscaro, "Estimi," p. 347.
16. See Appendix II, no. 2. At Volterra (*Stat. di Volterra*, p. 77), city
"domus et turres" were to be taxed only "media libra," in what seems an
attempt to ease the blow of the tax system on the value of urban property.

among the rural communes according to the number of their hearths. The city allowed the rural communes considerable freedom in the further breakdown of this impost; they could divide their portion not on the basis of their hearths, in terms of which their share had originally been determined, but on the basis of the wealth of their members, recorded in their own, local extima.[17] While this assured fairness within the rural communes, the contado as a whole could be made to bear a disproportionately heavy share of the taxes. At Pistoia in the middle 1280's, we can estimate that less than 400 rural hearths were taxed an amount equivalent to that paid by the entire city.[18] Moreover, the distribution of the communal debt between the corporations of knights and people respectively permitted a similar maldistribution in favor of the knights.

The crisis of the late 13th century brought to completion, under the commune of the popolo, the tendencies already in evidence the century before. The tax reforms then carried wiped out the distinctions between knights and people, between city and contado, and placed all on an equal taxation footing. Here as in debasement, the commune's acute financial need provided the pressure working for tax reform, but again the actual step comes with the democratic control of the commune. In 1240, probably for the first time in Italy, the popular party at Milan then in control of the commune carried a tax reform which incorporates the principles we have mentioned: equality between classes, between city and contado.[19] At Bologna

17. Cf. *Statuti di Bologna dall' anno 1245 all' anno 1267*, ed. L. Frati, Monumenti istorici pertinenti alle provincie della Romagna, Serie prima, (Bologna, 1869), p. 217 (1255), tax to be divided within rural communes "secundum facultatem cuiuslibet inter vicinos suos licet sit pro comuni bon. pro numero fumantium imposita."

18. Cf. *Statutum Pistorii*, ed. Zdekauer, p. xlviii, for calculations.

19. Discussed in Biscaro, "Estimi."

between 1245 and 1250 the anziani of the popolo were to
find a way "by which the lands of the Bolognese contado
should be put on an equitable basis in regard to the im-
position of taxes." [20] In Tuscany, too, the reformed libra
comes with the popolo. In 1259 the Florentine Primo
Popolo sought to extend the libra to the contado, but the
Popolo's overthrow the following year seems to have
squelched the attempt.[21] After the victory of Charles of
Anjou (1266), however, the effort was renewed. We have
the discussions from the commune of Prato leading to the
extention of the libra to the contado.[22] At Pisa sometime
between 1274 and 1283 the city quarters were lumped
together in single units with parts of the contado, although
during the tyranny of Ugolino the reform seems to have
been dropped.[23] With the renewed popular upsurge of the
late 1290's, however, the new tax system was reintroduced,
this time pretty much on a permanent basis.[24]

In an economic sense, the significance of this new tax
system is this: the full or partial tax immunity enjoyed by

20. Stat. populi Bononiae, in Statuti di Bologna, p. 7, "per quam terre
comitatus bon. adequentur de impositionibus collectarum."

21. Cf. Barbadoro, Finanze, p. 84, n. 4.

22. Piattoli, Consigli, p. 27 (1 June 1268) and p. 92 (29 Jan. 1276), "de
allibrandis terris et possessionibus forensium sitis in districtu Prati et
de datio imponendo dominis terrarum et possessionum ipsorum."

23. In 1274 (2516 15r, 13 Feb.) the city quarters were apparently still
being taxed independently of any section of the contado, but in 1283 (ASP
Alliata 13 July), accountants, following "formam brevis pisani populi," investigate the acts of the collector "in quarterio Foriporte et comitatum
ipsius quarterii assignatorum super exigendo datam libras LXXX milia
denariorum impositam in civitate et comitatu," and find that he has collected 16,065 pounds, 1 solidus, 3 denarii. However, in 1285 we hear again
of an assessment in horses, which suggests that the knights were again receiving tax considerations because of the special services they were per-
forming. See 2629 254v, 5 May 1285.

24. We have a complete extimum for the rural commune of Musigliano
in 2527. For the libra imposed, see below, n. 26.

urban property by virtue of its location or the social status of its owner was wiped out. Urban property was now assessed and taxed according to its value, as determined especially by its rental income.[25] Inflated city rents meant a proportionately higher capitalized value. For example, in 1299 at Pisa a tax rate of 25 per cent was imposed. If we may presume that rents were being capitalized at 12 per cent, a tax rate of 25 per cent forced the landlord to pay in taxes twice as much as he was receiving in rent. Such an astronomical rate turned urban property into a liability, and the more inflated the rent, the greater the capital value assigned the property, and the greater the liability. To be sure, the rate of 25 per cent imposed in 1299 was extraordinarily high, but in an age of recurrent crises, this was not the sole or the last time such a rate was resorted to. The reformed libra was throwing the booming costs of government predominantly on city landlords and their urban property with its inflated value. In 1299, for example, the minor sons of an urban landholder had not enough movable property to pay their tax, and some of their urban property had to be sold.[26] The result was to break the aristocrats' monopoly over urban property. More important, the reformed libra, as the libra originally, tended to deflate both property values and city rents while a simultaneous

25. As illustrated explicitly at Treviso, *Gli Statuti del comune di Treviso degli anni 1207, 1231–33, 1263*, ed. G. Liberali, Monumenti storici pubblicati dalla deputazione di storia patria per le Venezie, nuova serie 4, (Venice, 1950), 2, 243, "[Nemo debet pagare] coltam comuni pro domo in qua habitat nisi ex ipsa domo pensionem habuerit; et tunc pro tanto teneatur solvere quanta fuerit pensio."

26. ACA, no. 1110 (no date, but from context 1299); the procurator of two minors, sons of Andreas de Ebro, "pro dando et solvendo Francisco Upethini exactori date soldorum quinque denariorum pisanorum per libram nunc imposite in civitate pisana . . . cum dictus curator dicat ipsos minores non habere mobile ad solvendum dictam datam" sells land in the city to Henrigus Sismundus.

debasement of the coinage was butchering the real value of the rents received. At Pisa, the rent for an artisan's shop remained stable from 1264 to 1301 while in real value it was dropping by two-thirds.[27]

In combination with the new libra, therefore, debasement for the aristocrat and his urban property was partially confiscatory. As Chapter 8 will further show, against the peasant and his grain sales debasement in combination with market controls was a hidden but heavy tax. However, in this sense debasement's profits were not financing communal government but cutting the cost of urban living and hiking that of the countryside, in the sense of providing agriculture with less reward for its labor. It was in fact subsidizing urbanization and giving city industries a specialized yet cheap labor, the cost of whose support the aristocracy and peasantry were forced substantially to provide. Before, however, turning to a more detailed study of the impact of this labor subsidy and the process of urbanization, let us consider another type of communal taxes. For the reform of direct taxes forms only part of a broader revolution in city finances, which has in turn broader implications.

27. See Appendix II, no. 6. Cf. for Florence, A. Sapori, "Case e botteghe a Firenze nel trecento," *Studi di storia economica medievale* (2d ed. Florence, 1946), 371–418, in which it appears that rents remained virtually stable there too, at least for the later period 1317–66.

6. INDIRECT TAXES

Since for many years it has been the custom for the tariff collectors to do favors to men and merchants in return for that which they have had to give . . .

PROVISION OF THE *Curia Maris* (1245)

AS WITH DIRECT TAXES, the origins of the commune's system of indirect taxes antedate the commune itself, and are lost in the obscurity of the early Middle Ages. The right to exercise certain monopolies (as over the sale or purchase of salt, iron, and other commodities, or over the use of mills, furnaces, and so forth) perhaps derives ultimately from the "banal" rights exercised by the "chief" within the primitive community, as the concession of monopoly rights ("banalities") was an important means by which the community supported its chief and repaid him for the services he accorded it. In time these banal rights passed through many hands—kings, emperors, bishops, counts or their agents the viscounts—eventually being claimed by the urban communes. We can say, however, with greater certainty that consistently associated with the payment of indirect taxes in the earlier period was the concept that they were payments for services rendered: from tolls or tariffs for the maintenance of roads and bridges, or for the "weighing" of loads.[1] Of course, in practice this theory was seldom fully realized. Of course, too, it was modified during the period of growth in the late 12th century, in a manner we shall see. But its persistency too de-

1. Discussed in J. M. Kulischer, *Storia economica del Medio Evo e dell' epoca moderna,* trans. G. Böhm (Florence, 1955), *I*, 455.

serves emphasis. The "favors" which the tariff collectors provided Pisan merchants in the 1240's for their taxes were wine, the services of weighing their loads and perhaps judging their disputes. When Federigo Visconti was fighting for his tax collector's life against Pisa's popular regime, on the theory of service he built his case.[2] His sermon describing his Sardinian visitation in 1263—a trip with decidedly political overtones—is a running account of expenses incurred and paid with his own money in the commune's interest.[3]

The persistency of this concept of taxes as a payment for services is, however, revealed especially by the tax-collection system. Up to the late 13th century and the advent of the popolo, many if not most of the commune's indirect revenues remained the prerogative of private families or institutions to administer. As late as 1264, when cows were sold at Pisa's market place at the cathedral, the transaction took place "under the jurisdiction of the market of the cathedral, which jurisdiction belongs to the heirs of the lord Vettulus."[4] The archbishop collected tolls from the Arno's ford at Ricavo, at Bientina, Piombino in the Maremma, and at one time probably all the "ripa," the tariff, of the Pisan contado.[5] The Gaitani collected the

2. See "Sermo quem idem dominus fecit in maiori consilio pisano, ut revocarent statutum, quod fecerunt de auferendo iurisdictionem terrarum pisani archiepiscopatus," number fifty-one of the Sermones.

3. Printed in full by A. Matthaejus, *Ecclesiae pisanae historia* (Lucca, 1768), 2, 15 ff.

4. 2543 77v, 5 Feb. 1264.

5. Cf. Breve consulum (1164), *Stat., 1,* 39, "universum redditum ripae quem archiepiscopus detinuit." For the Ricavo tax, Davidsohn, *Forsch. 3,* no. 1, and ACA 26 April 1268 where Federigo Visconti leases his "passadium et pedagium de Ricavo tam per terram quam per aquam" for sixty-five pounds. For Piombino and "omnes redditus et proventus statere portarum sive riparum" owned by the archbishop, ACA 19 March 1282. For tax "aput Castrum de Bosco pisani districtus . . . apud Blentinam . . . contratam de Blentina," ACA no. 957 (1278).

duty for "weighing" the loads of the carters on the Florentine road, the Upezzinghi possessed the tolls from the Era
river, the house of Donoratico had the *patronatus* of Pisa's
Ponte Vecchio, and a whole group of nobles Pisa's Ponte
Nuovo.[6] Entire areas of the contado were under noble
jurisdiction, Maremma and Elba under the archbishop.[7]

The commune seems to have permitted its great feudatories to administer these taxes because the income from
them was considered payment for services rendered. For
the great lay families, it was compensation for the burden
of serving as horsemen in the communal army. For the
archbishop, it could be for a variety of services rendered
the commune in foreign negotiations or domestic charities.
These private incomes and jurisdictions were, however,
probably always subject to some degree of communal
supervision. In 1164 the Pisan commune ordered the archbishop to spend the income from the tariff to build a road.[8]
However, during the crisis of the late 12th century, when
the aristocracy's exemption from direct taxes was also being limited, the commune personified its power and interest in the figure of the podesta, who sat with these tax
collectors, imposed on them a semblance of discipline and
unity, and grew so important as to supplant the older
communal consuls. The podesta maintained a staff of tax
accountants, "modulators of the officials and the non-
officials of the Pisan commune," who, as their name suggests, looked into the administrations even of these private

6. Examples of noble jurisdictions could be multiplied here at will.
For noble jurisdiction over the carters and the boatmen of the Arno valley,
p. 62, n. 15. For the Donoratico house and the Ponte Vecchio, Toscanelli,
Donoratico, pp. 201–38. For patrons of the Ponte Nuovo (in 1258), parchment published in *Stat., 1,* 645.

7. Cf. Sieveking, *Finanzwesen,* p. 61, for the role of noble houses, and
especially the Visconti, as tax collectors at Genoa.

8. Breve consulum (1164), *Stat., 1,* 39.

collectors.[9] When in 1258 a new bridge keeper was invested with the Ponte Nuovo, the noble patrons of the bridge were present but the podesta received his homage.[10] We learn too that the tolls on the bridge could not be raised without the podesta's permission. Still, for all the podesta's supervision, the hand on the income remained the nobles'.

Simultaneously with the podesta appear new institutions, which modified importantly the system of indirect taxation; these were the *societates dogane,* the "customs-house companies," the nature of which at Pisa the complex and powerful curia maris (appearing in 1201) seems to have shared.[11] These companies administered certain important indirect revenues, especially monopolies; at Siena, for example, in the early 13th century, the commune was receiving "profits" from such companies which operated the mint and the "customs houses," probably monopolies, of iron, grain, salt, oil and fish.[12] From Siena, too, we have a contract by which one of these customs-house companies was created.[13] In 1203 the Sienese commune, the count palatine of Grosseto, and eight private entrepreneurs created a *societas dogane salis de Grosseto et dogane salis de Siena.* The company was to operate a salt monopoly—that is, buy all the salt mined in the contados of Siena and Grosseto and sell it to consumers at a profit. It was to operate four years

9. Modulators are mentioned by 1227, ASP Roncioni, 4 June 1233.

10. See parchment printed in *Stat., 1,* 645.

11. D. Herlihy, "Una Nuova notizia sull' origine della curia maris," *BSP,* 22–23 (1953–54), 222–7.

12. See *Libri dell' entrata e dell' uscita della Repubblica di Siena, 3* (Siena, 1914), 12, "lucrum" paid to commune by "Frederigo Petronchi et sociis dogane blade," and similar payments from the heads of companies concerned with the other commodities mentioned.

13. *Regestum senense,* ed. F. Schneider, RCI, 8 (Rome, 1911), 172, no. 416, 14 Nov. 1203.

"and longer as much as it pleases us." The commune, the
count, and the eight entrepreneurs were to divide all profits
equally. The private entrepreneurs, however, were to advance the capital necessary for the operation of the monopoly.

If we may consider this Sienese salt monoply as typical of
the many customs-house companies that appear throughout Tuscany in the late 12th century, we may make certain
observations on the significance of their appearance. One
is that the companies included new men of wealth, who
had no hereditary claim to serve as tax administrators but
who could advance money needed either for the actual
operation of the companies or for other purposes. The
commune's financial difficulties of the late 12th century in
that sense seem to have worked to limit the tax-collecting
prerogatives of the old noble houses (which, it appears, if
they were fortunate, were compensated for giving up their
tax rights to the new companies by being granted a share
in them). Conversely, these companies gave to new men the
chance to serve as tax administrators, and probably too provided the commune with much greater revenues than it had
formerly enjoyed.

We may note too that these customs-house companies,
partners more than agents of the commune, seem to have
acted quite as independently *vis-à-vis* the commune as the
individual nobles they sometimes replaced, and were supervised more than controlled by the podesta. The commune
of the podesta (late 12th to late 13th centuries) still seems
to have preferred that its revenues flow from source to ex-
penditure in autonomous channels which it supervised
only remotely. When extraordinary expenses were incurred over a long period—and such expenses at a time
when war was largely self-supporting were incurred chiefly
by public works—the commune set up or sanctioned the
existence of independent organizations: the *Opera sancte*

Marie maioris ecclesie, responsible for the construction and maintenance of the cathedral; the *Opera pontis novi de Spina,* the *Opera tersane,* and so forth.[14] These organizations were then endowed with revenues, from land or from imposts. In return for protection extended by Pisa's archbishop and the commune which stood behind him, Pisan iron workers contributed twenty solidi per year per overseas factory *(fabrica)* to the opera of the cathedral, and similar privileges entailed similar contributions.[15] The earliest tariff imposed on imported grain went to the cathedral, and in 1284 when Angelus Spina imported 1500 salme of grain from Sicily, he paid his taxes to the cathedral and not to the commune.[16] The cathedral took the revenue from the "stamp" tax, the sealing of measurements for carbon, wine, grain, etc., to guarantee their accuracy.[17]

In the late 13th century, however, the commune entered a new period of acute financial crisis, leading to new and important changes in its system of indirect taxes. The commune sought new sources of revenue partially at the expense of the aristocracy, in a sense carrying to completion the tendencies evident a century before. An attempt was made to expropriate all tolls and tariffs in the Pisan contado.[18] Both archbishop and cathedral chapter were stripped of their "lands," their feudal jurisdictions; and

14. On the nature of these operae, see N. Ottokar, *Studi comunali e fiorentini* (Florence, 1948), pp. 163–77.

15. Cf. *Reg. pis.,* no. 311 (1111), and *Stat., 3,* 891–2.

16. 2544 23r, 22 Nov. 1284.

17. ASP Coletti, undated parchment from the 12th century. Formula of excommunication to be used against those who robbed the measurements of grain from the cathedral's opera. Breve artis fabrorum, *Stat., 3,* 869, "quartuccium . . . sigillatum de sigillo Opere sancte Marie."

18. Breve potestatis (1286), *Stat., 1,* 80. "Pedagium aliquod . . . non patiemur . . . tolli . . . ab aliqua persona vel loco preter quam a communi vel pro ipso communi pisano." This entry may be dated after 1267, since in that year the Gaitani were collecting tolls from carters on the Florentine road. See above, p. 62, n. 15.

their protest is loud.[19] Even the cathedral—still of course
the city's pride—seems to have seen its stamp on measurements replaced by the democracy's proud eagle.[20] Those
nobles who had enjoyed the right to serve as patrons over
certain of the contado's *pievi,* baptismal churches around
which had grown subsidiary communes, were forced to account to the city for their stewardship.[21] They became virtually equivalent to the "captains" appointed by the commune over its own lands. After 1268 the "modulators of the
officials and the non-officials of the Pisan commune" become simply "modulators of the officials" since everyone
handling tax income was being reduced to a state function-
ary.

Further, from 1267, the commune began a sweeping sale
of revenues. In 1270, salt was sold twice, and again in 1275,
1279, 1282, and 1283.[22] In 1275 the "vein of iron" was sold,
as was in 1278 and 1284 the *modum pecudum et quartensis,*
an obscure tax on sheep.[23] In 1284 the *cabella,* the tariff, had
also been sold.[24] Ugolino's aristocratic tyranny seems to

19. See above, n. 2. In 1278 the archbishop petitioned the commune
"ea omnia et singula revocare et reduci in statum pristinum et ad ius
et proprietatem et possessionem pisani archiepiscopatus . . . ipsum domi-
num Ruggerium pisanum archiepiscopum pro ipso archiepiscopatu . . .
reponi et reduci [to the status enjoyed] ante alienationem concessionem seu
occupationem . . . que de predictis bonis facta dicitur fuisse a tempore
mortis bone memorie domini Vitalis archiepiscopi [1254]." ACA, 21 June
1278. See above, p. 59, nn. 8, 10.

20. Cf. above, n. 19, and Breve artis vinariorum, *Stat., 3,* 1107 and 1110,
"sigillo aquile pisani Communis."

21. The protest of nobles in investing money that the money comes
"ex industria sue persone et non ex aliquo beneficio quod tenet" shows
that the commune no longer permitted them to use their income from
feudal jurisdictions for personal use. Cf. 2515 40v, 21 April 1273.

22. Listed in Breve pisani populi, *Stat., 1,* 608, and Breve potestatis,
Stat., 1, 350–3.

23. Loc. cit. Pegolotti, *Pratica,* p. 216, describes a "diritto del quartino"
at Genoa as a tax of 3¾ per cent on salt.

24. 2545 143v, 2 May 1284, "in emptione cabelle pisani communis
vendite a communi pisano." See also 2544 18v, 31 Oct. 1284.

have tried to call a halt, but under Guido da Montefeltro (1288) iron was sold again, and probably salt.[25]

Frequently, these sales meant simply the alienation of a present income. However, particularly in the 13th century, the sale of a tax could mean something quite diverse, usually because the commune was "selling" an income it had never formerly enjoyed.

A parchment has fortunately preserved for us an accounting down to the last denarius of such a tax sale, which permits a unique insight into its workings.[26] In 1247 to build six ships for use against the Genoese, the commune imposed a special tariff, a *supraposita,* and promptly sold it to a corporation of bankers. In the accounting sheet of the following year, we learn that the tax had been sold for 22,100 pounds. For the period the sum is startling, particularly when presumably needed to equip six ships. However, the accounting sheet shows that the "sale" and the "price" were largely fictional. The bankers had lent the commune the money it needed to finance the ships—a more modest 500 pounds. In return they were assigned the income of the new revenue (though apparently not the actual collection, which remained under the curia maris). The money they received, as they received it, they consigned to two friars especially appointed for the purpose. After one year communal accountants, the modulators, audited their records. They determined that the bankers still owed the commune, for the tax purchased one year ago, 188 pounds ten solidi eight denarii. Indeed, the price for which the tax was "sold" was an accounting fiction utilized to audit what was in fact a year's administration—a price determined only after the year had expired. To be sure, the purchasers were allowed

25. Prohibitions against future sales in *Stat., 1,* 608. But cf. ASP Alliata, 20 Sept. 1290, "universitas emptorum doane ferri de Ilba." ASP Pia Casa di Misericordia, 31 Oct. 1290, money owed "a dovaneriis dovane salis."

26. ASP Alliata, 24 Nov. 1248. See Appendix III, no. 10.

to discount the amount of money they had advanced the commune—in 1247 not 10 per cent of the actual money handled—but everything they were collecting over and above that figure was being collected directly for the commune.

If we may consider this sale of 1247 as typical of the many that the commune resorted to in the late 13th century, we may say that these sales had certain implications in regard both to the tax-collecting system and to the revenues of the commune. The tariff of 1247 was again sold to new men of wealth, not members of the older families or even the older customs-house companies. It meant that the commune's financial need again was throwing open the ranks of its tax administrators to new blood, and we may presume that in a manner similar to this the customs-house companies had themselves originated the century before. It meant too that the tax-collecting prerogatives of the aristocracy and the older companies, such as the curia maris, were being severely restricted, as more and more they were reduced to serving as functionaries of the commune and the new companies of tax purchasers. Indeed, the curia maris, which in the early 13th century had rivaled the commune in power, by the early 14th century became little more than the commune's bureau for harbor administration. We might note in passing that even by 1300 the system of indirect taxes, still relying heavily on advances of revenue through tax sales and administration through semi-private companies, appears chaotic and discriminating. That should not obscure, however, the great extension of its system of indirect taxes, and the great increase in its revenues, which the commune achieved in the late 13th century.

For even the repeated sales of taxes, most of which seem to have involved new imposts rather than old sources of revenue, suggest a considerable growth in the financial resources of the commune. And indeed, for the six years 1227 to 1232, the commune's treasurers counted an average yearly income of 2,400 pounds—gleaned chiefly from court fees, the commune's castle of Ripafratta and others, and its chief tax, the *modum,* probably a kind of tariff collected from men and animals passing across those castles' territories.[27] The tariff on overseas trade sold in 1247 was valued at 22,100 pounds.[28] In 1288 the commune's treasurers counted nearly 40,000 pounds per year as the commune's regular income.[29]

This great new wealth was used not only for war, though war certainly claimed a gigantic share. It helped support the boom in bureaucracy of which, in the army of government notaries, we have seen something, and of which, in agricultural marketing controls, we shall see more. It helped make possible, too, the great upsurge in building and public works so evident in the late 13th century. And this in turn was of fundamental importance for Pisa's economic development. For the factors favoring immigration created by debasement, direct taxes, and market controls provide only a partial explanation of the city's great growth. That these pressures could work so effectively presupposes that it was now physically possible to provide food and work to cities of unprecedented size. It presupposes a revolution in communications.

27. ASP Roncioni, 4 June 1233. The commune's regular income from 1227–32 was 14,091 pounds, 8 solidi, 1 denarius. (Volpe, *Istituzioni,* p. 405, incorrectly thought that this was an auditing of the commune's income for one year when in fact it was for six.) Those investigated included "capitaneorum modi et eorum omnium qui pecuniam publicam per se vel per suum officium expenderunt . . . et castellanorum Ripafracte et aliorum castrorum."

28. See Appendix III, no. 10.

29. ASP Alliata, 28 Dec. 1288.

7. COMMUNICATIONS

In winter as you know men cannot flee from their enemies
because of the bad and water-filled road and because of the
bad and difficult fords, but it is only in summer that a man
can flee.

FEDERIGO VISCONTI

THE GREAT CHANGES in inland communications taking place in Tuscany in the late 13th century Johannes Plesner called a "road revolution." [1] In the early Middle Ages, the roads, wherever possible retracing the Roman, had like the Roman, followed mountain ridges. Less now for military reasons and fear of ambush, more because the river valleys were ill-drained, spotted with impassable swamps, and unhealthy, this favoring of ridges resulted in lengthy detours, slowness, and practical impassability for carts. The road revolution consisted in the directing of the chief roads through the valleys, in paving them, in permitting traffic in carts upon them, and in lending to them an unprecedented economic importance.

In inland communications, Pisa needed ties both with the sea and with the four inland areas she bordered—Versilia, Lucchesia, the Valdarno, and the Maremma. In the early Middle Ages the most popular routes were the rivers. Pisa in antiquity had stood at the confluence of two rivers, the Arno and the Serchio, the latter flowing down from the north, from Garfagnana and Lucca. However, in 575, to help his flood-plagued flock, the Irish bishop of Lucca,

1. "Una Rivoluzione stradale nel dugento," *Acta Jutlandica, 1* (1938).

Frediano, diverted (through a miracle, our source, Gregory the Great, relates) the Serchio to its present course, through Migliarino to the sea.[2] Pisa, however, could not be deprived of so convenient a highway. Throughout the Middle Ages and into the Medici period, a canal called the Auser continued to trace the Serchio's old route, from the river itself near Avena, along the base of the Monti Pisani to the baths of San Giuliano, and south across the Pisan plain to meet the city walls. There Pisa tried to divert the waters past the cathedral and so down to the Arnó, following the walls' outline and serving as a moat, but she faced considerable seepage through the city itself which made mud flats of important market places.[3]

The Auser provided Pisa's busiest road with the Monti Pisani. When the castle of Asciano needed brick, sand, and mortar for its walls, on the Auser they were carried.[4] On it, too, was taken marble from the Monti for Pisa's cathedral. By 1304 the canal was equipped with locks placed at the Porta Leonis near the cathedral, which could be closed, raising the water level so even marble-carrying barges could float upon it.[5] In 1299, barges from the Auser were at the Porto Pisano, so that harbor had a direct water link with the Monti Pisani at least as far as the baths of San Giuliano.[6] We do not know whether the Auser was navigable all the way to its confluence with the Serchio (some scholars have

2. Toscanelli, *Antichità*, 2, 630. For further discussion on the Serchio and the Auser, see Pedreschi, "Geografia," p. 120.

3. Cf. Toscanelli, *Donoratico*, p. 226.

4. 2523 28or (ca. 1300).

5. ASP Comune A 83, 47v, 25 Oct. 1304. Permission granted by commune "claudi facere Auzerem apud Pontem leonis vel apud sanctum Stefanum cum palata . . . ita quod aqua dicti Auzeris non labatur tantum abbundanter sed ex ipsa clausura intantum possit aqua crescere quod per eam possit dictus operarius reduci et portari facere ad civitatem pisanam lapides marmareos quos habet apud Montem Pisanum."

6. ASP Comune A 81, 50r, 24 July 1299.

even doubted that it did indeed flow from that river), and
whether it thereby provided an all-water route to Lucca.[7]
Later in the Middle Ages another all-water route to Lucca
was used, which skirted the Monti Pisani's opposite slopes
through the Arno, the Bientina swamp to the "port" of
Formica, and which until the 19th century served as
Lucca's link to the sea.[8]

Bound by the Auser to the Monti Pisani, Pisa was bound
by the Arno to the sea and the valley. Up the Arno came to
Pisa the wine- and grain-laden boats from the Maremma,
whose coast by 1300 was lined with signal lights.[9] Since the
lights, however, were intended to warn of "enemies" in the
vicinity, it is hard to know whether they indicate the increased safety of the route or its increased hazards, coming
with the decline of Pisa's maritime strength.[10] Pisan boats
penetrated deep into the river system of the Arno's plain,
the Cascina, Vicarello, the Era, and through Empoli to
Signa, Florence's barge harbor. At Pisa herself, wharves—
caricatoria, scale, gicte—stood within the city "between
the two bridges"; the phrase means the Piazza San Niccola,
where was unloaded the bulk of Pisa's overseas commerce.[11]
Likewise within the city the noble residences which lined

7. The statutes of 1286 (*Stat., 1,* 494) mention only traffic as far as the
baths of San Giuliano. In 1285, however, the commune of Avane was held
responsible for dredging the river, and Avane is very close to the Serchio.
The dredging, however, may have been for health purposes rather than
for navigation. Cf. 2629, 248v, 15 April 1285.

8. See Sardi, *Contrattazioni,* p. 105.

9. For a list of places having signal lights, ASP Comune A 82, 4r
(1299), and *Stat., 2,* 421 (1313).

10. "Pro faciendo signa . . . quando galee inimicorum essent vel non
essent in illis partibus." *Stat., 2,* 421.

11. Cf. Zeno, *Documenti,* no. 96 (1299), "in campo que est infra duos
pontes civitatis Pisarum." Ibid., no. 147 (1308), "infra duos pontes in
campo sancti Nicolai."

the banks boasted their private wharves.[12] The volume of
business squeezed wharves from both ends of the city-
embraced Arno. North of the city facing Florence, embracing both sides of the river, was the Piaggia; today a quiet
park on the Arno's right bank has kept the name.[13] There
boats were constructed and loaded; there, too, stood public
buildings, probably a customs house, just as west of the
city another *degathia* faced the sea.[14]

Traffic moved slowly on these inland waters; the trip to
Florence took six days, less than ten miles per day.[15] It
moved surely, however. In 1272 a Pisan at Barbaricina, a
sobborgo west of the city, could buy wood from Florentines
and allow fifteen days for the sellers to return home, load
their barge and deliver the wood at the Pisan's wharf.[16] To
carry salt to Florence in 1284 required one pound for every
staio worth three pounds ten solidi, a cost of over 25 per
cent of its Pisan price.[17] The barges, however, could be
ample. At once large enough to carry bulky grain, at times
even to risk the open sea on ventures of its own, small
enough to master the Arno's shallows, was the *placta marinara*, the sea-going barge. One built in 1299 was thirty feet
long and eight and one-fourth feet wide.[18] Another could

12. 2563 24v, 12 Sept. 1299. Boat leased "super ripa Arni ante geptum
heredum domini Ugonis Sclecti et consortum." For a barge at the family
wharf of the Laggius house, 2545 33r, 29 May 1301.

13. 2522 4v–5r, 11 March 1314, contract for the construction of a boat
drawn up "Pisis extra muros et porta de plagiis in domo pisana . . .
[illegible]."

14. 2545 57r, 1 Sept. 1301. "Actum Pisis in domo degathie pisani communis ubi exigitur dirictus degathie." 2545 45v, 24 March 1283, "barca . . .
existente nunc Pisis apud degathiam in flumine Arni."

15. Breve hominum viae Arni, *Stat., 3,* 1150 (year 1305).

16. 2515 118r and 136v, 15 Aug. 1272. Canceled 5 Sept.

17. Davidsohn, *Forsch., 3,* no. 120.

18. 2522 4v–5r, 11 March 1314.

carry one hundred thirty-five barrels of wine from Castiglione della Pescaia in the Maremma to the city, enough to satisfy the thirst of twenty-seven Pisans for one year.[19]

As frequently as barges, small boats, *barche,* are met on these waters. One constructed in 1314 was twenty-four feet long and four and one-half feet wide; its slim shape assured easy control in the river's shallows.[20] For equipment, a *scafa* constructed in 1306 possessed one "oar," probably a pole for shallow waters, and a tow rope, *alsana,* both illustrative of the boat's chief means of propulsion.[21]

So far as inland communications are concerned, however, in the late 13th century Pisa's chief energies, and the energies too of other Tuscan cities, were directed to road building. We may note in passing that even the building of roads seems not to have gone unaffected by the aristocratic-democratic feud. Probably because Pisa's Ghibelline popolo was more immediately concerned with warring against the Guelf hinterland cities than with trading with them, democratic regimes seem relatively negligent in improving the inland roads. Conversely, aristocratic governments, and especially the tyranny of Ugolino della Gherardesca, were especially energetic in constructing roads and building bridges.

Pisa's flat and ill-drained contado made land travel difficult, especially during winter. No matter where the destination, on leaving Pisa the traveler did best by taking the shortest route to the nearest ridge. Further, dependence on fords meant that during the flood season of autumn and winter, travel had all but to cease. Let us begin a trip to Florence, sometime before the 1260's, passing through only the section within the Pisan contado. We are leaving from

19. ASP Comune A 89, 165r (1322).
20. 2522 4v–5r 11 March 1314.
21. 2522 22r, 24 Feb. 1306.

Kinsica, Pisa's most populous quarter on the Arno's left bank. We first must ford the Arno at the river's great bend above the city where the water is shallowest, at "Guathalungo," the "long wade." We then strike out for the Monti Pisani, not because this is the direction to Florence but because by hugging the base of the Monti Pisani we can best hope to find the terrain passable. Then, not twenty miles up the Arno, we must ford the river again, this time to avoid the great swamps of Bientina, at Ricavo or Calcinaia.[22] Actually, these were fords only for low waters and only for horsemen. Early one morning, when St. Bona and a companion wished to cross at Guathalungo, her companion asked how it would be possible, since the ferrymen were not yet arisen.[23] One night, when two friars conversed with Bona and grew unmindful of the hour, they found they could not cross the river, since the ferrymen had gone home and to walk one-half mile through the darkened city to the Arno's one bridge was to risk their lives and, worse yet, to give scandal.[24] Both problems only miraculous intervention solved.

Little wonder, therefore, that in 1264 the guards at Pisa's busiest gate of Guathalungo were still called *ripuarii*, a name that reflects both their function as tax collectors (*ripuarium* means "tariff collected at a river bank") and how most goods arrived at Pisa.[25] The account book of Stefano Soderini, a Florentine merchant at Pisa from 1278 to 1279, shows a conspicuous gap during the winter months.[26]

In the latter half of the 13th century, however, Pisa had

22. Cf. Davidsohn, *Forsch.*, *3*, no. 1.
23. *ASS*, *20*, 149 B.
24. Ibid., 154 C.
25. 2514 35r, 6 Dec. 1264.
26. Edited in Castellani, *Testi*, *2*, 459–69.

embarked on an ambitious and extensive plan to improve
inland communications, her share in the Tuscan road revolution. The fourth book of Pisa's statutes (1286) presents
an imposing list of projects; the chartulary of Cherlus,
notary for Pisa's public works' director, her *operarius,* illustrates energy in execution.[27] Behind the plan and the
execution stands the figure of Pisa's tyrant Ugolino Gherardesca, who, if tyrants are always the best builders, seems
likewise to have appreciated the importance of roads for
Pisa if she was to retain her stature as Tuscany's favorite
mouth. The same year the Florentines ordered paved the
road to Pisa, they paved too the road to Pietrasanta, a potential rival in the Lucchesia to the north.[28]

To liberate roads from mountain ridges and build them
on the plains, drainage was the chief technical difficulty.
Over swampy land the road had to be elevated—*alsatum,*
elevatum, as the sources say.[29] Pisa's cart roads, *carrarie,*
thus often doubled as dikes. The dike on the Arno's left
bank east of the city provided a base for the new Florentine road made of gravel, and the road west of the city was
planted every four feet with trees to give strength to the
dike and permanence to the road.[30] To secure good drainage and overcome mud, pavement was essential, so that the
roads, as the statutes say, would be passable even in winter.
In the chartularies of 1285 and the statutes of 1286 the word

27. The public works described in the chartulary of Cherlus (2629) in
1285 are the following: 238v, "de fosso nuper faciendo iusta castrum de
Quoza"; 242v, "de fosso de Blentina"; 244r, "de gicto lapidum de Fagiano";
246r, "de silice sancti Marti"; 247r, "de factura sive actatura aut clausura
boccalis sive aggeris qui nuper est factus iusta Vicinaiam secus viam qua
itur Ascianum ex parte ganghii civitatis pisane"; 247v "de pontibus factis
apud Pappianam"; 247v, "de actatura et factura aggeris pedemontis"; 247v
"de mundatione et purgatione Auzeris."

28. *Consulte,* 2, 269, 299.

29. For example, *Stat.,* 2, 433 (1313).

30. 2629 246r, and *Stat., 1,* 491.

for the stone used for pavement, *silex,* is synonymous for the word for highway, *strata.*[31] The technique that used flint for pavement is as old as the Romans, perhaps the Etruscans; its wide application, however, seems peculiarly an accomplishment of the late 13th century. Common both in the chartularies and statutes after 1285, it is apparently unknown before. Such roads might be twelve to fifteen feet wide, enough for carts to pass.[32] And good roads meant large carts. Pisa's earliest carts, as seen from the contracts of 1263, were two-wheel affairs, and of the growth in load size we are better informed than of the growth in wheels.[33] In 1299 one cart could carry from Pisa to the Porto Pisano the great chain to be placed across the harbor's mouth. The weight of the chain can be appreciated from a piece of it (or one similar) contained today in the Camposanto; records show the entire chain weighed 2,500 pounds.[34]

Good roads, however, were little serviceable without good bridges. Up to the late 12th century Pisa had one bridge across the Arno which had apparently survived since Roman times. Its exact location has been a point of dispute among scholars.[35] At any rate, it was apparently destroyed

31. 2629 246r, 7 April 1285, "de silice sancti Marti." 2545 41v, 15 March 1283, "silex communis pisani de Poianis usque ad foveam communis pisani." *Stat., 1,* 491, 552. Siena seems to have begun a similar program of paving roads in 1241. Cf. *Cronache senesi,* p. 181.

32. *Stat., 2,* 410 (1313).

33. For sales of wheels, 2543 45r, 9 Aug. 1263, 62r, 3 Oct. 1263, and 2514 32r, 1 Dec. 1264.

34. ASP Comune A 82, 18r, 16 July 1299, "catena ferri quam fecit communi pisano ad opus pisani portus que fuit centenaria xxviii." Ibid., 38v, 22 Aug. 1299, "pro portatura catene ferri quam ipsi [carratores] portaverunt cum eorum curru et bobus apud Portum Pisanum," a fee of forty solidi is authorized.

35. For Pisa's bridges, see N. Toscanelli, "Il Quartiere di Kinsica e i ponti sull' Arno a Pisa nel Medioevo," *BSP, 4* (1935), reprinted in the author's *Donoratico,* pp. 201–38. Toscanelli's conclusions are, however, not beyond argument.

in 1179, and shortly afterwards two bridges were being built to link the two sides of the Arno. The Ponte Nuovo (perhaps so called since, according to some scholars, it was the old Roman bridge rebuilt) stood, as a contract says, "near the church of San Niccola," where today is the Via Santa Maria.[36] Further up the Arno, the Ponte Vecchio stood pretty much where the Ponte di Mezzo today stands. Begun apparently by 1192, it was carried to completion at a leisurely pace. In the life of St. Bona (d. 1207), the two friars who dallied too long at her house faced the possibility of walking "one-half mile" to the bridge.[37] Bona's house stood near the church of San Martino in Guathalungo and the Ponte Vecchio. Though the anecdote cannot be dated, the bridge was probably not passable much before 1200.[38] Like its famous counterpart at Florence, it supported shops and stores to help finance it, and its central location made those shops and stores important possessions. By the early 14th century Pisa's official weigher of florins, an important figure in the city's economic life, was stationed upon it.[39]

In the second half of the 13th century, Pisa constructed a third bridge over the Arno. The Ponte della Spina stood where today is the Piazza San Silvestro.[40] The bridge was meant to replace the ford of Guathalungo, and in fact forms part of an ambitious project to redirect the road to Florence. Work upon it started in 1262; it was, however, neglected by the popular regimes of the late 1260's and the 1270's, and only the energy of Ugolino's tyranny carried it to completion (1286).

36. 2516 2r, 28 Oct. 1273.
37. *ASS, 20,* 149 B.
38. ASP San Silvestro, 10 Nov. 1201, for a contract redacted on the Ponte Vecchio.
39. ASP Comune A 85, 47v, 29 July 1315.
40. 2514 11r, 5 Sept. 1264, "pontis novi qui sit vel fieri debet super Arno iusta sanctum Barnabam."

Of the growing network of Pisa's roads in the contado, naturally only the most important can here be presented.

The history of Pisan roads to the north is the history of her relations to the Via Francigena, the great pilgrim highway which provided Tuscany's link not only to Rome but to Lombardy and France.[41] In antiquity, Pisa had stood on Rome's chief road to Gaul, the Via Aurelia, built about 241 B.C. between Rome and Pisa, and its northern extention to Tortona and Liguria, built by the consul Emilius Scaurus in 109 B.C. and called the Via Emilia. In the early Middle Ages, however, when roads had to be self-maintaining, when the coastal plain was more swampy, unhealthy, and exposed to pirate forays, the road north, now the Via Francigena, retreated inland to the mountain ridges. In Tuscany it passed through Siena, followed the Elsa valley to cross the Arno near Fucecchio about twenty-five miles up from Pisa, continued on through Altopascio, Lucca, and Camaiore, and then went down to join the old Roman coastal route near Pietrasanta, about thirty miles north of Pisa.

Pisa's hope was ever to challenge Lucca's command of this road and the profitable pilgrim traffic that moved upon it, and perhaps to prevent the hinterland cities from using the highway as a link to the ports of Genoa or Venice. By 1162 she was building a road north across her plain to Pontaserchio, the first bridge over the Serchio river.[42] When St. Bona set out for Spain, she traveled on this road, and the saint even founded a church en route, San Iacomo in

41. For the road's Tuscan section, see Repetti, *Dizionario, 5,* 715; C. Sardi, *Vie romane e medievali in territorio lucchese,* Atti della accademia lucchese di scienze, lettere ed arti, 34 (Lucca, 1920); and P. Venerosi, *La Strada francigena nel contado di Siena,* Siena, 1933.

42. Breve consulum (1164), *Stat., 1,* 39. Breviarium pisanae historiae, *RIS, 6,* 170 D (year 1144) speaks of war between Pisa and Lucca "propter iniuriam similiter de strata Francorum."

Pozzo.[43] As the "Via podii sancti Iacobi" this road figures in Pisa's later sources. It passed through Vecchiano, Massaciuccoli, and met the Via Francigena at Quiesa. It made it possible, though Lucca ever sought to prevent it, for merchants from the north to by-pass Lucca on their way to Pisa.[44]

In the 13th century Pisa set about building another road to the north, retracing the old coastal route of the Roman Via Emilia. By 1233 we hear of a second bridge over the Serchio at Arbavola.[45] In 1267 when Frederick of Austria marched his army south, they came on this road.[46] And the road assumes considerable importance in the statutes of 1286, as part of Pisa's effort to colonize her maritime plain to the north.[47] In 1273 Guido of Corvaria, along this road, reached Carrara in three days, a speed of about twenty miles per day.[48] By the 14th century, a letter of exchange dated in Pisa May 24 could call for payment in Cremona by the middle of June.[49] Although travel was possible even at night upon it, it seems not to have been passable for carts.

To Lucca two roads ran. One climbed directly over the Monti Pisani, and while impossible for carts and difficult even for the old or weak, was the shortest and oldest road to Lucca. In the late 12th century, Pisa built a second road, skirting the Monti Pisani, through the half-mile wide gap of Ripafratta. It was longer but level, and by 1184 we hear

43. *ASS, 20,* 147 C.

44. See agreement between Pisan commune and consortery of Ripafratta, edited by Bonaini, *ASI, 6,* Pt. II (1845), p. 86, no. 24.

45. Constitutum Usus, *Stat.,* 2, 1003.

46. *RIS, 6,* 197 A.

47. *Stat., 1,* 287, for immunities offered to those willing to settle the area.

48. *RIS, 24,* 692 E.

49. 2521 175v, 24 May 1306.

of considerable traffic in carts upon it; it was, however, hardly passable during the rainy season.[50] In the late 13th century, St. Zita of Lucca set out from her native city through the gap of Ripafratta, along the banks of the Serchio to Pontaserchio, then to St. Bona's church of San Iacomo in Pozzo.[51] She continued down the Via San Iacomo to Pisa, four miles beyond Pisa to the church of San Piero a Grado. In returning home it was already vespers by the time she passed through Pisa, and she took the road across the Monti Pisani. Mountain hermits and custodians of castles warned her of the dangers, the wild animals and the robbers; she found the "covered bridge," closed at Pontetetto, where the road crossed the Serchio, but with miraculous help she reached Lucca. Her round trip to Pisa required twenty-four hours of continuous walking.[52]

To the Valdarno as well two roads ran. The oldest we have already mentioned; it set out from the Porta Calcisana on the Arno's right bank and provided Pisa's link with Calci, a town important for its waterpower, its mills, and its sheep, and with Buti, important, among other reasons, for its shale diggings. Most important, the road on the Arno's right bank, passing through Ghezzano and Mezzana, was the oldest road to Florence. Crossing the river in the early 13th century at the "pasagium de Ricavo," near Castello del Bosco not far from Montopoli, by the late 13th century it crossed at a ford near Calcinaia.[53] Near where

50. For tolls on carts passing through Ripafratta mentioned in agreement of 1184, see above, n. 44.

51. *ASS, 12,* 507 E–508 A.

52. Between 1286 and 1313 Pisans began building a more direct road to the Ripafratta gap, the "viam podii sancti Stefani, qua itur Ripafractam, a ponte Auzeris . . . usque ad ecclesiam sancte Marie de Pappiana." *Stat., 2,* 410.

53. Davidsohn, *Forsch., 3,* no. 1.

this road entered the city, Florentine merchants had their house. By 1286, however, it had been paved only its first six miles to Mezzana, although the statutes call for its completion through Vicopisano to Bientina.[54] The apparent neglect is explained by the fact that Pisa was building a better road to Florence.

And the Florentine road is an excellent illustration of the conquest of the river valleys, the great accomplishment of the 13th-century road revolution. The building of a new road on the Arno's left bank, the logical route to follow, faced a twofold handicap. The land outside the Gate of Guathalungo was especially swampy, as its name, "piaggia," suggests. And even if a road was built from Kinsica, Pisa's three other quarters on the Arno's right bank would still be dependent on Guathalungo's ford. In 1262 Pisa started its third bridge, Ponte della Spina, to replace the ford. Two years later, a contract tells us that Pisa was already "sending" a road on the Arno's left bank, that was to surmount a gravel mound to ensure protection from floods.[55] Initiated simultaneously as parts of a single plan, both bridge and road lagged in the democratic period. The Ponte della Spina was still uncompleted by 1286, and of the road the statutes refer to the "bad way which is there" and call for its repair "in that width as it was at the time that the highway was designed and built." [56] By the early 14th century it assured Pisa contact with the Valdarno that was independent of weather. By 1322 across it was carried not only Florence's industrial products but even spices from Venice and furs from the north, and it seems to have been Pisa's most important route to the northern

54. *Stat., 1,* 489.

55. 2514 32r, 1 Dec. 1264, "illius vie et strate que mittitur inter sanctum Martinum de Guassalungo et Fasianum."

56. *Stat., 1,* 489.

areas.[57] We hear of ambassadors making a round trip to Venice, presumably on this road, in one month.[58]

Leading south from Pisa, through Collesalvetti, crossing the Livorno hills to emerge into the Maremma at Rosignano, continuing south to the limit of Pisa's contado, Castiglione della Pescaia, was Pisa's own pilgrim highway, the Via Romea. Its importance, however, was incomparable with its inland parallel. When St. Bona set forth for Rome, she turned inland to the Via Francigena, and Conradin in 1267 in his march south followed her steps.[59] However, the road attracted considerable attention in the later 13th century. The statutes of 1286 say that it should be widened from "Vignali ad Scherlinum," a short section in the Maremma below Piombino, and the implication is that it had been widened in the sixty miles from Pisa even before that time.[60] In 1273 Guido of Corvaria could ride the fifty miles from Pisa to Piombino in two days.[61] An entry in a chartulary of 1308 shows that Pisa was attempting to pave the Via Romea from Rosignano to Castiglione della Pescaia, a distance of some seventy miles.[62] That the section of the road north of Rosignano to Pisa is not mentioned suggests that it had been successfully paved the years be-

57. See the impressive quantities of furs flowing through Florence to Pisa in 1320–21 in chart constructed by Ciasca, *Medici*, doc. XX, and the Florentine embargo on furs, spices and dyes going to Pisa in 1322 (Davidsohn, *Forsch.*, *3*, no. 777). For Florence's interest in the road to Venice, ibid., no. 808.

58. ASP Comune A 88, 40v.

59. *ASS*, *20*, 149 B; Ranieri Sardo, *Cronaca pisana*, ed. Bonaini, *ASI*, *6*, Pt. II (1845), p. 89.

60. *Stat.*, *1*, 481.

61. *RIS*, *24*, 682 B.

62. 2523 13v, 18 June 1308, "perticarum septingentarum trigintanovem silicis sive strate per quam itur Razingnanum ad mensuram pertice pisane contingentium communi Castilionis de dicta strata sive silice." The road cost to build eighteen solidi per pertica.

fore, and indeed the section figures as a model for a good road in the statutes of 1313.[63] This ambitious project seems an effort to replace Pisa's sea lanes, harassed by pirates who dared strip ships in the Porto Pisano itself, with safer bounds of inland communications.

Leaving Pisa at the Arno's left bank near San Paolo a Ripa d'Arno, following the Arno's left bank to San Piero a Grado, and swinging south across the plain ran the road to the Porto Pisano. In the late 12th century Pisa had bridged the swamps it had to cross and provided a hospital, San Lorenzo, at the Stagno inlet for the relief of weary merchants. Of three stone bridges, the largest across the Stagno was appropriately called the *Pons usione,* the bridge of departure.[64] The busiest of Pisa's roads, it was lined with hermits who lived from charities meted out by the rich merchants who passed; it was lined too with trees, every four feet. The road and its hermits figure most frequently in notarial wills. It was a good road too. When about 1260 a Tunis-bound merchant fell from his horse on the Stagno bridge, broke his leg, and had to be carried back to Pisa in ignominy, a cart could take him.[65] Over this road, too, was taken the one and one-fourth ton chain for the Porto Pisano.

And at the Porto Pisano converged the lines of Pisa's maritime communications.

Pisa's river harbor was miserable. When Federigo Visconti made his Sardinian visitation of 1263, to board his galley he descended the Arno to San Rossore. Upon his return in attempting to bring him to the city, the ship stuck in the mud immediately below its destination, San Pietro a Vincoli, "as if [the ship] were saying," relates the

63. *Stat., 2,* 431.
64. ASP San Lorenzo alle Rivolte, 3 Jan. 1154.
65. According to an anecdote told by Federigo Visconti, 59r.

archbishop, "you'd better get off here." [66] To be sure, the
ship had in fact reached the city; it was summer, too, when
the Arno was lowest. But for a galley, drawing little water,
built for speed and maneuverability, to have trouble is little compliment to the Arno's navigability. It measures how
far at Pisa the geological sequence characteristic of many
river ports had progressed: silting of the harbor, growth
of the delta, alienation of the sea, erection of and mounting dependence on a subsidiary harbor more accessible to
sea-going vessels. To be sure, smaller ocean-going ships
could still reach Pisa, but this honors more the mariners'
courage in taking petty boats to the open sea than the
Arno's success in floating large ships to Pisa.[67] Her subsidiary harbor Pisa found in the Porto Pisano, standing
south of the Arno's mouth very close to Livorno.[68] There
in springtime Pisa's fleets gathered to await the merchants
who, after a Sunday farewell feast with family and friends,
on Monday mounted their horses to ride to port, ship, and
adventures.

Of the larger ships, the chartularies give only one dimen-
sion, but that most important: cargo.[69] In 1283 the *San*

66. "Et sic pervenimus ricagnum sancti Petri ad vincula, et ibidem galea
addurata est quasi diceret descendendum est hic, et descendimus in nomine
Iesu Christi, amen." The sermon is printed in full in A. Matthaejus,
Ecclesiae pisanae historia, Lucca, 1768.

67. Cf. 2545 45v, 24 March 1283, a ship from Majorca bound for Provence, "existente nunc Pisis apud degathiam in flumine Arni."

68. P. Vigo, *Il Porto Pisano*, Rome, 1905. Cf. the anecdote told by
Federigo Visconti (59r) about a merchant who after making all prepara-
tions to set sail, while riding to the Porto Pisano broke his leg on the
Stagno bridge. For the handling of grain through the Porto Pisano, cf.
ASP Cappelli, 25 April 1278, where the grain was transferred from the
larger ships to "bone placte cum tendis cum quibus frumentum ab aqua
defendi possit" to be taken to the city.

69. 2544 23r, 22 Nov. 1284. The cargo consisted of "in salmis grani
ceciliani quadrigentis viginti quinque, uncias auri centum octuaginta;
in karlinis auri, uncias auri tredecim; et in tappetis quatuordecim, uncias

Niccola carried 1,500 salme of grain from Palermo to Pisa. Enough to feed 1,500 men for one year, the grain was not the only commodity carried. In 1299, another grain ship carried 2,500 salme; fifteen such could have fed all Pisa for one year.[70]

Efficiency, too, was an accomplishment. The *San Niccola* carried life's bulky staple the five hundred miles from Palermo to Pisa for 39 per cent of its Sicilian value. Cheaper was the transport on less bulky goods. Twenty bags of cotton and fourteen rugs were taken at a cost of 7 per cent of their Sicilian value.

If speed witnessed no revolution from the earlier Middle Ages, some figures are still interesting. On August 29, 1271, Guido of Corvaria left Pisa, and three days later, on September 1, he was in Corsica.[71] A whole Pisan fleet, with assorted ships to retard them and Genoese pursuers to spur them on, made the Porto Pisano from Genoa in five days.[72] Most remarkable, in 1303 the crew of a galley which had made a round trip to Sardinia was paid for one week, and if this was not an overtime payment—and silence makes it unlikely—the galley averaged about 100 miles a day.[73] In 1263 Federigo Visconti took eight days to reach Sardinia, but the archbishop paused in the Maremma ports to greet his flock and hire a crew.[74] The archbishop himself in an anecdote tells how a ship left Pisa, was sacked by pirates south of Sicily on the way to Tunis, and fifteen

---

auri quatuor et tarenos auri sex; et in libris decem sendadis viridis, uncias auri septem et tarenos sex; et in cantaribus duobus casei ceciliani et in vino ceciliano salmis tredecim cum aliis rebus minutis, uncias auri tres."

70. Zeno, *Documenti*, no. 90.
71. *RIS*, *24*, 676 B.
72. Ibid., 692 B.
73. ASF C 462, 70v, April 1303.
74. Matthaejus, *Historia*, 2, 14.

days after the ship's sailing, Pisa heard the sad news.[75]
Leaving Naples on July 6 in the evening, ambassadors in
1271 were back in Pisa on July 25, and the fact that they
left in the evening makes it likely, although the chronicler
does not say it, that they came by water.[76] By the early 14th
century embassies could visit Sicily, transact their business,
and be back in Pisa in forty-five days.[77] In 1270 ambassadors made a round trip to Tunis in two months, and in the
12th century, a voyage from Pisa to the Levant took sixty
days.[78]

However, not over speed but over the seasons was the
period's impressive victory. About 1260 when a Tunis-
bound merchant broke his leg in the springtime, his wife
wailed that they would make no money "this year." [79] In
the earliest chartularies and even in 1272–74 trade follows
heavily the rhythm of the seasons. However, changing
times are evident. In 1264 a ship could set off in early
November for Sicily, but the two weeks needed for the
trip would bring her to port before the mare clausum.[80]
In 1270, ambassadors could start out for Tunis in mid-
November.[81] By the years before Meloria, the seasons'
rhythm are without sharp impact on the chartularies. On
December 20, 1282, a ship was ready to sail for Palermo,
another, on November 24, 1283, for Montpellier.[82] In 1284

75. Visconti, 59r.

76. *RIS, 24,* 676 B.

77. ASP Comune A 84, 23r (1311).

78. *RIS, 24,* 676 E, 677 E. *ASS, 24,* 344 B.

79. Visconti, 59r. The lady protested, "O dominus, feceram celebrari
tibi missam pro viro meo et ecce quanto bene me exaudisti, confundens me
et domum meam totam quia nichil lucrabitur hoc anno . . ."

80. 2514 26v, 1 Nov. 1264. See also 2514 20r, 13 Oct. 1264, for a ship
ready to go "Pisis in Pulliam et de Pullia in Alexandriam."

81. See n. 78, above.

82. 2545 26r, 20 Dec. 1282; 100r, 24 Nov. 1283.

a merchant was "prepared . . . at once to make" a trip to North Africa on January 31.[83] On December 7, 1301, a ship sailed for Castiglione della Pescaia and on January 24 another for Corsica.[84] On January 10, 1308, a boat was ready to sail for the Maremma.[85] This list could be continued; but enough has been given to show that if captains still respected the winter waters and preferred port during the bad months, the seasons had lost their overriding significance.

Greater efficiency in handling volume and independence of the seasons were further supplemented by regularity of contact. By 1286 Pisa's podesta could be ordered to seek justice against those who injured Pisan citizens within the following periods: for Corsica and the "parts" of Genoa, one month; for Sardinia, Sicily, Naples, Apulia, Provence, and Catalonia, two months; for Tunis and France, three months; for the Byzantine Empire, Syria, Egypt, and Armenia, six months.[86]

By the late 13th century, commerce could become fully the handmaiden of large cities and industries. Of wider economic changes, it is in part the gauge, in part the cause.

83. 2545 114v, 31 Jan. 1284.
84. 2545 98r, 7 Dec. 1301 and 15r, 19 Feb. 1302.
85. 2523 256v, 10 Jan. 1308.
86. *Stat., 1,* 552.

8. AGRICULTURE

This Count Ugolino was a man of such a type that he caused
the people of Pisa to die of hunger and at his time, although
he had a great abundance [of grain], was so cruel that a staio
of grain cost seven pounds at Pisa . . .

PSEUDO-BRUNETTO LATINI

THE MASS IMMIGRATION to the city and its growing
size, favored by the new taxation system and made possible
by the age's new communications, had, for Pisa's economy,
this significance: certain segments of that economy were
being forced to pay for the rapid expansion of others; especially, agriculture was being saddled with the cost of a remarkable growth in urban crafts and industries.

In grain production, while Pisa's own plain was too
swampy for extensive or efficient cultivation, the Maremma
south of the Livorno hills had been one of urban Italy's
breadbaskets. The chartulary of Bartholomeus for the year
1284 illustrates the Maremma's importance as a grain producer. This was at a time of aristocratic rule in the commune, when interference in the grain market was kept at a
minimum.[1] In the late summer of that year, Bartholomeus
traveled approximately once every two weeks to the Maremma, to the little town of Bibbona about forty miles
south of Pisa. The reason why Bibbona needed another
notary—it already had several of its own—was that in the
fall at the nearby monastery of Maggio a fair was held, at

---

1. 2544. For the Maremma's importance as a grain producer in the
earlier period, see Volpe, *Istituzioni*, p. 77; Schaube, *Handelsg.*, p. 623.

which grain was of course the principal item. A measure of the fair's importance was that all Bartholomeus' clients were Florentines. And other Florentines in other chartularies show a similar interest in Pisan grain, and their presence betrays a lively export.[2]

In the late 13th century the commune interfered decisively in the grain market, and the history of Pisan grain production becomes very nearly a study of the nature and impact of this communal interference. To be sure, the Italian commune had evinced interest in grain long before this. Even before the end of the 12th century numerous cities were exercising considerable supervision over the production of and trade in grain.[3] However, this interference could spring from two quite diverse motivations. The commune could establish a monopoly over, or taxes upon, grain as it did with other commodities (oil, fish, salt, iron, etc.), utilizing it as a source of revenue. Or it could attempt to hold down the price of grain even to the extent of spending its own money to subsidize consumers.

Naturally, the nature of the grain policies of any particular commune was greatly influenced by its own economic position and needs. If the commune raised grain for export, it was more likely to utilize this trade as a source of revenue, since the added cost was shifted largely

2. 2544 7r, 11 July 1284; 9r, 9 Sept.; 9v, 12 Sept., four loans involving the Florentine Amfiossus Malesicchi and sons; 11r, 1 Oct. 1284, for another Florentine, Bindus Codenaccius. Cf. also 2545 14r, 26 Sept. 1282, where Beldimodo quondam Salmonis de Quarantula comitatus Florentie invests ten pounds in a company that will purchase in the Pisan contado "ligna oleum granum bladam et bestias." In the chartularies of Ugolinus and his sons (2543, 2514, 2515, and 2516), the Florentine Gerardus quondam Rigoletti is particularly active in transactions involving grain.

3. H. C. Peyer, *Zur Getreidepolitik oberitalienischer Städte im XIII. Jahrhundert* (Vienna, 1950), while it does not include Tuscany, is an excellent study of the administrative aspects of the commune's interest in grain.

onto foreigners. Conversely, if the commune had to import grain, it was more apt to supervise rigorously its own
production and even help pay for the cost of foreign grain
in order to assure adequate supplies and hold down the
price. In the earlier period, controls on grain seem predominantly of the first type, intended to provide communal income and not a consumers' subsidy. However, in
many cities, as crafts and industries expanded and grain
consumers grew in number much more rapidly than grain
producers, pressure on the commune mounted to have it
assure the urban consumers adequate, cheap grain supplies,
if necessary to change controls originally established as a
source of revenue into controls directed toward pegging
the price of grain.

Over fifty years ago, G. Salvemini studied this revolution
in the communal grain policies at Florence in the later
13th century and related it to the class struggle within the
city.[4] According to Salvemini, the aristocratic faction, the
"magnates," represented the large agricultural landowners
and the important producers of grain. With large quantities of grain to sell, the magnates fought any effort to im-
pose a ceiling on the price of grain or any export embargoes, if that meant an artificially depressed price at home.
Conversely, the *popolani* defended the interest of the consumers and favored both export embargoes and rigid grain
controls, both to cut the price of urban food and to under-
mine the wealth and political power of their aristocratic
enemies. Salvemini doubtlessly exaggerated by equating

4. *Magnati*, p. 165. Salvemini's interpretation is discussed and rejected
by Davidsohn, *Forsch.*, *4*, 307, and especially by N. Ottokar, *Il Comune di
Firenze alla fine del dugento* (Florence, 1926), but has recently secured
partial confirmation from Peyer, *Getreidepolitik*, p. 49. On the general
problem of the commune's relations with the contado, see most recently
E. Fiumi, "Sui rapporti economici tra città e contado nell' età comunale,"
ASI, *114* (1956), 18–68.

the magnates so exactly with the grain producers; he tended further to discount the fact that any city government had, after all, to assure its citizens sufficient food. In the conflict between the aristocracy and democracy, it would be fairer to say that this dispute over grain was only one of many sources of friction, stemming from many efforts on the part of the democratic commune to hold down the cost of urban living. Still, for all its exaggeration, Salvemini's interpretation has an important kernel of truth that research in the grain policies of towns other than Florence has recently helped confirm.[5]

For Pisa herself, we have little information from chroniclers or treaties that would permit us to set the beginnings and evaluate the importance of the commune's interference in the grain market. While we know that Siena by the early 13th century had a *dogana blade,* some sort of grain tax or monopoly operated for the commune's and not the consumers' profit, Pisa seems to have insisted only that in the sale of grain a tax should be paid to the *opera* of the cathedral.[6] In 1268, however, we hear of an embargo placed on the export of certain commodities from the Pisan contado, which commodities, as the Florentine treaty of 1270 stipulates, were salt and grain.[7]

A much fuller record of the commune's grain policies is provided by the behavior of grain prices in the face of debasement and in comparison with prices on the free market.[8] Thus a staio of grain sold from 14 to 16 solidi in the years 1263–64. In 1273 in the midst of debasement it maintained a still stable sixteen, and we are probably safe in concluding that the embargo on grain exports in 1268

5. See above, n. 4.
6. See above, p. 85, n. 16. 2544 23r, 22 Nov. 1284.
7. See Volpe, *Istituzioni,* p. 363; *Relazioni,* no. 198.
8. See Appendix II, no. 7.

signified a broader effort to peg the cost of grain, though the money was being debased. By 1277 when the Pisan denarius stood at one-half its value of 1263–64, the price of a staio of grain had risen only about 25 per cent, to twenty solidi. Only after the democratic period, when debasement had been halted, does the grain price shoot upward, suggesting that with the new stability in the money had come, too, an end of an artificially imposed ceiling on the price of grain. And that Florentines in 1284 could freely buy Pisan grain confirms that grain had been returned to a free market. In 1283 it stood at forty solidi a staio when sold to consumers, and in 1286 under Ugolino's tyranny it reached a staggering fifty. Pseudo-Brunetto Latini's complaint about the cost of grain at Pisa during Ugolino's tyranny, which we have quoted at the beginning of this chapter, is not without some basis in fact.

After Ugolino's overthrow, as the pendulum moved toward popular government, the grain price fell, showing that the commune was again restoring market controls. In 1291 the commune itself was selling grain to its citizens for twenty-nine solidi per staio. We can estimate that this cost was less than the free market value of Sicilian grain, and that the commune had begun absorbing a loss in its purchases of imported grain and hence was subsidizing the consumers.[9] In 1299, the cost of a staio of grain was evaluated in a rural commune at fifteen solidi. To summarize a long story, in 1322 with the Pisan denarius at a third of its original value, the commune was selling grain to consumers at twenty solidi the staio, only 25 per cent more than its cost in 1263–64. To compare this with the

9. From 2544 23r, 22 Nov. 1284. Sicilian grain cost twenty-nine solidi per staio (in Pisan money and measures) in Sicily and another nine to bring it to Pisa, in all thirty-two solidi. If this price held for 1291 too, the Pisan commune was absorbing a loss of two solidi per staio of grain it sold.

price of a commodity on a free market, a cow, worth about six to eight pounds in 1263–64, cost about eighteen pounds in 1302, an increase that corresponds pretty well to the extent of monetary debasement.[10]

The office through which the commune came to control the grain market was the *canova*, the grain administrators, *canovarii*.[11] The canova was the deposit, an open warehouse of grain from which the city lived between harvests and for the protection of which guards were stationed. The canova itself seems a consolidation of various offices set up by the commune to buy Sicilian, Sardinian, or local grain, but of its administrative development we know little. Further, how old was the canova's organization—an organization of which only the early 14th century's fuller sources can illustrate—will probably never be known. We do know, however, that in pegging the price of grain the canova was successful, and that for this success certain operations were indispensable.

One was that the canova should purchase enough grain for Pisa's population, whether from the peasants or from importers from the contado or from overseas. The price paid depended on the bargaining strength of the grain seller. Over her own merchants, the commune insisted that all grain taken from Sardinia be taken only to Pisa, an indication that she was forcing on them a debased price.[12] The result was to drive Pisa's own merchants from the grain market—depending of course on the state of the

10. See Appendix II, no. 9.

11. Discussed in G. Rossi-Sabatini, *Pisa al tempo dei Donoratico (1316–1347)* (Florence, 1938), pp. 54–60.

12. See for instance ASP Comune A 89, 108v, 29 July 1322. A Pisan merchant carrying 3180 starelle of Sardinian grain was forced by one Arthithuccius Romanetti to carry the grain to and sell it at Portovenere, "dicentes se indigere frumento et quod dicta terra erat in maxima necessitate frumenti." The merchant asks the anziani that he not be punished for not bringing the grain to Pisa.

free market and the canova's policies.[13] From 1290 the
commune's agents were buying grain in huge quantities
from Catalonian importers or from the great Florentine
houses, the Bardi and Peruzzi, whom the commune could
not coerce.[14]

Over the peasant, however, the canova could exert better
control. Rural communes could sell grain only to the
canova or its agents, of course at the canova's price. Probably the canova profited enough from these semirequisi-
tions to mitigate its deficit from the purchases of imported
grain. By the early 14th century, if a commune did not
deliver its allotted quota, the canova's legal arm could
proceed against it by prosecutions and seizures.

In attempting to evaluate the results of this policy on
Pisan grain production, we should not presume that the
effects of this depressed price were immediately or necessarily disastrous. It is entirely possible that at first this
policy "thinned the herd" of the marginal farmers, forced
them to sell their land to more efficient producers, and
therefore helped create a more productive system of agriculture. If this be true, however, Pisa's sources do not
establish it. What they do establish is that the policy of
forcing agriculture to subsidize urban living was pursued
with a ruthlessness that by the 14th century did result in
an impressive decline in Pisan grain production. By then
rural communes found it easier to turn their land to other
pursuits and buy their grain on the free market, which
explains the prevalence of Sicilian grain in local transactions and signifies the withering of local production.[15] In

13. For a Catalonian selling Sicilian grain in 1290, ASP Alliata, 30 June
1291.
14. Cf. Rossi-Sabatini, *Donoratico*, p. 55.
15. To stop this practice, which resulted in more land falling out of
grain cultivation, the commune by the early 14th century even forbade one
rural commune to sell grain to another. See Rossi-Sabatini, *Donoratico*,
p. 56. For the decline of the Maremma's grain production, see also Volpe,

1290, for instance, one Catalonian merchant sold the commune 18,212 staia—enough to feed over 5,600 Pisans for one year.[16] In the poor crop year of 1322 Pisa had to buy in overseas markets 80,000 staia, enough to feed for one year 18,000 of her people.[17] By that time, even the Maremma communes could not feed themselves. The growing importance of imported grain over the local crop meant a growing financial strain on the canova, which more and more had to be subsidized "for the welfare . . . both of the commune and of individual persons and especially the poor." The subsidization had to be provided by taxes which weighed as much on the city as on exhausted agriculture. The policy of forcing agriculture to subsidize the cost of urban living and hence of industrialization was by the early 14th century at Pisa clearly failing.

This marked decline in Pisan grain production suggests that agricultural land was falling out of grain cultivation, and raises the problem of what use that land was being turned to. While we have no statistics, perhaps we can establish the trend by considering the importance at Pisa of a second agricultural pursuit: the raising of animals.

The profession most immediately reflecting the importance of animal husbandry at Pisa is of course the butchers. Because of Pisa's wet terrain and the abundance of fodder, butchers had always been an important profession. They are one of the four earliest artisan guilds, and even for this earlier period show considerable affluence. One in 1196 had investments involving eleven donkeys and parts of three others, a goat, and two sheep.[18] Their court claimed

---

"Pisa," p. 311. See also ASP Commune A 85, 16r, 24 May 1315, for five rural communes which had to petition for permission to purchase grain from the canova.

16. ASP Alliata, 30 June 1291.

17. Rossi-Sabatini, *Donoratico*, p. 58.

18. ASP Roncioni, 15 Dec. 1196, inventory of possessions of Guiccionus tabernarius.

jurisdiction over all contracts involving cattle, and the volume of their business is illustrated by a special cattle market with its own consul, and imports of animals from inland Tuscany.[19]

Further, butchers in the later 13th century were becoming still more numerous. In comparison with the vintners, the butchers had an index of 0.79 in the oath of 1228, and in the *Breve Antianorum* from 1289 to 1300, that index has jumped to 1.24, an increase of 60 per cent as against a profession that was itself hardly atrophying. With the exception of the notaries, butchers are more frequently elected anziani than any other artisans.

Simultaneously, in the extant contracts the number of *soccide,* investments in cattle, grows until by 1300 they are more numerous than the *societates maris* and *societates terre* combined, and the *mezzadria,* the land lease, has vanished.[20] Significant too is a shift in the type of animals raised. The division of the butcher's investments in 1196 (fourteen donkeys, two sheep) is typical. Sometime before 1150, fees for letting beasts graze on the Calci hills were paid by "ass-keepers." [21] After 1260, however, the numbers of sheep which appear make even their unquestioned importance in earlier years seem slight by comparison. In 1271, we hear of a flock of 1,000 "and more" coming down from the Lucchese Garfagnana to graze on the Pisan "plain of the port" and to trample grain and wine fields on the way.[22] In 1270 Pisa had to compose those long chapters

19. *Stat., 3, 105.* 2629 253r, 20 April 1285, "consul mercati bestiarum."
20. In 1301–02 in the chartulary 2545 there are almost thirty guardie contracts (a variation of the soccida) and not a single mezzadria contract.
21. *Reg. pis.,* no. 421.
22. ASP San Lorenzo alle Rivolte, 10 Nov. 1271. For the earlier period, see document of 1156, published in *ASI, 6,* Pt. II (1845), p. 23, "turmas pecorum de Carfagnana" feeding in the forests near San Rossore. Constitutum Usus, *Stat., 2,* 1017, official stationed at Ripafratta "super pecudum redditus constitutus." However, up to 1257 San Miniato was using

which her statutes of 1286 have preserved, *De dampnis et guastis, De guardianis, De guardianis vinearum,* meant to protect Pisan agricultural land from the sea of animals that was coming to surround it.[23] In 1284 members of a Pisan noble house, the Masca, and a Lucchese formed a "company of sheep." [24] The Lucchese was to raise the company's flock in the Garfagnana for six months, presumably summer, the Pisans for the other six months on the Pisan plain, presumably during the winter, and profits after five years "and more" were to be evenly divided. Reference to a "custom of the society of beasts" shows that this was no isolated contract. Indeed, in 1283 the Pisan nobleman Albertus, son of Uguiccione Pandulfi, had an estate in Lucca that went by the expressive name of "the farm (*podere*) of the beasts from Pisa." [25] In 1298 we hear of a flock of 2,000 sheep and goats going from the Garfagnana to winter on the lowlands of Grosseto.[26]

Did this increase in sheep raising and decline in grain production, this growth of the urban and fall of the rural population, mean that there was taking place in the Pisan

---

Pisan measurements for linen and Lucchese for wool, showing that the Pisans were behind the Lucchese in wool production. Davidsohn, *Forsch.,* 2, 749.

23. ASP, San Lorenzo alle Rivolte, 10 Nov. 1271. Flocks had damaged cultivated land, "contra formam banni pisani communis inde missi ab octo mensibus citra." The Breve potestatis (1286), *Stat., 1,* 238 ff., contains these or similar capitula.

24. ASP Cappelli, 23 April 1284. The members of the Masca family involved were "dominus Bonaccursus Masca iudex et Guilielmus Masca germani filii condam Bernaduccii Masche pro se ipsis et Uguiccione fratre eorum . . . et Galganus Mascha filius condam Bonaccursi Masche." Bernaduccius Masca was a consul in Alexandria and had been exiled along with the Guelf nobility in 1270, but in the later 13th century the family passed over to popolani status. See Schaube, *Konsulat,* p. 165.

25. 2545 38r, 8 March 1283.

26. ASP Archivio Montarelli della Volta, chartulary of Pepus of Fucecchio, 28 Oct. 1299.

countryside an "enclosure" or "engrossing" movement on the part of Pisa's powerful landowners? If so, what motivated them to it? Was it that steady population growth in the contado had resulted in excessive subdivision of holdings and critical underemployment of agricultural workers, so that the movement was a response to an agricultural depression? Or was it that the growing Tuscan wool industry held out to landowners possibilities for profit in sheep raising they could not ignore? These are basic questions, the answers to which our present knowledge cannot provide. Suffice to state that at Pisa the evidence is considerable that an enclosure movement of significant proportions was occuring in the late 13th century, although we cannot yet explore fully the factors behind it.

Pisa, with her wet plain and precious fodder, was an area where enclosures in the interest of sheep raising would be early felt. The important regions are the two areas which could play a role in a system of transhumance, the Pisan "plain of the port" for winter pastures, and the Valdarno, Piemonte (Calci), and the Val di Serchio, summer grazing lands or the gateways "beyond the mountains" to the Lucchese Garfagnana.

From the "plain of the port" we have a long series of parchments dealing with the land operations of the founder of one of Pisa's new houses, Falcone. Of Iohannes Falcone's own background we know little. Professionally he was a *pannarius,* a cloth salesman. Did he perhaps come from the Valdarno, the Val di Serchio, or Piemonte, like so many other *pannarii?* [27] At any rate, the family he

27. Iohannes was at Pisa by 1248 (ASP Cappelli, 5 Feb. 1248 and ASP Primaziale, 1 Oct. 1252), where he was renting a shop from a noble of the Gualandi family. For land purchases of Iohannes Falcone in Colognole, ASP Cappelli, 5 Feb. 1248, 16 March 1248, 30 Sept. 1249, 17 Nov. 1250, 17 Dec. 1253, 8 Oct. 1256, 12 May 1261, 20 Dec. 1262, 6 May 1264, 17 Dec.

founded is one of Pisa's most prominent. By 1302 another Iohannes Falcone, probably his grandson, had risen through the aristocratic ranks of the curia maris to become consul of the sea.[28]

But apparently the family won its start not by commerce but by agricultural or industrial ventures. Between 1240 and the 1260's Iohannes purchased upward of one hundred pieces of land in Colognole, embracing part of the Livorno hills and the plain of the port, mostly from needy members of the noble consortery which controlled the area, the *domini de Colognole*.[29] By the 1260's, a majority of the land purchased bordered property Iohannes already owned.

Most interesting is Iohannes' relation to the institution known as the *curia* or *guardia* of Colognole. The curia was simply an estate or manor, the area of land surrounding the noble manor house or castle which had been the controlling family's patrimony or fief. Such estates might be held in fee simple, others were fiefs especially from the archbishop. The nobles who possessed these curiae possessed numerous feudal prerogatives over the land or people: jurisdictions, the right of advowson over the churches, the right to collect tolls, and so forth. However, the seigneurial prerogative which seems to come most into prominence in the late 13th century was the *pascuum,* the right to graze flocks on the curia's forests and waste lands. Many nobles found it profitable to lease these grazing rights. The lessees paid for the privilege of serving as *guardiani* or *cafadarii* in these areas, with the right of grazing their own flocks but the obligation of protecting agricultural lands.

1266, 5 Feb. 1267. See also ASF C 462, 39v, 5 Aug. 1302, will of Falcone notarius filius condam Iohannis Falconis filii condam Upetini Falconis.

28. ASF C 462, 27r, 11 Feb. 1302. Iohannes Falconis, Michaelis Pedone and Gottifredus Sampantis consuls of the sea.

29. Above, n. 27.

The value and importance of the office are perhaps best illustrated by the stringent regulations the statutes of 1286 place upon it.[30] A guardianus could serve for only one year, and only in an area where he did not himself own land, and neither his son nor his grandson could succeed him if anyone else could serve. All instances of crop damage by his flocks had immediately to be reported to communal officials. In the sheep centers of the Pisan contado —the Serchio valley, the Piemonte and the Valdarno— these guardiani had to assemble every eight days before the communal captain to make this strict supervision a reality. But before the rights of the pascuum, agriculture seems to have verged on helplessness. In 1271 when a flock of over 1,000 sheep trampled grain and vines and the owners sued, the sheep raisers appealed to seigneurial prerogative, and the case was dismissed.[31]

Besides obtaining through leases the right to graze their flocks, sheep raisers could also purchase control of curiae outright. In 1248 Iohannes Falcone bought from a needy noble one-sixteenth of the curia of Colognole, in 1264 he purchased another one forty-eighth, and another one twenty-fourth in 1266. And of course, our contracts are fragmentary.

30. *Stat., 1,* 238–48. Cf. 2545 41v, 15 March 1283. Members of several noble consorteries lease for one year for four pounds fifteen solidi "guardiam predictorum consortum" and nominate the lessees "guardianos cafadiarios et custodes cum omni iure et actione." The guardiani are to graze their animals as determined by the "forma brevis et ordinamentorum pisani communis" and are responsible for all "dampnum et guastum" they cause. See also 2545 95r, 10 Nov. 1283.

31. ASP San Lorenzo alle Rivolte, 10 Nov. 1271. The plaintiff was asked "si scit vel credit quod curia et pascuum de Oliveto plani portus [est] pro medietate pro indiviso dominarum Omnium Sanctorum Hospitalis ecclesie sancti Leonardi de Stango et pro quarta parte Henrigi comitis de Portu et pro octava domini Pellarii et pro alia octava parte Uguiccionis Amascii quondam Bernarducii Rosselmini."

What Iohannes, whose profession was the sale of cloth, wanted with these contiguous lands and grazing rights would seem to be evident. Important to note is that Iohannes' career is hardly isolated.

There is Lucterius or Terius Agnelli, De Agnello, or Dell' Agnello.[32] Another parvenu of obscure origins, Terius was the ancestor of one of Pisa's most important families, which even, in the 14th century, gave the city a tyrant, Giovanni Dell' Agnello. Terius' father was professionally a notary, but of him we know only that he was living in the city by 1252.[33] Terius himself seems consistently associated with the democratic regimes. He first appears as anziano in 1290 and 1291 when Guido da Montefeltro compromised the aristocratic reaction of Ugolino Gherardesca, and again in 1294. After the revolt of 1295 he was anziano again in 1296 and prior in 1298. In the early 14th century, he was anziano in 1301, 1303, 1304, and 1306. During the last Ghibelline upsurge that heralded the arrival of Henry VII (1310) he was appointed an official in Sardinia. In 1315 under the tyranny of Ugione della Faggiola, he was prosecuted for behavior in that office. The prosecution almost certainly had political overtones. In 1319, "languishing in body," he was probably near death.

As one of Pisa's new capitalists, Terius had close ties with commerce. In 1285 he had in his possession Genoese prisoners and, like Iohannes Falcone, served as consul of the sea.[34] His family in the 14th century was prominent

32. See Bonaini, *Famiglie*, p. 820. Bonaini errs, however, in giving credence to the oath of 1188, according to which the family was already in the city in that year.

33. ASP Primaziale, 1 Oct. 1252, "Tedicio notario quondam Agnelli."

34. For Genoese prisoners sold as exchanges to Pisan families with relatives imprisoned at Genoa, 2529 276v, 12 Sept. 1285; 277r, 12 Sept.; 277r, 12 Sept.

in the new-found Majorcan and Catalonian trade.[35] As
with Iohannes Falcone, from the earlier period we hear
nothing of commerce, but much of land. In 1284 he is en-
gaged in extensive land exchanges in the upper Serchio
valley; he is buying up property from needy peasants and
lends money to needy communes. Most interesting, he had
married a daughter from the old house of Assi, the Casassi.
Either before or because of the marriage he came to control six fiefs held by that family from the archbishop. In
1287 at the height of the aristocratic reaction, Terius had
to renounce these fiefs. The renunciation was ineffectual;
in 1310 he still controlled them. Two other pieces of land
Terius was administrating for the noble house. These fiefs
were located at San Piero a Grado and at "Del Falda" and
had given Terius grazing land in the plain of the port.
The others were at Settimo and Fagiano in the low and
wet Valdarno. Of two we know the type of agriculture
thereon practiced: *terra campi, terra pratata,* pastures.

How much other land Terius or his father had gained
we do not know. Their interest in land, however, is better
explained: Terius married his son with a wool merchant's
daughter. The dowry, 1,000 pounds, was the kind that
evinced strictures from Dante and Villani. The name of
the wool merchant is new, another of the then parvenu

35. For the family's commercial activities, see M. Luzzatto, "Rapporti
tra Pisani, Amalfitani e Catalani nel secolo XIV," *Rassegna Storica Salernitana,* 22 (1951), 108–225. For land operations of Terius, 2629 243r, 24
March 1285 (Serchio valley); 2629 283v, 30 Oct. 1285 (Serchio valley); and
Terius' will, 2525 37r, 24 May 1310. For loans to rural communes in the
Serchio valley, 2629 245r, 3 April 1285, and 246v, 9 April 1285. For his
service as "rector ville ecclesie de Sardinea," 2525 34r, 29 April 1310. For
his wife, "Getta filia condam Iacobi Tanfi de Casassi," 2521 39r, 16 Dec.
1305. For the marriage of his son with "domina Contissa dicta Teddia
filia Iacobi dicti Puccii lanarii de cappella sancti Laurentii de Rivolta
condam Bernardi Aiutamichristo," 2521 203v, 17 Oct. 1307.

families with a long history awaiting it: Aiutamicristo.

Careers like Terius Agnelli's could be reproduced here at will. For completeness, that of Ranuccius son of Guido Rossi is valuable.[36] He came perhaps from Vico in the Valdarno, and purchased himself a fief from a nobleman in the plain of the port, perhaps for winter pasture. He was the partner of a *lanarius,* the father-in-law of a Paganellus de Vico, later a frequent anziano during the popular regimes, and the father of an overseas merchant.

The chartularies show too that this zeal in acquiring land was often coupled with an effort to force the peasants from the soil. Ranuccius in 1285 ordered the peasant Martinus de Noceto "who lives on the estate of Ranuccius," to "leave the farm or piece of land . . . on which the same Martin is living." [37] Chellus Afferra was a Lucchese, but related to another of Pisa's new houses, the Sciancati.[38] Within his estate, he forced out the peasant Paulus de Montigiano and in his will of 1310 wants the land he seized returned. His operations in the hills above the Serchio ran up a list of extortions against peasants and rural communes, which, for charity, we shall let rest in his unpublished will. In 1299 from the area of Musiliano which then

36. Ranuccius owned grazing land, "in suis pratis et palude" near the Monti Pisani and Vico, "positis apud Vicascium," 2629 255v, 29 May 1285, and his daughter married Paganellus de Vico, 2629 275v, 12 Sept. 1285, "Paganellus iudex de Vico generus meus." For his land in the plain of the port, 2629 275v, 12 Sept. 1285, "tenere et usufructum petii mei terre de Colognole quod emi a domino Gottifredo Guintavallis." His partner (2629 280r, 9 Oct. 1285) was "Bacciameo quodam Strenne lanario de cappella sancte Cecilie." For his son, 2629 278r, 13 Sept. 1285, "Coscium filium meum qui est in Tunithi."

37. 2629 242v, 20 March 1285.

38. His will, 2525 42v, 28 May 1310. He returns as unjustly taken "filiis et heredibus Pauli de Montigiano sive eis ad quos legiptime pertinent omnia petia terrarum que fuerunt dicti Pauli que sunt infra podere meum de Schiava in loco dicto al pagio." Rainerius Sciancatus was his "nepos."

had a population of sixteen, we have five orders directing peasants to leave the land.[39]

And the peasants, almost without protection from the powerful landowners, were willing to go. By 1309 two of the Valdarno's three *pievi*—San Lorenzo alle Corti and San Casciano—with an area of about twenty square miles of level country, counted 196 heads, less than ten persons per square mile, less than five persons left for each of the forty communes which had crowded the area.[40] Little wonder that of San Lorenzo's nineteen churches, eight no longer exist, of San Casciano's twenty-one, thirteen have vanished. Little wonder too, that of the population of urban San Cristofano in 1272, 50 per cent were recent immigrants.

We do not, however, have to leave entirely the professions directly associated with agriculture to find one that seems to have profited from the pegged prices and restricted markets associated with the democratic commune. That profession was the vintners.

At Pisa, the vintner was not primarily a vine-cultivator. The statutes of the guild rule that a vintner had to own either a shop or a boat, and the vintner's apprentice swore to serve him "on land or sea."[41] The reference to boats would seem to indicate the peculiar strength of the Pisan vintners: profiting from Pisa's admirable location and easy

39. 2527 9v, 24 Sept. 1299; 9v, 10r, 10r, 10v, 10v, and one renunciation of land, 46v, 9 Oct. 1300. Three renunciations in Cherlus, 2629 270v, 15 Aug. 1285; 271r, 29 Aug. 1285; 271v 30 Aug. 1285. See *Stat., 1,* cap. 150, De refutationibus et prohibitionibus terrarum.

40. 2523 209v, 27 Jan. 1309. San Lorenzo taxed for seventy-eight "heads" and San Casciano for 118 in financing a dike on the Arno. On the constituent communes, see *Tuscia, 1,* 186, nn. 3727–39; 2, 240, nn. 3680–99; and Repetti, *Dizionario, 1,* 809. In 1299 one of San Lorenzo's communes, Musiliano, had sixteen persons, 2527 1r.

41. *Stat., 3,* 1106; 2543 80v, 21 Feb. 1264.

access to sources both of foreign and Tuscan wine, the vintners were able to build strong marketing organizations serving areas beyond Pisa's own borders. Indeed, their extensive commerce on both fresh and salt water brought them very close to the domain of the curia maris, the bastion of Pisa's mercantile aristocracy. Serving a mass consumption market, vintners had always been numerous; in the oath of 1228, they were eighty. However, only with the ascendancy of the popolo did they gain independent status. There were other fruits, too: the right independently of the curia maris to export or import wine, and subservience to their guild of the *homines vie Arni,* the carters and boatmen along the Arno valley.[42] In fact, the guild seems to have usurped the authority over the carters formerly exercised by the noble house of Gaitani. It even imposed taxes, "for expenses," on rural communes with which Pisan vintners contracted for deliveries of wine.[43]

Moreover, the vintners seem to have profited from the debasement of Pisan money in a sense more strictly economic. Wine, unlike grain, was left on a free market (although, we might add, during the 14th century it became increasingly loaded with excise taxes so as to provide the commune's chief source of indirect revenue). Debasement meant, therefore, rising wine prices.[44] The vintners possessed, however, a strong enough marketing monopoly not to be required to pass this increase along to the grape growers.

Vintners at Pisa are among the richest of artisans. In-

42. See p. 62, n. 15, and p. 82, n. 6.
43. "Et quod quilibet . . . sensalium communium terrarum de foris pisani districtus et Sancti Miniatis et eius curie habentium pacta cum arte vinariorum teneatur . . . dare omni anno . . . in adiutorium expensarum suprascripte artis, libram unam piperis." Breve artis vinariorum, *Stat., 3,* 1115.
44. Cf. Appendix II, no. 8.

deed, they were able to become, to an important extent, the wine purveyors for inland Tuscany. In 1295, when Florence faced a wine shortage, she contracted with Pisans to alleviate it.[45] To Florence, Pisans carried even Sienese wine.[46] Their importance at Florence in the early 14th century is revealed by the protests of Florentine vintners as to their presence.[47] To the over-all pattern of Pisan economic subjection to the hinterland, the vintners provide a brilliant exception.

However, the most important result of communal policies in regard to agriculture was that the countryside was made to subsidize urban residents; profiting most from this subsidy were the urban crafts and industries.

45. See G. Arias, *I Trattati commerciali della Repubblica fiorentina* (Florence, 1901), p. 454, document dated 6 Dec. 1295.

46. Davidsohn, *Forsch.*, *4*, nos. 758, 830.

47. Ibid., no. 725.

9. CRAFTS AND INDUSTRIES

> I saw Bellincione Berti going bound
> with leather and bone, and coming from the mirror
> his wife without painted face;
>
> And I saw those of the Nerli and of the Vecchio
> content with uncovered fur . . .
>> DANTE, *Paradiso* 15:112–16, DESCRIBING
>> THE SIMPLICITY OF OLD FLORENCE

THE SUBSIDIZATION of urban living resulting from the policies of the democratic commune did not affect all urban crafts and industries equally. Crudely put, the larger the labor force employed, the greater the profit that the industrial entrepreneur stood to gain from the democratic policies. But this in turn meant that the older crafts established in the city (at Pisa, especially, the production of iron and luxury leather), which were relatively simple in organization and worked with small labor forces for restricted markets, reaped little from the new policies, the benefits of which accrued rather to the new industries, which employed more labor and produced for wider markets, at Pisa especially the industries of cheap leather and wool.

According to the numbers of artisans appearing in the oath of 1228, Pisan economic efforts in that year were distributed approximately as follows among five sectors: [1]

---

1. *Caleffo, 1,* 365 ff. Under "Food" I am including fornarii, vinarii, tabernarii, olearii, vinaioli, casciaoli, piczicaioli, speciales, to mention the most important. Under "Building and metallurgy" are included the artisans concerned with construction, metal or armor work (fabri, ferrarii, cultel-

Professional (notaries, lawyers, doctors)	147
Food (grain, wine, meat)	346
Building and metallurgy	289
Leather and skins	305
Textiles (linen, wool, dyeing, tailoring)	101

The importance of "building and metallurgy" at Pisa is the importance especially of one group, the *fabri*, who in 1228 constituted at Pisa the largest single profession (125 participants in the oath).[2] One of the oldest occupations to appear in Pisa's sources, the fabri were likewise one of the four earliest artisan guilds. Originally workers both in wood and iron, they labored at Pisa during the summer, and in the winter they would go by sea "to Elba, Giglio, and Alma, and in all other places from the mouth of the Arno to Rome and Corsica."[3] There they would remain until the feast of Santa Cristina in May, working "as is the good custom and the good tradition in the guild of fabri."[4] In those areas they maintained *fabricae*, factories, both for wood and especially for iron. They therefore devoted the winter to gathering raw materials and the summer to making finished products. Indeed, the "good custom" which closed their factories after May betrays appreciation of the health hazards of a Maremma summer.

The chartularies of 1263 and 1264 present an interesting

larii, tappiaoli, metellarii, muraioli, scudarii, arcarii, aurifices, again to mention the most important). For a breakdown of the most important groups under "Leather and skins" and "Textiles," see below, p. 135.

2. On Pisa's iron industry, see *Mostra autarchica del minerale italiano. Miniere e ferro dell' Elba dai tempi etruschi ai nostri giorni*, (Rome, 1938), and Pintor, "Elba." Neither, however, makes use of the chartularies, the richest source on the 13th-century iron industry, and hence are sketchy for our period.

3. Privileges granted by the archbishop to the fabri for protection in these overseas areas from 1094 to 1274 are printed in *Stat., 3*, 891 ff.

4. 2543 35r, 4 June 1263; 2514 1v, 14 Aug. 1264; 2514 14r, 23 Sept. 1264; 2514 23r, 24 Oct. 1264—all contracts in which workers are hired "ab inde ad festum sancte Christine mensis madii."

series of contracts regarding the winter migration of the
iron workers and the men they hired to help them.[5] We
hear of *opera de supersalliente de casa, opera de ceppaiolis,
opera de menafollis, opera delo scaldatore*. The "supersalliens de casa" was probably a guard to protect the factory in its still wild surroundings against attacks by pirates
or natives as depicted in the life of St. Rainerius.[6] The
man hired for the job does not call himself a *faber* and his
pay is half what a skilled master would receive. A job likewise for the unskilled worker was "opera de ceppaiolis";
almost certainly it involved the working with logs (*ceppe*),
probably the preparation of charcoal. "Menafollus" suggests *menare*, "to lead out," "to produce." Of *folles*, Federigo Visconti remarked once that the good priest "should
stand devoutly in the choir without putting one foot on
the seat like an iron worker holding one foot on a rod of
folles." [7] It was a bellows operator. "Scaldator" probably
ran the furnace.

By the 1260's, however, this specialization had not
reached the stage where there had appeared a division between mine operators, owners, or lessees, and the mine
workers. The contracts rather illustrate that the operator
of the mine himself worked in it and participated in the
yearly migration.[8]

An obscure question concerning the operation of the
mines is the relationship of the fabri with the feudal suze-
rains of the areas they mined, especially the archbishop,
and, perhaps too, the cathedral chapter. The iron workers
donated to the cathedral twenty solidi per year per fabrica,

5. On the following terms, "supersalliens," 2543 35r, 4 June 1263; the
"ceppaiolus," 2514 23r, 24 Oct. 1264; the "menafollus," 2514 1v, 14 Aug.
1264; the "scaldator," 2514 14r, 23 Sept. 1264.

6. *ASS, 24,* 375 C.

7. Visconti, 2r.

8. Thus 2514 1v, 14 Aug. 1264, worker promises faber that he "ibit cum
eo in eius fabricam quam habebit in Ilbam vel alibi."

in return for the archbishop's protection in their migrations. They seem, moreover, to have made other payments to the cathedral chapter and probably also to the archbishop, perhaps in return for the privilege of mining their lands.[9]

In 1274, another privilege granted by the archbishop to the fabri is apparently the last reference to their yearly migration. Evidence of it vanishes from the contracts as well, and when the guild statutes (1305) cast a flood of light upon the industry, they have lost all trace of the "good custom" of working the mines from autumn to May, and of the tribute formerly given by the fabri to the Pisan cathedral. On Elba, mine workers are now simply *cavatores;* in Pisa's iron industry, the fabri seem no longer to have controlled nor even worked the traditional iron centers.

The disappearance of the "good custom" suggests that in the later 13th century year-round exploitation of the mines had begun. It argues, too, a reorganization of the industry in a manner usually called capitalistic, in the sense of a dichotomy between the mine operator and worker. In this reorganization, the coming of the democratic commune, the acute financial crisis of the late 13th century, and the temporary loss of Elba to Genoa were surely important factors. By 1269 and again in 1275, Pisa sold the "vein of iron."[10] Simultaneously with these sales, the commune had

9. ASP Primaziale, 26 Dec. 1265. Leonardus archipresbiter with the consent of the canons and the canons themselves for their chapter and Rainaldus operarius sancte Marie maioris ecclesie collect "a fabris et qualibet persona facientibus et habentibus fabricas vel cathormas in ysula Ylbe vel alibi" twenty-nine solidi for each fabrica and nineteen solidi four denarii for each cathorma. See also Dal Borgo, *Raccolta*, nos. 8 and 9 (1289), where the podesta orders the communes of Elba to present every year falcons to the archbishop, which they have not done for over ten years.

10. ACA, 22 May 1269. Federigo Visconti "ad preces Calmangiaris de Folle camerarii hominum qui emerunt dovanam et venam ferri a communi pisano concessit . . . quod vena ferri quod flumen Arni possit libere

taken from the archbishop and cathedral chapter their
feudal jurisdictions, including Elba.[11] After Meloria, Elba
fell under Genoese control, so that in 1291 Genoa sold the
iron of Elba to one of her own citizens.[12] Though Pisan
control over the island was restored in the Genoese treaty of
1300, the Genoese capitalists retained a permanent interest
in the island's mines. In 1305, the head and probably a
majority of the members of the company that operated Elba
for the Pisan commune were Genoese.[13]

Exactly when Pisa and, in 1291, Genoa were exploiting
Elba's "vein of iron" as a rich source of revenue, the "good
custom" of mine operation only from autumn to May
vanishes. That the two developments are to be related
would seem a plausible presumption. To gain as much
profit as possible, the commune would naturally favor
year-round production. In our period, Elba's output was

---

portare" will be charged a toll at Ricavo of two instead of the usual
eighteen solidi, "et hoc fecit de gratia propter magnas expensas quas
pisani faciunt propter guerram." For the sale of 1275, Breve pisani populi,
Stat., 1, 608.

11. As reflected by the fact that about 1278 the communes of Elba had
ceased to give the archbishop his falcons. See above, n. 9, and p. 59, nn. 8,
10.

12. See Iacobi Aurie Annales, anno 1291, (MGH, Ss, 18, 335), "Federicus
Aurie emisset in callega a comuni Ianue venam ferri de insula Elbe pro
uno anno pro libris 8500 Ianuinorum, quia tunc temporis comune Ianue
eam tenebat et possidebat . . ."

13. ASP Comune A 83, 54r (1304). "Guillielmus Palavigini de Ianua
procurator mercatorum ianuensium et pisanorum habentium venam ferri
de Ylba." ASP Comune A 84, 33v, 19 Aug. 1311, iron to be assigned to
"mercatoribus ianuensibus pisanis habentibus ea in conpera a communi
pisano ut moris est." See also R. S. Lopez and I. W. Raymond, Medieval
Trade in the Mediterranean World (New York, 1955), p. 191, n. 97, for a
Genoese contract of 1308 dealing with an investment in the "vein of iron"
in Elba. For Lucchese investing in the "vein of iron," ASP Alliata, 20
Sept. 1290; for Florentines, 2524 30r, 25 Feb. 1308, Fettus condam Ubertini
de Florentia and Laurentius Cannuccini de Florentia operators of a "vein"
in Lunigiana.

indeed stepped up; by the early 14th century Pisa's "vein of iron" constituted the largest single source of income from her own contado.[14] The penalty was that the mine workers, the cavatores, became subject to the financial exploitation of the iron purchasers and the even worse health hazards of the Maremma summer. In the later 13th century the stage was set for that picture of Elba's misery— poverty, disease, and class warfare—which the *Provvisioni* of Pisa's anziani from 1299 on first bring fully into light.[15]

As producers of iron products, Pisa's fabri had enjoyed all the advantages which easily available raw materials could give. We hear of Pisan iron at Genoa in 1140, and in the early 13th century Frederick II had invited Pisan fabri to make armor in the Regno.[16] When in 1285 Parma needed a new bell, "for lack of metal" she could not strike it herself.[17] In view of the 1,000 pounds she was willing to pay, a Pisan faber came to strike it, disposing "of new metal, in great supply, as abundantly as he wished." To the Parmesans he displayed such pomp and pride as to seem "a great baron." And the bell he cast was of such grandeur as to tempt the Lord. The Lord replied, our source, Fra Salimbene, tells us, to this metallic expression of human arrogance by dulling its tongue, so that the great bell could hardly be heard!

However, even before Meloria, Pisa's iron industry was showing weaknesses. In 1284 a contract mentions *corettum pisaneschum de mallea,* and the reference to "Pisan" shows that the writer was conscious of other armor in his city not

14. Cf. Volpe, "Pisa," p. 310. *Acta Henrici VII Romanorum imperatoris,* ed. F. Bonaini (Florence, 1817), 2, 96, no. 9. From Elba Pisa was drawing 60,000 florins and from taxes and fines in the city and contado, 50,000.
15. Discussed in Pintor, "Elba."
16. Schaube, *Handelsg.,* pp. 491, 623. *Codice diplomatico della Repubblica di Genova,* ed. C. Imperiale (Rome, 1936), no. 102, "ferri pisaneschi."
17. Salimbene, *Cronica,* 2, 314.

of Pisan manufacture—perhaps Florentine, whose armor makers thought their product the best in the world, or "Lombard," Milanese, whose presence at Pisa can be documented for the period after Meloria and whose industry was perhaps being supplied even with Elba's iron by the Genoese.[18] The statutes (1286) sternly forbade Pisans to trade with the rival ports of Talamone or Motrone; one exception was permitted, however: the vein of iron could be carried there.[19] The exception was evidently allowed, since from the sale of iron the commune profited immediately. The entry shows, too, that the policy of selling raw iron to foreign industries rather than monopolizing it for Pisa's own had prevailed. In a table of Pisan-Florentine trade constructed by R. Ciasca for the year 1320–21, Pisa exported to Florence predominantly raw iron and imported iron products.[20] In comparison with the number of vintners, the number of *fabri* drops from an index of 1.33 in the oath of 1228 to 0.33 in the Breve antianorum from 1289 to 1300.

Pisa's iron industry, therefore, suffered heavily from the commune's growing need for money without gaining much from the policies that money was partially supporting. A different picture emerges from an analysis of Pisa's industries of leather (in the oath of 1228 her largest) and textiles, both of which we may consider under the general heading of clothing material.

Thirteenth-century clothing material came from three sources: animal skins (leather and furs), vegetable fibers (linen, cotton, and hemp), and animal hair (wool). "The clothes of my back," says a contract of 1272, "of wool and

18. 2544 6v, 11 July 1284. For Lombard iron, 2525 140r.
19. *Stat., I*, 391–2.
20. Ciasca, *Medici,* doc. XX.

of linen and of skins." [21] In 1228 the four industries associated with clothing material (leather, furs, linen, and wool) had the following distribution: [22]

Tanners (excluding shoemakers)			
coriarius		44	
ervarius		19	
pellarius	13		
cordovanerius	1		
beccuniere	6		
conciapellis	2		
		22	Total: 85
Furs			
pellicciarius		64	Total: 64
Wool			
lanaiolus		3	Total: 3
Linen and Hemp			
tesitor (also wool)		12	
banbacarius		10	
canaparius		4	Total: 26
Miscellaneous and General			
sutor		9	
talliator		4	
pannarius		11	
tinctor		29	

The distribution shows that for clothing material, furs and leather were the first, and by 1228 still the only, industries to be what we shall call urbanized. Indeed, if we add to this table the other artisans associated with leather (shoemakers 112, belt makers 28, saddle and rein makers 15, shield makers 30, and so forth), we may conclude that in 1228 leather and furs supported more Pisans than any other industry.

And in discussing urban industries, let us clarify our

21. 2515 124r, 2 July 1272.
22. *Caleffo, 1,* 365 ff.

meaning of the term "industrialization" which we shall use
so frequently. Medieval industry was and remained, of
course, predominantly a household industry. The production revolution of the 12th and 13th centuries did not take
production out of the household but moved the household
to the city, and this in turn made possible, even within the
household, a greater specialization and professionalization
of productive processes. Urbanization, and in this sense
industrialization, came to Pisa in two waves. The first was
during her crisis of the closing 12th century and concerned
leather and furs. The second came after 1250 and was of
wool.

In 1298 Pisa's leather industry was divided into two
groups on the basis of technological process: hot-water
guilds and cold-water guilds. The history of Pisan leather
is very nearly the history of these two technologies.

In all, we know the names of eight guilds at Pisa which
tanned leather: two shoemakers' (*calthularii* and *calthularii
de vacca*) and six tanners' (*coriarii aque frigide de Fori-
porta, coriarii aque calde de Spina, coriarii* or *pellarii de
Ponte Novo, coriarii* or *erovarii de carraria et cappella
sancte Marie Magdalene, cordovanerii de Ponte Novo,
pellarii de campo sancti Niccoli*).[23] Unfortunately, their
guild statutes are mutilated. Of the two shoemakers' guilds,
we have nothing from the calthularii de vacca. Of the six
tanners' guilds, we have the chapter headings or rubrics of
all, but the complete statutes only of the first three given
in the above list. The text of these leather-guild statutes as
published by Bonaini has another curious error. In 1298
Pisa's tanning guilds together formed a *sotietas* embracing
the whole industry.[24] The instrument of union contains the
rubric "instrument of the society of seven arts of tanners."

23. Rubrics published in *Stat., 3,* 899–910, statutes 911 ff.
24. *Stat., 3,* 901 ff.

In fact, only six guilds drew up the union. In copying the statutes before him, the 14th-century scribe made his error because he did indeed have seven guild statutes, although he copied out fully only the rubrics, and not the complete statutes, of the seven. In fact, however, one of these statutes —called in its rubric but not in its text *Breve coriariorum aque frigide*—is not that of any participating guild in the union of 1298.[25] In it the consul calls himself simply *consul coriariorum pisane civitatis,* and pretends to speak for all of Pisa's tanners. Moreover, this statute can be approximately dated. It refers to *potestatis vel rectoris vel consulum.* It comes therefore from that twilight period in Pisan governmental history when the consuls were disappearing and the podesta assuming their powers, from the early 13th century. It may further be associated with a privilege we know was granted to the tanners "by the consuls of Pisa," who do not appear at Pisa after 1234.[26] Although containing later entries, this *Breve* may be considered the oldest of Pisa's artisan statutes to have survived. We have in it a priceless record of the organization of Pisa's leather industry which was changed, indeed revolutionized, by movements which led to the union of 1298.

Next to the fabri, the tanners are the oldest artisans to appear in Pisa's sources.[27] However, not until the closing 12th century do we find trace of an organized guild. In an

25. *Stat., 3,* 928 ff.

26. *Stat., 3,* 928, "et ad honorium potestatis vel rectoris vel consulum qui pro tempore fuerint." For reference to the privilege, *Stat., 1,* 347, and Volpe, *Istituzioni,* p. 248. The Breve mentions the Breve pisani populi (*Stat., 3,* 942) and the captain of the people (ibid., p. 928) and hence was being revised even after 1254. However, the fact that this guild was so disrupted in the late 13th century and the Breve itself finally replaced by the new union of 1298 has preserved it from later changes; it is therefore the best preserved of Pisa's artisan statutes, all of which were further revised in the early 14th century.

27. *Reg. pis.,* no. 270 (year 1116), 466 (1160), and 558 (1188).

inscription that may be dated from 1186 to 1223, we hear that the tanners had already six captains.[28]

When the tanners first secured the commune's recognition sometime in this period, they were divided into three guilds: the *ars pellariorum vel cordovaneriorum,* the *ars coriariorum,* and a shoemakers guild, the *ars calthulariorum de vacca.*[29] It is a safe presumption that at the head of each of these three guilds were two captains, so that the six captains mentioned in the inscription reflect further the existence of these three earliest tanning guilds. The precociousness of their appearance, their early organization into and the number of their guilds, are all testimony to the importance of tanners at Pisa, even in the 12th century.

The oath of 1228 permits us to locate the guilds in the city, in order to give a topographical index of their development. The pellarii were concentrated around the Piazza San Niccola, the city's market place for overseas imports, and one of the oldest sections of medieval Pisa.[30] The piazza's church a contemporary parchment calls San Niccola in Pellaria.[31] By the union of 1298, this guild had split into three: the two guilds of pellarii and the one of cordovanerii. Without surviving rubrics or statutes, the calthularii de vacca are more difficult to locate. However, almost certainly they are identical with the *erovarii,* the tanners in 1228 already numerous in the parish of Maria Magdalena.[32]

28. The inscription originally from the Camposanto is published in *Stat., 3,* 926; for its date, Volpe, *Istituzioni,* p. 243.

29. *Stat., 3,* 928.

30. Out of 116 conjurors, San Niccola had ten pellarii and eight coriarii.

31. ASP Primaziale, 1 Feb. 1236.

32. Out of seventy-four parishioners, nineteen were ervarii. The word itself is of obscure origin. It is probably associated with "erba," a bark from which tannic acid was extracted. "Erba buggiea" was apparently a bark exported from North Africa used in the preparation of morocco leather. See Pegolotti, *Pratica,* p. 418. That the ervarii are to be identified with the calthularii de vacca seems shown by the following. The cal-

That parish stood on the other side of the Ponte Nuovo, almost directly opposite from the Piazza San Niccola. The third guild was "outside the gate," in the quarter of Fuoriporta, in the parishes of Sant' Andrea and Santa Lucia.[33] Topographically, the first two guilds would seem to be the industry's oldest. As their name shows (pellarii and de vacca), they were producing a supple luxury leather. The name of the third guild "outside the gate," the ars coriariorum, suggests that it concentrated upon producing a tougher, cheaper leather (corium). By the time the leather statutes were redacted, however, it was the industry's most important.

Significantly, all three of Pisa's earliest leather guilds used the cold-water process. Their statutes bear even the rubric coriarii aque frigide, although significantly too, the reference does not appear in the text, since that might indicate the contemporary existence of a hot-water guild. Our topographical index show rather that in 1228 the hot-water guild was still to be organized. It was later to be concentrated in the "Spina," in the parishes of San Silvestro and San Barnaba. In 1228, San Silvestro had one tanner out of 115 conjurors; San Barnaba, among its fifty-four, had none.

Curiously, we no sooner have a full picture of Pisa's leather industry than we find it in difficulties. Our earliest statutes have already imposed severe production restrictions. A master could cure sixteen skins per year, his ap-

thularii de vacca were members of the first union of leather tanners but not of the second; the erovarii were not members of the first union but were of the second. Yet the erovarii formed a numerous profession during the time of the first union, and the calthularii de vacca were still in existence and according to the Breve calthulariorum, they enjoyed an independent status during the time of the second union (Stat., 3, 1031). The problem of what happened to the calthularii de vacca is solved by identifying them with the erovarii.

33. Sant' Andrea had thirteen coriarii and two conciapellis out of 116.

prentice only eight.[34] Moreover, only the guild could decide when leather could be lifted from the tanning vats,
which means that the sixteen-skin quota was a maximum
not always permitted. Probably during the 1270's, the
pellarii fractured into three guilds. From one of the splin-
ters the statutes have fortunately survived, so the motivations of the split can be examined. The tanner of the
"pelarii de Ponte Novo" pugnaciously refers to his right
to tan any leather in any color he wishes "as we have tanned
. . . since twenty years." [35] The guild statutes, dating from
the late 1290's, would seem to suggest that these tanners
had had an independent guild since the 1270's at the latest.
The pellarius calls himself "coiaio de l'acqua calda"; he has
shifted to the hot-water process.

Moreover, even the coriarius of Fuoriporta by 1298 was
making hot-water leather as well. He was required only to
inform the purchaser of the type of leather he was selling.[36]

During this period, hot-water tanners secured their own
guild, that of the *coriarii aque calde de Spina;* the effort to
find room for this important new guild seems to have led to
the reorganization of the leather guilds of 1298.

In the late 13th century in Pisa's leather industry, we
thus have to do with the rapid rise of a new process for
treating leather and new groups of artisans connected with
it. We are poorly informed concerning the fate of the cold-
water process, nor can we judge how much it lost in importance; we may probably presume that it continued to be
utilized for certain types of luxury leather. What we can
say with certainty is that relatively, in terms of rapidity of
growth, the making of cold-water leather lagged behind a
new branch of the industry, which concentrated on pro-

34. *Stat., 3,* 936, 938, 939.
35. *Stat., 3,* 981.
36. *Stat., 3,* 953.

ducing leather of a different type and was based on a new technology.

Technologically, the difference between cold- and hot-water leather may be expressed as follows: the cold-water process sacrificed speed and volume to quality; the hot-water began by sacrificing quality to speed and volume, then perfected itself to where it could rival the older.[37] The skins coming to tanners of both types would either be fresh if from local flocks or dried and salted if imported from overseas. The latter skins had first to be soaked for three to seven days, but otherwise they had no special treatment. Naturally, the skin carried much waste material—hair, dirt, meat, and so forth—which had to be removed. The whole skin was therefore first placed in a bath of lime and alum, which loosened the dirt. Then it was lifted out, scraped clean of the wastes, and returned to the tanning vats proper. How early these three natural divisions—first soaking, cleaning, second soaking—were distinguished into specialized operations cannot be known. At any rate, by the 13th century each was performed by a specialized work-man: the *addobbator* for the first bath, the *mectitor ad ferrum* or *scarnator* for the cleaning, and the *servitor caldarie* for the tanning.[38] The cleaning bath lasted for large skins about one month. The scarnator then took the skin to the Arno, scraped it clean, and beat it down with myrtle. The servitor caldarie handled the tanning vat proper, and in this, the heart of the process, was the difference between

37. The following reconstruction of the leather-tanning processes is based on the "Libro di Girolamo Bertucci cominciato all' anno 1570 addi primo di Gennaio," ASP Pia Casa della Misericordia, no. 460. While late, the book serves to explain the terminology used in the 13th-century statutes.

38. *Stat.*, *3*, 921, "et quod addobbator, mectitor ad ferrum et servitor caldarie . . ." Liber Bertucci, 2v, "volui tre lavoranti adobatore scarnatore et servitore."

the hot- and cold-water processes. The cold-water tanner let the skin soak in myrtle and only in cold water. To have the skin absorb the acids better, he would lift it occasionally and rub and beat it down with myrtle. The hot-water tanner, on the other hand, first boiled the tanning mixture so that the water would better take the acids, then while the water was still hot—not so hot, however, as to cook a yet crude skin—he would pour it into the vats.[39] This he did twice a day. The tannic acid used may also have distinguished the processes. Cold-water tanners used myrtle—expensive and slow, but producing an excellently supple leather. Hot-water tanners seem to have used first myrtle—which tanned the skin partially but throughout and helped prevent its cooking in the hot water or forming an impervious crust under the stronger acids—and then, in subsequent soakings, lime or alum.[40] The succession of stronger baths is much as leather is tanned today. For complete tanning, cold-water leather took six months; the hot-water process could do it apparently in as little as ten days, depending of course on the type of leather desired (the tougher, the shorter time).[41]

39. Liber Bertucci, 4v, "mettene una buona corbella di mortella in caldaia cosi la sera come la mattina e la facci bollire una ora perche bollendo assai cava meglio la sustanza della mortella e poi mez' ora la lasci posare e di poi la temperi con l'acqua di tina avertendo che quando la gitta in tina non sia troppo calda perche scotere le quoia."

40. Breve coriariorum aque calide de Spina, *Stat.*, *3*, 967, "et che alcuno . . . non possa . . . conciare alcuno cioame . . . se in prima non fusse concio in mortella in de la citta di Pisa." Ibid., p. 959, "Io coiaio de la Spina, conciante le cuoia in calcina et mortella."

41. *Stat.*, *3*, 933, for the six-months' minimum. At Pistoia too (Zdekauer, *Statutum*, p. 121) in 1296, leather of calf, cow, horse or mule had to be left in the vats for six months. The ten-day period for hot-water leather seems illustrated by the following arbitration settlement between two hot-water tanners, ASP San Marta, 1 April 1326: "in qua concia coriaminis posita Pisis . . . dictus Dinus [coriarius] misit hiis diebus et habet adobbas decem coriaminis sive plures pro conciando . . . et quod finitis decem

The growth in importance of the hot-water process was made possible by the perfection of its technique, to the point where it could rival even in the making of expensive leather its ancient predecessor. Still, technological change always suggests a shifting demand to prod it. To review all the changes in the uses of and the demand for leather over the late 13th century would be to write a book on Pisan private life and the material impact of the Renaissance upon it. Suffice to note that according to its use leather both declined and prospered. In part leather declined before something better: expensive parchment to paper, oil-soaked leather for windows to glass, the *fiascum incoriatum*—the leather-lined wood bottle—to earthenware, glass, and metal.[42] In part it suffered from more luxurious tastes and the economic prosperity that made them attainable, as for silk or linen in purses and shoes. In those areas where it stood firm (containers of all types, reins, saddles, and so forth), the demand was for tough leather and for volume, speed, and economy in its manufacture—for the hot-water process.

The two fields of largest single importance for the leather industry were armor and clothing. Leather as body armor was dying a slow death in the 13th century. The chief battle had been lost during the preceding centuries; the *corettum*, cuirass, once of leather as its name suggests, in the 13th century seems to have been exclusively of mail.[43] Curiously,

---

diebus incipiendis in connumeratione die sabbati proximi Guido scriptus [coriarius] . . . mittat . . . adobbas decem coriaminis in dictam conciam pro conciando . . . et sic de decem diebus in decem dies . . . a die sabbati proxime ad annos quinque proximos."

42. Parchment makers were under the coriarii de sancto Niccola, *Stat., 3*, 993. For oiled parchment as glass, L. Zdekauer, *La Vita privata dei Senesi nel dugento* (Siena, 1896), p. 37. The fiascum incoriatum is common in notarial inventories.

43. For example, 2543 96v, 98r (1264), and 2544 6v (1284).

leather fared better in helmets and especially in those parts of the body where mobility was essential: thighs, legs, arms.[44] The slow perfection of metal armor, which by the early 14th century made it possible to dress entirely in iron, was offset by the growing demands of war.

And in meeting that demand, leather in shields had full advantage of the booming market. The *targie* and *pavenses* were shields of wood, "of fig or willow" says one description, and this wood was covered by leather, *incoriati, incollati,* one time with "two good ass or horse skins, one outside and the other inside," another time with leather of "mules or asses or horses or cows." In two contracts Charles of Anjou ordered upward of 4,000 such shields from Pisans.[45] Here, too, the demand was for toughness, volume, and economy—for the hot-water process.

For this market, the pellarii had little to offer. Their product was meant for clothing, and in clothing the tide ran the other way. In the early 13th century, leather hats are quite common, but by the end of the century we find them no more. Universally worn in the early period was the *corrigium* or girdle.[46] A *locus communis* of the period speaks of coming "with your girdle around your neck"— to come seeking forgiveness.[47] When Dante speaks of old Florence's nobles "bound in leather," he referred, presumably, to the girdle.[48] And when he contrasts modern Florence with the old on this point, the inference is that the moderns wore it no longer. By this period the *corrigiarii* were belt makers.

---

44. Cf. Zdekauer, *Vita privata,* Appendix, doc. of 1202, "unum elmum corii." ASP Primaziale, 22 May 1314, "par unum cosciaronorum de corio, unum gambaronorum de corio, par unum cosciaronorum de corio."

45. *Relazioni,* no. 735 (1276) and no. 811 (1282).

46. Among the 135 mercatores in the oath of 1228, eleven are corrigiarii, the same number as the spice salesmen.

47. Cf. *ASS, 12,* 516 E, Life of St. Zita of Lucca.

48. *Paradiso* 15: 112–13.

A further blow to the industry of soft leather was the declining use of those long leather stockings or pants, the *osa, hosa,* or *caligae.* Brought to Italy with the Germanic and especially the Lombard invasions, these might be considered the buckskin breeches of Italy's frontier age.[49] Made of soft leather, they were often dyed in bright colors; in what is perhaps our earliest record of woad at Pisa, it is being used to color leather.[50] Still, produced so slowly and expensively, leather garments could not meet the competition of quality cloth, and had to give ground especially to wool.

The importance of skins as clothing in this early period is further illustrated by the importance of a near relative to leather, of whose uses we have perhaps even a fuller picture: furs.

What articles of clothing did men wear in the 13th century? [51]

Underwear was apparently not universally worn, although the rules of religious houses sometimes insist upon its use. It consisted of two parts, the *interula* or *camicia* above, and the *femorale* below.

The suit proper (*indumentum*) consisted in full of three garments. The *tunica* or *gonnella* was sort of a long shirt, reaching on men not quite to the knees and on women to the ground. Over this, for greater warmth—necessary too,

49. See E. Salin, *La Civilisation mérovingienne d'après les sépultures, les textes et le laboratoire,* (Paris, 1950–52), text no. 12, p. 455, citing and discussing Paul the Deacon's description of the Lombards.

50. Breve coriariorum aque calide, *Stat., 3, 959,* "et facciendo del bianco nero et vermiglio et iallo et arancino." ASP Primaziale, 7 Nov. 1238, Gratianus cordovanerius buys woad from Eiotisalvus quondam Gottifredi of Florence.

51. On clothing, L. Muratori, "Dell' arte del tessere e delle vesti de' secoli rozzi," *Dissertazioni sopra le antichità italiane* (Naples, 1752), no. 25, is old but richly documented and still useful. For further bibliographical guidance, see Castellani, *Testi, 2, 933.*

the period's moralists tell us, for decency—was commonly
worn a shortcoat. The shortcoat might be called variously
pelliccia, pelliccio, renonis, or *marzucca.* The first three
names are as old as the Germanic invasions, the last is associated with Sardinia, drew comment from Cicero and is
worn even today. Actually, these names might mean any
garment of fur, and apart from the material seem always to
have been somewhat nondescript. They might be worn
under the tunic, serving as a sort of girdle, hugging the
waist quite tightly with the fur side out. More usually,
however, by our period they seem to be outer garments,
worn with the fur side in, and functioning much as shortcoats. Other types of shortcoats were the *guarnacca* and
argoctum, concerning which we can say only that they were
often but not always made of fur, perhaps with sleeves and
certainly were considered more elegant than the above-
mentioned garments. Varieties of overcoats were the *mantellum, pelles, par pellium, chlamys,* often with a *cappu-
tium* (hood). They could be wrapped around the body and
joined by a single buckle at the corners over the right
shoulder (to keep the hand free). However, the use of the
word "par" in relation to them probably means they could
be made of two pieces joined at each shoulder, to permit
maximum freedom of movement to both arms.

As for the material of which this clothing was made,
undergarments were of cotton or linen, for the rich the soft
linen of Alexandria or the Levant and cruder varieties for
the poor. For the poor, too, a cloth known as *pilurica* was
used, of which we know only that, as its name suggests, it
was hairy. It was probably a crudely woven wool, much like
that rough wool cloth *cilicium,* a favored penitential garb.
For the *gonnella* we may presume that linen, wool, and
perhaps silk found application. However, in the outer garments, furs ruled the field. The *pelliccie* and *renones* were

of course of fur, and usually the more elegant *guarnacca*. The mantellum was likewise; in the Genoese chartulary of Giovanni Scriba it is always of fur.[52] A Venetian source of 1202 describes the suit as "gonnella, guarnacca, et pelles," in the sense of ". . . et mantellum." [53] The Pisan statutes of 1313 speak of "mantellum vel pelles," although by then only the function, not the material, was identical.[54] When St. Zita gave her chlamys to a beggar, she told him, "Take these furs." [55]

Up to about 1150, the furs going into this clothing were principally from wild animals; the mantella in the chartulary of Giovanni Scriba are of rabbit, fox, squirrel, and *varium;* the pelles to be given a monk of San Ponzano at Lucca in 1135 were to be of fox, hare, or rabbit; a *marzucca* worn in 1146 by a Pisan was not of sheep skin as traditionally described but of fox.[56] *Varium,* used so frequently in relation to furs, is, strictly speaking, a color not a type. Still, both from the way it was measured, always in *miliaria,* by the thousands, and from its price, about two to three times that of rabbit, in this earlier period it was probably ermine.

Of course, sheep skins were also widely used. They were, however, used only by the poorest classes, were locally made and of scant commercial importance. The discomfort of

52. *Il Cartolare di Giovanni Scriba,* ed. Chiaudano and Moresco, DSSCDI, 1, (Turin, 1935), nos. 47, 130, 971.

53. Cited in Castellani, *Testi, 2,* 934.

54. *Stat., 2,* 366, 434.

55. *ASS, 12,* 506 E.

56. "Unum mantellum de coniculis coopertum de scarlata, unum mantellum vulpis . . . una pelle vaira pellatos," (*Giovanni Scriba,* no. 47); "duos mantellos varios" (ibid., no. 130); "mantellum ermellinum et mantellum grisium," (ibid., 971). ASL San Ponziano, 28 July 1135, "duo guarnella et duas camisias et duo paria bracum . . . parium unum de calthari . . . et de quarto in quarto anno unum parium de pellis vulpinis novis et pilicione de conillio vel de lepre . . ." ASP Primaziale, 28 May 1145, "mastrucana vulpine pelli."

sheep skins the rules of a women's religious house of 1225 make clear.[57] Each nun was to be given every two years a pelliccia "of fox, hare, or even sheep." If the nun "out of higher devotion," should choose sheep, she was to have every year two linen coats, "superpelliccie." The concession seems not intended to hide the horror of a visible and un-lined sheep skin; the nuns, or at least their superiors, were not looking for elegance. It seems rather aimed at affording the nuns both comfort and modesty in the Italian summer. The picture of the clergy stripping to camicia sleeves under Italy's sun is a common one in the 13th century.[58] To flour-ish as a fur, sheep skins had first to give way to lamb pelts, and this in turn demanded access to large herds for the young animals needed.

The opening up of the central Mediterranean, espe-cially Sardinia and North Africa, brought the first of two revolutions to the fur industry; the wide use of the lamb pelt. In the 13th century, furs from the less valuable wild animals—rabbit and foxes—lose their importance, while lamb pelts with the strength of quantity if not of quality, storm the market. The shift from the products of the chase to commercially raised furs seems associated with the pro-fessionalization of the furrier, both to cure and to sell skins.

57. "Qualibet monialis habeat in anno tres camisias singulis duobus annis unam pelliciam, de vulpibus, leporibus, vel etiam agnis. Si aliqua voluerit altiori devotione agninis pellibus uti, habeat etiam quolibet anno duo superpelliccea." Cited in Muratori, "Vesti," p. 303.

58. For example, Visconti, 2r, "primo, ut [sacerdotes] intrent ad altare ad celebrandum divina cum habitu honesto, coctas vel capa sive camisia superna et quod existens in choro sit cum capa vel cocta de pellibus vel mantello extenso . . ." Ibid., 21v, "et recordamus quod quando dominus hostiensis episcopus venit Pisas legatus qui papa fuit Gregorius IX fecit congregari omnes cappellanos fraternitatis in ballatorio archiepiscopatus nostri et cum vidisset eos ita honeste vestitos videlicet cum mantellis et camiseis supernis quia erat tempus estivum dixit, 'Benedicat vos dominus.' "

While their profession is an ancient one, pelliparii do not appear in Pisa's sources before this revolution; their numbers in the city must have been small. When Pisan furriers appear for the first time to get themselves a church in 1193, they had three captains.[59] From their statutes, that section of the industry which processed and sold new furs had two consuls, the sellers of old furs one.[60] In 1193 that division is already in evidence with the furriers' three captains. Their growth in numbers has already been alluded to: twenty-three in 1193, they are sixty-four in 1228, without estimating the absentees.[61]

Moreover, of the industry's staple, the Sardinian and Corsican lamb pelt, we even have some idea of the output.[62] Workers were forbidden to clean more than 200 lamb pelts per day intended for the guarnacca, or 150 per day for the pelliccia. A production restriction, this looks like a sign of decline. It is likewise a level of production, which, if the sixty-four furriers of 1228 took advantage of it, would give a daily and monthly production output no medieval economic historian would dare print.

However, after 1250 furs like leather are showing signs of decline. The rules of Pisa's Nicosian canons (ca. 1268) show both the late survival of furs and the pressures of a new age.[63] For undergarments, the friars may wear linen,

59. Document published in *Stat., 3,* 1092.
60. *Stat., 3,* 1074.
61. See p. 37, n. 8.
62. *Stat., 3,* 1075, "Et quod aliquis pelliparius . . . qui faciet scarnari coriamen . . . non ponat . . . alicui scarnatori . . . plus quam cl agnellinas a pellicciis, vel plus quam ducentas agnellinas a guarnacciis." For lamb's importance, ibid., p. 1070, "aliquas agnellinas, vel aliquod aliud laborerium dicte artis," and p. 1064, "quod pellicia sardischa et corsesca dici possit una et promicti pro sardischa."
63. Published in *Stat., 1,* 664 ff.

though not soft linen. The tunic was of wool, not "ultra-montane" or "sumptuous" but purchased with an eye to durability rather than looks. In 1268 the canons are still wearing their two coats of fur: the pelliccia and pelles, of course of sheep skins. In the summer, however, they could wear instead of the furs a coat of linen. Most interesting, the skin side of the furs had to be "uncovered." For the Nicosian canons, the covering, not the furs, was the luxury item.

Indeed, Dante contrasted old and new Florence not because the moderns had renounced furs—of course, they had not—but because they came to insist on covered furs.[64] To this the *Ottimo Commento* adds that if anyone dared appear in public with *pelle scoperta* he would be ridiculed. Yet according to Villani, as late as the 1260's uncovered furs could be found in volume at Florence.[65] Of course, covered furs even in the earlier period were far from unknown.[66] To hide them another garment could be worn on top; this was the *superpelliccia*. However, the more common means was simply to cover the fur with a piece of some other material—wool, linen, perhaps silk. The importance of the contemporary literature's emphasis on uncovered furs is that it illustrates the relative output of the fur and wool industries. The disappearance of the uncovered fur was made possible by the triumph of industrial wool. Of course, the ever more active trade with the Champagne fairs and Flemish wool contributed to this

64. *Paradiso* 15: 112–17.

65. *Cronica*, 2, 96, "e molti portavano le pelli scoperte sanza panno."

66. Some examples, 2515 114r, 30 Dec. 1273, "et unum par pellium panni parisii pionbati cum penna veccha variorum desubter"; 2516 26v, 21 March 1274, "unius paris pellium maschilium de Provino virgato cum penna agnellina nigra"; 2545 121v, 1 March 1284, "unius argocti [panni virgati de Ypra] foderati una penna angnelli taccata."

sophistication of taste.[67] Such wool is common in the chartularies. More nearly, however, local industries first produced the volume which reversed the relative output of furs and cloth and made unlined cloth more common than uncovered furs.

Were older furs and new wool competitive? Rather they were complementary. To cloth garments, furs by the later 13th century provided the *penna,* the lining, an interesting variant, apparently, of the word *pannus.*[68] And as a lining, furs were rather the first phase in the manufacturing of clothing to be urbanized, and only later the urbanization was completed as one by one the other processes—dyeing and finishing, weaving, spinning, combing, and washing— followed the march of furs to the city. And yet in one respect furs and wool were competitive. Both used the same staple, sheep skins. In 1198 in Lombardy, whose wool industry was probably fifty years ahead of Tuscany's and whose artisans were chiefly responsible for introducing it, merchants at Susa could not purchase sheep skins or sheep but only wool.[69] The purpose was to stimulate wool production over fur, as the efficiencies of the former gave shepherds a greater profit. Moreover, the lamb pelt as fur was crude, and faced competition both from the luxury furs which greater wealth made possible or from *sendadum,* silk. The declining importance of furs is a tendency which Zdekauer noted also at Siena.[70] More precisely, furs as a luxury item held their ground, but the one-time staple of the industry, the lamb pelt, could not please the

67. Besides Ypres and Provins in note 66 above, common are cloths from Cambrai (2516 26v, 21 March 1274) and Paris (2545 34v, 22 Nov. 1284, "indumentum meum de Parigio").

68. See above, n. 66, and C. Du Cange, *Glossarium ad scriptores mediae et infimae latinitatis,* ed. Favre (Paris, 1883–87), *sub verbo.*

69. Schaube, *Handelsg.,* p. 335.

70. *Vita privata,* p. 81.

Renaissance's richer tastes or meet a demand for volume. Pelliccie survived longest as the garment of the poor and the religious; in the luxurious inventories of the rich, by the 14th century they are seldom met.[71]

Moreover, to call furs and wool competitive is to do injustice to the magnitude of the revolution in the wool industry in the late 13th century. The real contrast in Pisan life under the impact of this revolution is not the replacement of furs by cloth, but the replacement of simplicity and paucity by luxury and wealth—trends which confirm Dante's characterization of his own age.

At Pisa, the study of the growth of the wool industry is an effort to evaluate and balance two factors: the extent to which this revolution was born of local skills, and the extent to which it was imported, either by foreign artisans or unfinished foreign cloth to nourish its rise. Bonaini in a series of editorial notes, Volpe, and especially Silva have emphasized the age and importance of Pisa's local industry.[72] Silva in particular has presented a picture of a flourishing industry challenged and eventually surpassed by the upstart Florentines. He concedes that our sources on the early wool industry are desperately scarce—a blame he would lay more on the sources than on the possibility that a wool industry of importance had not yet become estab-

71. A monk in 1301 was still wearing a "pellicione de angnello albo," 2545 6ov, 26 Sept. 1301.

72. On Pisa's wool industry, see notes by Bonaini, *Stat., 3,* 680, 690; Volpe, *Istituzioni,* p. 234, and "Pisa," p. 235; Silva, *Gambacorta,* p. 13, and especially P..Silva, "Intorno all' industria e al commercio della lana in Pisa," *SS,* new ser. *1* (1910), 329–400. All, however, were misled by the oath of 1188 and the "consuls of the art of wool" that appear in it. The fullest study on a medieval wool industry is A. Doren, *Die florentiner Wollentuchindustrie vom vierzehnsten bis zum sechszehnsten Jahrhundert* (Stuttgart, 1901), but Doren has little to say on the industry's origins. For a study of the Genoese industry, see R. S. Lopez, *Studi sull' economia genovese nel Medio Evo,* DSSCDCI, 8, (Turin, 1936), pp. 65–181.

lished in that focal point of historical consciousness, the city. Sources on the leather industry, for instance, reveal no comparable paucity. To illustrate the early importance of wool production at Pisa, Silva points out the presence of "consuls of the art of wool" in an oath of 1,000 Pisans taken in 1188. The oath, however, has since been shown to have been a later fabrication—as fantastic a work as ever to mislead historians.[73] He further alludes to the presence of *sagu pisanu* in Cagliari. However, the source is not 12th century as Silva says, but 13th.[74] He speaks of "huge quantities" of wool exported from North Africa in 1202, but his statement finds no basis in the source he alludes to.[75] In fact, as the following chapter will illustrate, trade in raw wool was at this time considerably behind trade in leather and furs in importance.

Silva further points out that Volterra hired a wool worker from Pisa in 1245. The document refers, however, to the worker with the formula *qui moratur Pisis,* proof that he was not a native of the latter city.[76]

The oath of 1228 presents a better picture of the early wool industry; in it there are three *lanaioli* out of 4,700, and twelve weavers to be divided among linen, wool, and hemp—not half the number of girdle workers (28).[77] Of

73. See Cristiani, "Osservazioni," on the oath of 1188.

74. See R. Carta Raspi, *L'Economia della Sardegna medioevale. Scambi e prezzi* (Cagliari, 1940), p. 171, n. 1.

75. Amari, *Diplomi arabi,* ser. 1, nos. 14, 15, 17, 18, 20, and 21.

76. Published in *Stat., 3,* 742.

77. The manufacture of cloth in the contado is a common Tuscan phenomenon and in the late 13th century many cheap cloths seem to have been still manufactured in their entirety there. See for example *Stat. di Volterra* (1210–24), p. 23, "De burnellis et albasiis." As a result, consuls of an independent wool guild are comparatively late in appearing: at Siena, not until the 1240's; at Lucca, not until the early 14th century. Florence is exceptional in having an ars lane by 1212 and consules artis lane by 1218. See *Documenti dell' antica costituzione del comune di*

course, the use of wool in garments was not that trivial; the figures show that in 1228 the production of wool cloth, behind that of leather and furs, was yet to be importantly professionalized and urbanized.

These figures, too, serve the better to illustrate the rapidity of this urbanization. In the chartularies of 1263, it is the industry most in evidence. By 1266 Pisan wool cloth is being sold in South Italy.[78] By 1268 we hear apparently for the first time of "consuls of the art of wool," and by the same year the "art of wool" has won place alongside the "orders" of sea and land merchants.[79]

The chartularies emphasize, too, how much imported foreign skills figured in this urbanization. During this period the *Humiliati*, the order of brothers who lived by cloth manufacture, can be found at Pisa.[80] Perhaps more important are the Lombard weavers. Every weaver who appears in the earliest chartularies and many thereafter is a Lombard.[81] Willing to take advantage of the great de-

---

Firenze, ed. P. Santini, Documenti di storia italiana . . . per la Toscana, 10 and 15 (Florence, 1895 and 1952), *1*, 190, 376. However, the Florentine guild consisted of merchants importing especially wool thread from the countryside and having it finished into cloth in the city. Santini, *Documenti*, *1*, 376 (year 1212), "de stame filato de ea arte [lane] devetato undecumque fuerit et evenerit aut de Lucca aut de aliis locis." They appear, therefore, to be equivalent to the contemporary mercatores lane, lanarii, at Pisa, who, however, remained subject to the curia mercatorum. At Pisa, by the time the ars lane was recognized in 1267–68 it had developed into a guild of workers manufacturing the cloth and especially the thread formerly imported from the contado. Of the guild's three consuls, all had to be "quelli che fanno panni, e uno almeno sia stamaiuolo; e lo terso consule sia vel stamaiuolo vel che faccia panni vel che faccia tondere," *Stat.*, *3*, 651.

78. *Cancelleria Angioina*, *1*, p. 105, n. 5, "de panno pisano pal. V."

79. See above, pp. 61–2.

80. Cf. *Stat.*, *1*, 294 ff., and Bonaini's notes.

81. Some examples: Azzinus lumbardus textor de Carrara Gonnelle, 2543 54r, 14 June 1264. Baldinus lumbardus de civitate dicta Dardona filius fratris Berlingerii promises to Rufinus lumbardus rumpitor et

mand for their skills, these Lombards took apprentices and
so implanted a tradition. The supposition seems safe that
this Lombard influx which carried skillful weaving to Pisa
carried it also into other Tuscan towns, and both from
Prato and Pistoia we have explicit reference to such an
immigration.[82] The history of Tuscan wool production is
not that of Pisa's ancient industry challenged by the Florentine, as Silva would have it, but of simultaneous and
rapid development in all the Tuscan towns.

Yet if Lombards perfected the Pisan wool industry, they
did not create it. Their presence shows that the local industry had developed sufficiently to demand their skills.
The Lombard influx is only part, albeit integral, of the
broader pattern of Pisa's industrial development: urbanization.

For where was the woolen cloth industry first developed?
It was born outside of the city, independently of Pisa's

accator lini filius quondam Alberti Peverade de Pavia to become his apprentice, and among witnesses is a Iacobus lumbardus de eadem arte lini,
2543 64r, 18 Oct. 1263. Anselmus dictus Anselminus lumbardus filius
Manuelli Pancaldi de Bosco districtus Alexandrie, 2543 83r, 3 March 1264.
Armanninus de Cremona textor, Guilielmus textor filius quondam Stefani
de Pavia, 2514 18r, 9 Oct. 1264. Filippus testor de Pavia, Ambrosius textor
de Bergamo, Iohannes textor de Pavia, 2525 49v, 13 May 1273. Picchinus
testor de Cremona, 2515 91v, 9 Nov. 1272. Iacobus de Asti, 2515 152r, 25
Sept. 1273. Ventura testor, Iacominus testor lombardus quondam Simonis
de Arasso, 2516 2v, 29 Oct. 1273. Iacominus testor quondam Gherardi de
Cremona, 2629 270r, 14 Aug. 1285. Ugolina uxor Riccardi testoris et filia
quondam Henrici lombardi, 2545 39r (1283). From the early 14th century,
2523 40r (testor de Venetiis), 2524 39r (from Cremona), 49v (from Pavia),
50r (Pavia), 2525 88v (Parma), 132v (Cremona), 2521 125r (Milan). Emigration of these skilled workers out of Lombardy was brought about importantly by the fact that many were involved in heretical movements and
subject to persecutions. A similar influx of skilled Lombard workers marks
the early years of the Genoese wool industry. See Lopez, *Studi*, pp. 65 ff.

82. Zdekauer, *Statutum*, p. 239, wool workers "de Verona et . . . de
Lombardia," (1296). At Prato, Piattoli, *Consigli*, Appendix VII, p. 482, 14
Jan. 1270.

great commercial tradition and her great commercial families. Specifically it was born in the Piemonte (Calci), the Valdarno, and the Val di Serchio. The recruitment of Pisa's wool workers predominantly from Calci has been noted by G. Volpe, but his interpretation of Pisan wool development was led astray by the spurious oath of 1188 and the "consuls of the art of wool" who appear in it.[83] Apparently the first fulling mill Pisan sources reveal was at Calci, although we may presume that some of the many mills found there since the 11th century were in fact used for fulling.[84] The first sale of alum and dyes we find was made to men from this area.[85] The first sale of wool cloth took place not at Pisa but at Santa Maria a Monte.[86] The one member of the only wool company the chartularies of 1263 reveal whose origins can be traced was from Montemagno above Calci.[87] Pisan wool was also born in inland areas—not the cities but the contados. From the late 1260's

83. *Istituzioni*, p. 237. See also Breve dell' arte della lana, *Stat., 3, 739,* where two men are to be sent twice yearly to investigate the washing of wool at Calci. Cloth salesmen in particular seem associated with these areas. Henrigus apothecarius pannorum . . . filius Aliocti de Fasiano, 2514 27v, 13 Nov. 1264. Simon apothecarius . . . quondam Guidonis Actaviani de Pectori, 2545 101r, 26 Nov. 1283. 2545 70v, 19 Aug. 1302, Bonaiuncta venditrix pannorum filia Conventi de Calcinaia. Robertinus apothecarius quondam Tedicii de Rilione, 2514 4v, 23 Aug. 1264. Bencivenne quondam Baraccii de Fasiano as a buyer of wool, 2516 31r, 10 April 1274.

84. ASP San Lorenzo alle Rivolte, 9 Oct. 1259.

85. ASP Primaziale, 22 April 1222. Gainellus de Vico quondam Ranuccini Riccardi et Malvicinus de Cisano quondam Ildebrandini de Cisano confess to Matheus de Seta quondam Soffredi de Seta that they owe him seventy pounds for five cantars "alumen castile" and 80½ pounds "indici de Bacadeo."

86. In the diocese of Lucca but hotly contested between the two cities. ASP Primaziale, 1 Oct. 1248. Bartholomeus quondam Bonavacce sells 31½ canne "panni saivellorum (?)" and eighteen canne less two pounds "panni coloris viridis et biadecti lane," for thirty-six pounds. "Actum in castro sancte Marie montis in domo dicti Bartholomei."

87. 2543 36r, 5 June 1263. See above, n. 83.

from the fringe areas of the Pisan contado and especially
from San Miniato came to Pisa an influx of men calling
themselves *merciadrii*.[88] In fact they were cloth salesmen.
The more far-sighted of native Pisans consigned them huge
sums (for that age) "in the art of wool."

More precisely, the history of the industrialization of
wool is that of the successive urbanization of the processes
connected with it, working in reverse order from the backs
of men to the backs of sheep.[89] Furs as an early stage in
this process we have already seen, and of course the *sutores*
and *talliatores,* the tailors, were urbanized equally early.
In 1228 the finishing processes, dyeing and clothes manufacture, had been largely urbanized, as shown by the number of *tinctores* (29), more than twice the number of
weavers (12), in the oath of that year. In 1263 the finishing
processes are still most in evidence, the dyeing of wool
and the making of hats. To this finishing industry, wool,
already spun into thread or even made into cloth, was
carried from the countryside.[90] Sometimes this cloth bore

88. "Iacobus filius Guidonis de Cantone mercidarius" has investment
"in arte lane," ASP Primaziale, 22 Oct. 1272. Martinus merciadrius de
sancto Miniato, Grimaldus merciadrius de comitatu Pistorii, Bertuccius
de comitatu florentino, Lellus merciadrius de curte sancti Miniatis, 2544
3v, 30 June 1284. Rainerius merciadrius de comitatu Pistorii et Bom-
filiolus merciarius de comitatu Pistorii, 2545 13v, 24 Sept. 1284. Nutus
merciarius quondam Ciapuli de Gratula comitatus florentini, 2545 19r, 2
Nov. 1284. Bonaiuntus merciadrius quondam Henrici de Casanova curie
sancti Miniatis, 2545 20r, 13 Nov. 1284. Balduccius merciadrius de Carmignano (in Pistoia), 2545 56r, 19 Dec. 1283.

89. Cf., for Lucca, T. Bini, *I Lucchesi a Venezia* (Lucca, 1854), p. 27,
where the author notes that in contrast with dyers, spinners appear much
later in Lucchese documents, showing that there too not all the processes
connected with wool manufacture were urbanized simultaneously.

90. From the early 13th century, the Breve mercatorum includes brevia
for hat makers, dyers, and tailors, but not for weavers, although the profession was then subject to its court. The absence confirms the evidence
of the oath of 1228 that the weaving industry had not yet become professionalized to the extent of the other three in the early 13th century.

the name of the rural district where it was made, as "carfagnini" from the Lucchese Garfagnana.[91] To bring it to the city was the function of the early lanarii, pannarii, and merciadrii. In this period they seem always migrants, with one foot in the city and one in the sheep centers of the Pisan contado.

Of course this finishing industry has been most frequently associated with the importation of unfinished Flemish and French wool from the Champagne fairs. And yet this foreign cloth, like the Lombard weavers, we must call supplementary without questioning its importance. The type of wool sought in these overseas areas—finished or unfinished cloth, carded, combed, washed, or raw wool —like the type of wool sought in the contado, was always a function of the urbanization and hence of the perfection of the local industry. Of this the important social correlative is that at Pisa the sheep raiser, industrialist, and importer of Flemish cloth or Catalonian wool was frequently one and the same man.

In 1263, the number of Lombard weavers at Pisa shows that weaving was being urbanized and professionalized.[92] Unfortunately we cannot know if the thread sold in these earliest contracts was spun in the city or in the contado.[93] The urbanization of spinning, the heart of the wool process and of the "art of wool"—weavers at Pisa always worked half in linen—seems achieved peculiarly during the late 13th century. The rise of the "art of wool" to one of Pisa's major guilds (by 1267/68) is testimony to its rapidity. With

91. *Cancelleria Angioina, 1,* 105, n. 5, "de carfagninis can. CIIII et pal. medium."

92. See above, n. 81.

93. 2543 55v, 19 Aug. 1263. Iohannes Laggius quondam Bernarduccii Laggii confesses to Michaele lanarius that he owes him twenty-three pounds for the price of "unius centenarii staminis filati," to be paid October 1.

spinning moved to the city, the guild could restrict the working of wool in the countryside; by 1305 it had forbidden the operation of any wool shop in the contado.[94]

But if industrialization at this period meant urbanization, the factors that encouraged or obstructed it are importantly those bearing upon the cost of urban living. The chartularies of 1263 help illustrate a principal block in the road to urbanization.[95] In 1263, Lazarius Talliapanis, a man of whom more will be seen, was having wool hats made in batches of 100. We have enough documents to figure his relative investments. For the wool Lazarius was paying 56 per cent of the total cost; for labor, 44 per cent. However, precisely on the cost of city living and hence of city labor all the changes Pisa's democratic regimes wrought —taxes, debasement, the partial expropriation of the aristocrats and the fuller exploitation of the peasantry—were being brought to focus. Between 1266 and 1300 democratic policies had cut the cost of living to one-third the amount of 1263. The aristocracy's monopoly of city rents had tended to keep the production of wool cloth distributed in the contado and penalized urban labor. This the democracy reversed by penalizing labor in the contado and subsidizing it within the city. The result was to favor the influx of labor into the city such as the demographic history of San Cristofano reveals.

The importance of this urbanization, of the slashing of labor costs by from one-half to two-thirds, can hardly be overemphasized, and a booming wool industry was the result. We need hardly point out, however, that all urban industries involving labor gained too. Of the tremendous economic upswing in the late 13th century, wool provides

94. *Stat., 3,* 679, "di non fare bottega d'arte di lana fuore de la citta di Pisa."

95. For the contracts illustrating the following, see Appendix IV.

the most brilliant but by no means the only example. The prosperity made the episcopacy of Federigo Visconti Pisa's golden age of Camposanto and Baptistry, of art and Renaissance. Of course, this shining coin has a reverse side. The peasant slid downward into depression and misery that dim peculiarly the city's glory.

However, in industry as in demography, Tuscany has an example of yet more vigorous growth. Before 1300, Florentine wool cloth had penetrated down the Arno valley to the very gates of Pisa.[96] By the early 14th century, the Pisan industry was struggling to compete even within its own city.[97]

To explain this differential growth turning into dependence is again a difficult search for diversity in similitude. Pisa's failure to keep abreast of Florence was partially due to her geography: the convenience of the sea undoubtedly drew her energies and capital into foreign commerce, to the partial neglect of her home industries. It was partially due to her agriculture. Urbanization tapped agriculture in a double fashion: for labor and food. Pisa's contado, however, for all its wealth, was about half the size of Florence's, and much of the coastal region was given over to swamps. She did not have an agricultural base comparable to her rival's. By the early 14th century, her agriculture was clearly not supporting the strains that had been laid upon it. Social factors, too, contributed to her failure. Pisa's precocious rise had saddled her with a powerful aristocracy unwilling to sacrifice their rents and status to industrialization. Historical factors figured, also. Pisa's economic efforts had been so long oriented to, and so successful in,

96. "Pannus florentinus" is common in the chartulary of Pepus of Fucecchio, ASP Archivio Montarelli della Volta, 23 Nov. 1297, 24 Dec. 1297, Feb. 1298, etc.

97. Discussed in Silva, "Lana."

the southern trade and the production of leather and furs
that she was probably reluctant to take risks on new commercial and industrial ventures. Probably most important,
however, was Pisa's unhygienic living conditions, which
set a limit on her growth, racked her with plagues, and
debilitated her energies when that limit was challenged—
and which blocked the growth of a labor force that could
bring industrialization on the Florentine scale.

10. COMMERCE

As you know, ever since our galleys have been making trips
to Provence, our commune has been drawing much profit . . .
PETITION OF ANDREAS GAMBACORTA AND
BECTUS SCIORTA TO ANZIANI, 1325

P ISA'S crisis of growth during the last decades of the 12th
century brought with it an ostensible contraction of her
commerce. The disturbances accompanying the Fourth
Crusade dealt her colony at Constantinople a severe blow,
and it never regained its erstwhile importance.[1] Acre, the
center of Pisa's Levantese trade, had two consuls up to
1192, three from 1192 to 1248, and from then on only
one.[2] By that time, too, all her colonies in the Levant, with
the exception of Armenia, had disappeared, leaving only
the Acre outpost. Moreover, Pisa, which once had consuls
in Damietta and Alexandria, by the late 13th century seems
to have used Venetian facilities, and after the 1280's we
are without record of Pisan trade with those cities.[3] As

1. See Heyd, *Commerce, 1,* 472–4; idem, *Le Colonie commerciali degli
Italiani in oriente nel Medio Evo,* trans. G. Müller (Venice and Turin,
1886), *1,* 370; and Borsari, "Rapporti." However, for Pisans involved in
trade between Constantinople and Acre, see the interesting contract (ACC,
6 May 1279) drawn up "at Acre in the church of St. Peter of Pisa."
Georgius Cofinus the executor of the will of Guido Bizarra now deceased
confesses to Guido condam Martini de Constantinopoli that he has received from him for himself and Baialardus Bonaiuncte and Gregorius
Corsochefali from the goods of the late Guido Bizarra "dragmarum viginti
octo milia berethet (?) in auro et in variis . . ."

2. Rossi-Sabatini, *L'Espansione,* p. 21, and Schaube, *Konsulat,* p. 161.

3. For evidence of Pisans participating in trade between Alexandria and
Armenia, see ACC, 17 Aug. 1264, a contract drawn up in the presence of
Iacobus de Morella, the viscount of the Pisans in Armenia, at Laiatium in

early as the early 13th century the goods moving through Pisa were divided roughly one-third from the Levant, one-third from Sardinia and the Regno, and one-third from "Garbo," Africa—a remarkable reflection on the Levant's decline *vis-à-vis* these other areas.[4]

Does this fading importance of the Levant mean Pisa's commerce was declining?

As for the importance of Pisa's port as the mouth of Tuscany, there can be no thought of a decline. The value of the tariff of 1247—22,100 pounds—bespeaks a flourishing trade.[5] We possess a discussion leading to a similar tax imposed the year before (1246) for the provisioning of four ships (the tax in 1247 was for six), and the highest rate suggested was six denarii per pound.[6] On the assumption that this was the tax rate for 1247 too, the value of goods flowing through Pisa's port in 1247 was 884,000 pounds. We may estimate further (though unstable coin values make it uncertain) that this was about 15 per cent greater than the value of goods moving through Genoa in 1214, and about 40 per cent less than the value of goods moving through the same port in 1274.[7] If merchants may be assumed to have realized a profit of 20 per cent on the goods

---

Armenia, in which Giraldus de Masese confesses that he has received from Bartholomeus de Pansero "tot pannos de Alexandria, zucheram, stagnum et mastica que omnia ascendunt in summa bisancios mille nonigentos quadraginta unum sar[acinatos] Syrie ad bonum et iustum pondus Syrie."

4. Breve curiae maris, *Stat., 3,* 383. The curia maris had nine sensales (brokers), "quorum tres sint extimatores haveris Levantis et Romanie tantum; et tres haveris Regni et Corsice et Sardinee, et de aliis partibus marinis; alii tres haveris Garbi."

5. ASP Alliata, 24 Nov. 1248. See Appendix III.

6. ASP Comune A 81, 2r, 7 April 1245, "et ut omnes qui vadunt debeant iurare dare per libram denarios vi et illi qui veniunt similiter dare."

7. Our knowledge of the value of the goods moving through Genoa derives from the records of the Genoese tariff, the *collecta maris.* See Sieveking, *Finanzwesen,* p. 67. Lopez, *CEH, 2,* 314.

at Pisa, the wealth produced by this commerce was 176,-800 pounds, or about enough to support over 42,000 men for one year. Of course, much if not most of this volume represents inland Tuscany's trade too, but it does help show that whatever the fate of Pisa's marine, her port kept its stature.

Of this commerce, at least 50 per cent was carried by foreign merchants, Saracens, Italians from Savona near Genoa, Provençaux, or South Italians. Between 33 per cent and 40 per cent of all commerce and about 90 per cent of the portion carried by foreign merchants was in the hands of South Italians. The figure helps emphasize how thoroughly oriented was Pisan trade to the South. Still, even in this Southern trade, the predominance of merchants from the Regno suggests a specialization. It shows how much Pisa had concentrated her trade on two areas: Sardinia and Africa. Indeed, the "captains of the ports of Sardinia" at this time sat alongside the consuls of the sea in the guild and even in communal government.[8] Pisa's principal market place for overseas imports, the Piazza San Niccola, "between the two bridges," was the responsibility and prerogative of the Sardinian merchants to administer. The consuls of Tunis and Bugia—some of whom stayed at Pisa, some overseas—enjoyed an importance in Pisan councils surpassed only by the Sardinian captains and merchants. Not even Sicily nor the Regno, the strategic gateway to Africa and the Levant, the source of grain and wine, had anything similar.

And let there be no doubt of Pisa's commercial primacy

8. ASP Comune A 81, 4r 4 Dec. 1245, "et ut consules maris et consules portuum Sardinee et consules de Tunithi et Bugea debeant securare eis naulum . . ." Dal Borgo, *Raccolta*, p. 195, for the composition of Pisa's communal council in 1262, which included "consulum et capitaneorum portuum Sardinee."

in these two areas, however much her trade faded in the Levant before the Genoese and Venetian. "No other Christian merchant may enter [the ports of Tunis and Bugia]," says a privilege of the Hafsids in 1264, "but only those whom the Pisans want." [9] "That place," says a Genoese source of 1285 in reference to North Africa, "few Christians visit, unless only the Pisans." [10]

Of the factors which led to this intense concentration on Sardinia and Africa, an important one was geography. These areas were closer to Pisa than to either Genoa or Venice; Pisa undoubtedly found it easier to maintain her commercial position there than in the competition-racked Levant. Should we even look at this trade as something of a second choice, pursued because Pisa could no longer compete in the Levant on equal footing with Genoa and Venice? To a significant degree, yes. But we would be wrong to write off this westward swing of Pisan trade as no more than the mark of Pisa's own commercial weakness. The competition in the Levant, embittered the more by the presence of French and especially Catalonian merchants, was having visible effects upon Genoa and Venice too. With the collapse of the crusading movement, Italy's commercial energies swung to the West and North, to the establishment of all-water routes to England and Flanders.[11] Even for Genoa and Venice, interest in this new frontier had become such as to drain men and money from the Levant, where commercial endeavor seems to have reached the point of diminishing returns. Or at least, this was not the area where growth is most evident. Almost simultaneously, when Venice in the later 13th century instituted her

9. Amari, *Diplomi arabi,* ser. seconda, no. 29.
10. See Lopez, *Zaccaria,* p. 261, document of 1285.
11. For the establishment of the water route north, see Lopez, *CEH,* 2, 314.

yearly fleets to Flanders, she imposed a ceiling on the amount of money her citizens could invest in trade with the Levant.[12] Perhaps for Pisa, her growing weakness made her the more sensitive to the falling returns of the Levantese trade. But her behavior becomes so much the more a vane in recording the direction of the period's economic forces.

Pisa's interest in Sardinia and Africa seems, therefore, an early manifestation of a general westward swing of the center of gravity of Italian trade. Let us explore the process at Pisa in more detail. Of course, Pisa found in those areas large markets for products in which her contado was especially rich. Pisa had Tuscan wine and oil, both of which she carried to the Regno and Africa.[13] Hemp and flax from her plain gave her another product for overseas export.[14] Most important, however, Pisa had four com-

12. Cf. G. Luzzatto, *Studi di storia economica veneziana* (Padua, 1954), p. 74.

13. ASP Roncioni, 17 Oct. 1278. Will of Lupus filius domini Gerardi Rosssi de domo Lanfrancorum. "Item iudico et relinquo medietatem vini quod ego habeo in fundaco maiore pisano cabelle vini de Bugea ita et tali modo quod si quis habuit partem in dicta cabella a quinque annis circa habeat et habere debeat suam partem sicut ei evenerit." For oil, "item iudico et relinquo pro remissione peccatorum meorum universitati Turcimannorum et ipsis Turcimannis de Bugea omnes et singulas quantitates denariorum et rerum quas et que ego recipere habebam . . . pro oleo et occasione olei . . ." Wine to the Regno, 2543 17r, 30 April 1263. Melior vinarius receives "in societate maris" ten pounds from Bencivenne quondam Gualfredi and ten from Paulus olearius, to be taken "in mercantia vini" from Pisa to Naples or Scalea in two ships for one-third of the profit. Because of the two ships, I would interpret this "mercantia vini" as the sale rather than the purchase of wine.

14. ASP Roncioni, 17 Oct. 1278 (see above, n. 13) Saiectus saracenus of Bugea owes Lupus Lanfranchi two debeni "pro una canno panni bladicti." The cloth could have been either of linen or wool. Saracens were also in debt to the Pisan "pro pannis et sendadis," i.e. silk. See also ASP Roncioni, 17 Aug. 1236. Riccus vinarius quondam Corsi confesses to Lucchese calafatus that he owes him 100 solidi, "pro pretio . . . certi petii de drappis et rebus quas ipse Riccus recepit . . . a dicto Lucchese pro vendendis apud Neapulim."

modities: salt to some degree, wood, iron, and silver. Wood
provided ships, and in 1248 Salimbene was impressed with
Pisa's feats as a shipbuilder.[15] Merchants from Marseilles
in the 1240's had ships built at Pisa with such frequency
as to argue a common practice.[16] Pisa's merchants would
often sell in overseas areas their ships as well as their car-
goes; to favor such sales, wood-scarce Tunis exempted them
from taxes—the only commodity so honored.[17] In exchange
for trade privileges, Tunis was granted the right to draft the
Pisan ships in her harbors whenever need should dictate.
Wood and iron also meant arms, and their manufacture
made for considerable export to Islam. Federigo Visconti
complains bitterly of Pisans, whom the world once thought
Christians, carrying arms.[18] At the Council of Lyons the
archbishop thought the Holy Land could be conquered
by an economic blockade: "A force of twenty-five galleys
[should remain] in Saracen waters until the recovery of
the Holy Land for two reasons: first, to prevent the Saracens from taking food from Sicily . . . secondly, to prevent false Christians from carrying wood and iron." [19]

Sardinian silver, too, struck either into Arabic or Pisan
coins, was a valuable item of exchange for trade with North
Africa.[20] However, the importance of Sardinia and Africa

15. *Cronica*, p. 771. Salimbene says the Pisans built 100 ships, which,
however, should be compared with ASP Alliata, 24 Nov. 1248 (Appendix
III), "supraposita duarum navium et quatuor galearum."
16. Many in L. Blancard, *Documents inédits sur le commerce de Marseilles au Moyen Age* (Marseilles, 1884–85), nos. 407 (1248), 777, 933, 934,
939, 978, 997.
17. Amari, *Diplomi arabi*, ser. seconda, no. 29.
18. Visconti, 116v, "in mercatoribus et sacerdotibus et aliis habentibus
proprium et hec per avaritiam scilicet defraudando entecam suam sotiis
suis vel dando ad usuram vel subtrahendo pupillis et nepotibus suis vel
eundo in cursus vel deferendo arma ad saracenos contra excommunica-
tionis sententiam quod est tote civitati ignominiosum cum consueverit
mercatores pisani homines catholici reputari per mundum . . ."
19. Ibid., 144v.
20. See Schaube, *Handelsg.*, p. 298.

is explained not only by the market abroad but also by the market at home. About 1200, more than any other Tuscan town, Pisa had urbanized and industrialized leather and furs. The industrialization created at home a market of unprecedented size for raw materials. The areas nearest Pisa where large-scale flock raising was economically feasible were Sardinia and Africa. The trade pattern which emerges from this period—two-thirds to Sardinia and the South, one-third to the Levant—however much influenced by Genoese or Venetian competition in the Levant seems more nearly a response to Pisa's own industrialization of furs and leather.

From the late 12th to the late 13th century, Pisan trade predominantly involves Sardinia and Africa, and leather and furs. In 1173, to illustrate the inflation caused by a famine year, the Pisan chronicler Maragone gives prices for some typical commodities.[21] Except for food items, spices, and a scarlet cloth of unstated material, they are furs—ermine for the richer market, rabbit for the poorer. In 1181 Ubaldus, archbishop of Pisa, appealed to the sultan of Tunis to lift a ban forbidding Pisans to export skins.[22] In 1202 when Leonardo Fibonacci gave directions for loading ships at "Garbo," Africa, he stated that the unity of weight should be the cantar of skins.[23] "From olden days," ships in North Africa placed alum in the ship's bottom, skins in the middle, and *beccune,* skins of calves or mutton, on top. The oft-quoted figures of the numbers of lamb pelts Pisans were taking from Tunis in 1201 are worth quoting again. One letter between Pisans and Saracens refers to 5469 sheep skins purchased at Tunis.[24] Another speaks of

---

21. *Annales,* p. 60, anno mclxxiiii.
22. Amari, *Diplomi arabi,* ser. seconda, no. 14. Schaube, *Handelsg.,* p. 354.
23. Leonardo, *Liber Abbaci,* p. 117. The *Liber abbaci* dates from 1202.
24. Amari, *Diplomi arabi,* nos. 14, 15, 17, 18, 20, 21.

2978. A company of Pisan merchants is found buying 1485 lamb pelts, and we hear further of sales of 500 and 491.

These figures show the intensity of the African skin trade developing simultaneously with the urbanization of the production of leather and furs. And this African output Sardinia surpassed, if seen only in the statutes of the guild of furriers.[25]

We should point out, too, the absence of wool in all these transactions. No better example can be found of the still secondary importance of the wool trade than Leonardo's *Liber Abbaci* and the mathematical problems drawn from actual business life he gives.[26] Besides the influence of the Levantese trade—spices and Alexandria's linen—the examples are skins and furs. Wool is rare. Only when local sheep had built the local industry was commerce enlisted as a servant.

Absent, too, is any record of Pisan trade with Catalonia. Even trade with France, as shown by the lack of any special brokers (*sensales*) for it, seems to have lacked vigor. Indeed, in 1325 the establishment of *viaggi* to Provence was still in men's memories, and the fact that members of two of Pisa's new houses, Gambacorta and Sciorta, were making the statement we have quoted suggests that such new houses were the pioneers in establishing it. To be sure, the record of Pisan trade with Provence is impressive in its age. However, the Provençal trade, as indeed the Levantine, seems from the late 12th century to have become obscured in our sources by the great gains made by the traffic with Sardinia and Africa. Not surprisingly, up to about 1270 the inland Tuscan trade with the Champagne fairs was predominantly an overland trade.

25. See above, p. 149.

26. Some examples: corium (p. 88), panni (p. 89), miliarium variorum (p. 90), rotuli 1,000 variorum (p. 90), beccune in Garbo (p. 93), linum in Suria vel Alexandria (p. 94), fustaneum (p. 113), cotton (p. 117), beccune (p. 118), panni (p. 178), linum (p. 180), and wool (p. 276).

In the late 13th century we can point to two important trends in Pisan commercial development. One is that the areas with which Pisan commercial exchange is most rapidly growing are still further to the west, France and Catalonia. The second is that Pisa's aristocratic merchants, and the Sardinian and African trade upon which they lived, entered into a period of economic decline.

In 1273, apparently for the first time, we find Pisans at the Champagne fairs.[27] For a new trade, new men: the Pisan merchants are from the capitalist families of Cinquina and Buonconte. From 1272 we hear, apparently for the first time, of a Pisan consul at Marseilles; and her other consulate at Montpellier, which we find again after a long silence in 1283, was restored even after the interruption of the Melorian war.[28] To be sure, until well into the 14th century Cagliari in Sardinia was the principal gateway to Majorca and Catalonia, and it is not always easy to distinguish a Sardinian from a Catalonian venture.[29] Still,

27. ASP Olivetani, 5 Oct. 1273. Provins. "Iacobus olim Benincase dictus Cinquinus civis et mercator pisanus nomine suo et Guiscardi Cinquini Banduccii Boncontis et aliorum sociorum suorum civium et mercatorum pisanorum" promises "pro cambio centum et nonaginta librarum bonarum provinium fortium Francie quas confessus est . . . in presentibus nundinis sancti Aygulphi de Provino apud Provinum recepisse . . . a Cursetto Arrigi . . . pro se ipso et pro Falco Bonaccurso, Duccio Davizini et aliis suis sociis" to pay "in civitate Florentia infra octo dies ab intrante mense Novembris proxime futuro libras dlxxvii solidos viii denarios iiii bonorum florenorum parvorum in bonis florenis grossis argenteis de duodecim minutis absque aliquo cambio supercomputando in illis." ASP Olivetani, 4 Dec. 1273. Florence. Florentines acknowledge payment.

28. See P. Pitzorno, "I Consoli veneziani di Sardegna e di Maiorca," *Nuovo Archivio Veneto*, new ser. *11*, Pt. I (1906), 93–106. 2545 100v, 24 Nov. 1283, "Vivianus Panatelli consul pisanorum in Monte Pesulani," and Schaube, *Konsulat*, p. 107.

29. ASP Comune A 83, 61r, 10 Oct. 1304, "pro satisfactione et restitutione librarum mille cccc lviiii soldorum octo et denariorum unius denariorum pisanorum minutorum in una parte que fuerunt exacte pro communi pisano ab ipsis catalanis apud degathiam predictam pro eius

our first record of Pisans in Majorca in the 13th century
(1245) shows they went there on a ship owned by a Lombard.[30] When we find a Pisan in Catalonia (1275), a
Pistoiese owned the ship.[31] In the late 13th century the
French trade first and the Catalonian hard behind are
booming, and in the contracts dealing with them both can
be found a whole list of Pisa's new houses: Gambacorta,
Agliata, Sciorta, Cinquina, Buonconte, and so forth.[32]

Another change too occurs in Pisan commerce. In 1275
during the democratic regime the Catalonians had a consul and rectors at Pisa—apparently over 100 years before
they had one at Genoa.[33] By 1283 for the first time Venice
too had a consul at Pisa, probably dating from about the
same time as his Catalonian counterpart.[34] For all her com-

---

drictu et cabella et librarum ccc xlvi solidorum xvii denariorum ii aqui-
linorum parvorum in alia parte que exacte fuerunt pro communi pisano
a dictis catalanis in Castello Castri pro dirictu duorum per centenarium."
2630 171v, 11 Feb. 1311, a societas maris "a Pisa in Castellum Castri et de
Castello Castri Maioricam."

30. ASP Coletti, 29 Aug. 1244. The ship belonged to Ardiccione de Alexandria de Palea (?) Lombardia and was rented to fourteen Pisans in
Majorca.

31. ASP Trovatelli, 12 March 1277. Legal dispute over "viadio quod
fecit Maioricam et in Barcellonam" two years before, "in navi Franci de
Carmignano." The cargo carried by the Pisan involved was 150 cantars of
cotton, probably reexported from Sicily. See also ACC, 16 May 1270, a contract drawn up in Majorca dealing with the sale of a ship. However, it is
difficult to know who were the Pisans involved in the transaction.

32. For Cinquina and Buonconte in Provence, see above, n. 27. For
Gambacorta and Agliata, see Volpe, "Pisa," p. 299. For Sciorta in Provence
and Catalonia, 2545 134v, 8 April 1284 (Provence) and 2630 4v (1316–24, a
list of Bectus Sciorta's investments in the Catalonian trade). For more on
the Catalonian trade, below, n. 38.

33. See Pitzorno, "Consoli"; Schaube, Konsulat, p. 241; and M. Luzzatto,
"Rapporti tra Pisani, Amalfitani e Catalani nel secolo XIV," Rassegna
Storica Salernitana, 22 (1951), 108–225.

34. 2545 85r, 27 Sept. 1283, "Leonardus quondam domini Rainerii de
Venetiis nunc consul Venetorum in civitate pisana."

mercial importance, Venice had never before succeeded in penetrating into these western waters, and the Catalonians won an importance they were not soon to relinquish. Of course, let us not imagine that Pisa's own new capitalists were not themselves overseas merchants, or that they had particular fondness for foreigners. In building trade to new overseas areas, however, they were building beyond the limits of Pisa's old and great maritime tradition; they needed these foreign ships.

Even the Battle of Meloria, while a disaster for Pisan merchants generally, gave added impetus to this westward movement of Pisan trade by injuring the old houses more than the new. Tradition has emphasized and recent research has confirmed the role played by Pisa's aristocracy in the Melorian catastrophe.[35] "A great part of the Pisan nobility" the oft-quoted Genoese inscription heralding the victory says of Pisan prisoners. The new houses, whose diversified interests were not so immediately tied to shipping and to the fate of Pisa's marine, possessed a certain immunity from the full blow of Meloria. Through subterfuges and the help of foreign captains, they could pursue their economic endeavors even in defiance of the tight Genoese blockade. A series of contracts from 1283 illustrates one way it could be done: [36]

1. Baccione Tiniosi sells two-thirds of his ship, the *Sant' Antonio,* to the Venetian Rainerius, "now the consul of

35. E. Cristiani, "I Combattenti della battaglia di Meloria e la tradizione cronistica," *Bollettino Storico Livornese, 1* (1951), 165 ff., and 2 (1952), 18 ff. The inscription is reprinted in Lopez, *Zaccaria,* p. 127, n. 68.

36. 2545 85r, 27 Sept. 1283, "Actum Pisis Kinthice in domo dicti Baccionis posita in classo de regio cappelle sancti Cristofori." 2545 85v, 27 Sept., "Actum . . . in scripta domo scripti Baccionis." 2545 86r, 27 Sept., "Actum in scripta domo . . ." 2545 86r, 1 Oct. 1283, "Actum Pisis Kinthice in apotheca solarioli turris Balneatorum de pede Pontis veteris." Cf. Lopez, *Zaccaria,* Appendix V, regarding Venetian-Genoese relations and the Genoese blockade.

Venetians at Pisa," and Iohannes the Paduan for 200
pounds.

2. Rainerius sells two-thirds of the ship *Sant' Antonio*
and Iohannes the Paduan one-third of the same ship to
Baccione Tiniosi for 200 pounds.

3. Iohannes the Paduan admits to Baccione Tiniosi that
he has received "in accomanditia" the ship *Sant' Antonio*
to be taken wherever he wishes for two-thirds of the profit.

4. Rainerius leases two-thirds of the ship *Sant' Antonio*
to Iohannes the Paduan, already owner of one-third, to
be taken wherever he wishes for two-thirds of the profit.

To explain this bewildering series of contracts—numbers three and four flatly contradict each other as to the
ownership of the *Sant' Antonio*—they must be taken in
two groups, one with four, and two with three. According
to numbers one and four, the *Sant' Antonio* was a Venetian ship, commanded by a Venetian captain who owned
it jointly with no less a personage than the "consul of the
Venetians" at Pisa. As such it enjoyed the privileges of a
neutral. Numbers two and three however assured the
Pisan that he could establish the ownership whenever he
wished. Not only by such means could the Genoese blockade be broken, but the ship could also escape the Pisan
draft of her own ships. The close participation of Pisa's
capitalists with foreign captains gave them an immunity
from war's losses that the aristocracy could not enjoy.

After Meloria, it is easy to illustrate a continued and
even vigorous Pisan trade with France and Catalonia.[37]

37. See above, n. 32. Some further examples: ASP Coletti, 8 Dec. 1293,
for a Pisan, Bonusvicinus quondam domini Turrexani, selling spices, sugar,
and copper at Paris. ASP Cappelli, 9 Sept. 1297, Petrus Segarra de Maioricis
confesses to Ligus quondam Mathei pisanus civis that he has received 635
brachia of linen cloth and "ballam unam" of wool cloth from Milan, to be
taken in the ship of Berlingerius Albertonis de Valentia to Castellum
Castri, there to be consigned to Ligus' partners. 2545 45v, 24 March 1283,

The Sardinian and African trade, and Pisa's commercial aristocracy, saw no such revival. In the chartularies of 1283 Simon de Silva is an active merchant concentrating on the skin trade with North Africa. In 1301 he was bankrupt and his four sons watched their clothes taken from them.[38] In 1301 Cortingus Marti returned to the scene of Pisa's former triumphs: Tunis. He borrowed money for the venture from some of Pisa's new capitalists: in 1305 he died bankrupt.[39] The fall of Pisa's old families from "great status and great power" to a position "as other families" is easy to illustrate in terms of foreclosures, renunciations of inheritances "more costly than profitable," the sale of wives' dowries "for reason of need." [40] For trade with Africa and Sardinia had entered upon hard years. After the 1280's the Sardinian captains figure no more in the

---

Guilielmus Cuthacchius of Majorca contracts to carry woad to Marseilles. 2545 134v, 8 April 1284, letter of exchange with France involving 1,000 florins. 2545 143v, 2 May 1284, Pisan merchant bequeaths a statue to the "ecclesie sive loco in quo beata Maria Magdalena penitentiam suam fecit vocato Alabialma vel aliter de comitatu vel districtu de Marsilia." 2545 81v, 1 Sept. 1302, 1,350 florins invested in voyage "in Provinciam et de inde in Franciam et in Campagnam." 2630 171v, 11 Feb. 1311, 1,700 florins invested in voyage "in Castellum Castri et de Castello Castri Maioricam.

38. 2545 32r, 1 Feb. 1283; 30r, 15 Jan. 1283; 32v, 1 Feb. 1283—all sales of "coriorum barbarescorum bovum et vaccarum." 2545 37r, 31 May 1301. Procurator of the Monastery of San Stefano is given possession of land and clothing of the heirs of Simon de Silva "ex forma et tenore unius carte compangnie terre" drawn up 7 May 1299.

39. 2545 12r, 13 April 1301 and 2521 14v, 8 Nov. 1305.

40. For the citation see below, p. 176. A few examples of families in trouble: 2563 42r, 14 April 1300, among those warned to pay delinquent debts to a banker from Pistoia, are Gualandus de Comte, domina Duccia, Albiscuccius domini Nerii Picchini de Stateriis, domina Frandina uxor Nerii Carlecti, Nichola camerarius domini archiepiscopi. 2545 17v, 19 Feb. 1302, Iohannes de Balneo filius condam Pancoli de Balneo sells land "occasione necessitatis." 2545 40r, 8 June 1301, judgment against the property of dominus Bartholomeus Pilistris de Casapieri. 2545 27v, against an Assopardi; 2524 59v, against comites de Bizerno.

councils of the Pisan commune. By the early 14th century the Sardinian merchants, we are told, are in "weak state" and in the contracts Sardinia appears most frequently as a post on the road to Catalonia.[41] By 1286 the number of captains at Bugia and Tunis has dropped from two to one, and we hear no more of them in the 14th century.[42] The needs of a new industry and the attraction of new areas have triumphed.

41. See Schaube, *Konsulat*, p. 190, "debile statu . . . de li mercatanti che in Castello di Castro concurreno." Cf. the composition of the commune's great council given in n. 8 above for the year 1262 and the composition in 1277 (document in *Stat.*, *1*, 53), where the "consules et capitanei portuum Sardinee" have disappeared.

42. They are not found in the redaction of the Breve curiae maris of 1346.

11. THE CAPITALIST AND
THE ARISTOCRAT

> [These old Pisan families] were of great status and of great
> power in olden days. And although they still exist, yet they
> have fallen much; they are as any other.
>
> FRANCESCO DA BUTI *

THE DYNAMIC ELEMENT which worked for change in so
many fields of the economy of 13th-century Pisa we have
called the urbanizers of production, the capitalists. Precisely, it was a group of families which in the late 1240's
began to appear at Pisa and by 1300 have won a position
of dominance retained for centuries: Gambacorta, Agliata,
Buonconte, Cinquina, Delle Brache, Pedone, Aiutamicristo, Papa, Fauglia, Sciancati, Sciorta, Griffi, Rau, Gatti,
Dell' Agnello, Del Mosca, Falcone—and the list goes on.
Of course, let us not pretend that this was the first influx
of new families into the ruling circles of the city; particularly in the crisis of the late 12th century, of which our
period is in so many ways a repetition and continuation,
new blood had surged upward, to become fused in the
calmer years that followed with the old blood to form a
new aristocracy. Nor, for the late 13th century, should
we suggest that the break between Pisa's new and old

---

* Commento di Francesco da Buti sopra la Divina Commedia (Pisa, C.
Giannini, 1858–62), 2, 831; cited in G. Volpe, "Pisa, Firenze, Impero al
principio del 1300 . . ." SS, 11 (1902), 202. The commentary is from the
late 14th century.

houses was complete. It is easy to show some of Pisa's aristocratic houses—Seccamerenda, Lanfranchi, Laggii, Murscii—sharing the newcomers' interest in local sheep or playing a major role in the new trade with Spain.[1] Nevertheless, more numerous, more active, and more interesting are the *novi homines* who pioneered the changes in a change-packed half-century and who had no direct connection with Pisa's commercial families or economic connection with the commercial revolution that went before.

What sparked these families' success is dark, since they are new arrivals in the city and since beginnings are the obscurest things. Their later activities are of little help. The Gambacorta family, for instance, imported wine from Naples and grain from Sicily, and were prominent in the French and Catalonian trade.[2] These manifold activities show they had the strength of capital to expand in all directions without affording a hint of their origins.

Through a fortunate survival, however, the chartularies of 1263–64 present a relatively full and unique picture of one of these new capitalists freshly arrived from his rural home.[3] The richest figure in these early chartularies, the only man who from volume of transactions and network of interests deserves the title capitalist, is Lazarius Talliapanis. To be sure, Lazarius was childless and no line carried his name. But in the rapidity of his rise at a time when Pisa's

1. See ASP Primaziale, 22 Oct. 1272, for Donatus Seccamerenda and an investment of 500 pounds "in arte lane." 2545 134v, 8 April 1284 and 2545 81v, 1 Sept. 1302 for the Murscii and trade with Provence. 2630 171v, 11 Feb. 1311, for the Laggii and trade with Majorca. 2630 4v for the Lanfranchi and an investment in a Catalonian venture. For sheep and the house of Masca, see p. 118, n. 24.

2. Cf. *Cancelleria Angioina, 6,* 230, n. 1227 (year 1270–71), for a ship of Iohannes Gambacurte carrying cloth and other commodities to Naples, sacked by the Genoese. Cf. also Zeno, *Documenti,* no. 13 (1298); ASP Alliata, 3 Oct. 1294.

3. For what follows, see Appendix IV.

other new families were also rising, his story is valuable.

Like these families, Lazarius was a new arrival at Pisa. His home was San Miniato in the Valdarno; he had no economic connection with Pisan commerce or social connection with Pisa's old commercial houses. The critical point is his relation to San Miniato, for with that rural home he never broke. By 1263 Lazarius was a large landowner; he was a sheep raiser. In his will he forgave his brother-in-law some money entrusted him for the purchase of sheep. He gave money to the monastery of Altopascio, located between the Arno and the great sheep runs of the Garfagnana. Neither the land nor the sheep seems to have been his patrimony, however. He refers to "poor relatives" back home and was himself a man without family; Lazarius, it seems, was a parvenu in land and sheep as he was in industry and commerce. Lazarius' business consisted of bringing wool from the countryside to the city. Probably it came chiefly from his own sheep, though we find him buying it also from a Sienese wool merchant. This wool he had made into hats. While Pisan commerce and Pisan aristocrats were still occupied in relatively petty sums, Lazarius was having hats made by the hundreds and exported overseas by the thousands. The direction of his investments was such as to favor the growth of the wool industry, which in agriculture he was simultaneously pursuing. These hats he did not sell in Tuscany but exported overseas to Sicily. Because of the valuable exchange he took three-fourths of the profit. From goods shipped back to Pisa in payment he had all the profits. Lazarius' meteoric rise gave him a wealth outstanding for the age. Though a parvenu, a man who had avoided paying tithes to his native parish of San Genesio, in 1263 he was rich and pious enough to wish these old obligations erased; to the churches of San Miniato he gave silver chalices so that after his death, at mass, he might be remembered daily. In his honor the poor of Pisa's hospitals ate a meal of bread, meat, and wine; on his rural estate, three beds stood ever ready for the poor, the pilgrim, the drifter. When he died, over 1400 masses were to ring forth in Tuscany.

Although his hats were moving in the traditional channels of Pisan commerce, Lazarius was feeling his way in a new direction. In his will he grants a bequest to the monastery of "sanctus Bartholomeus de Alpibus." Had Lazarius himself been to this station on the overland road from Italy to France? We know he was making local wool into hats. Was that interest in wool sending him to France for better cloth or better wool?

Clearly, to call Lazarius Talliapanis primarily a sheep raiser, an industrialist, or an overseas merchant is impossible. So, too, to suggest that any of Pisa's new men were exclusively sheep raisers, industrialists, or overseas merchants is to do an injustice to the revolution they were working. Wool was bringing equally a new agriculture, a new industry, and a new commerce, and with the newness, not with any particular aspect, are these men to be associated. Further, to write the hard and fast rules for success is as difficult for the 13th century as it is for today. But it is both permissible and instructive to let Lazarius' story provide a context for our fragmentary information about some other men whose careers more permanently impressed Pisan history.

The remarkable aspect of all Pisa's capitalists is that, like Lazarius, they could appear in the city with a rural background and so rapidly win pre-eminence. That which distinguishes them sharply from Pisa's older houses seems to be the peculiar relation with their rural homes. As to what those contado roots were, we have one precious hint: the areas in the countryside from which they came. As far as scanty sources can inform us, they come to a surprisingly large extent from the Valdiserchio, the Piemonte, and the Valdarno—areas all economically similar to Lazarius' San Miniato in the Valdarno. The Agliata house, unique because of the clarity in regard to its origins, came from Calcinaia in the Valdarno and moved to Pisa about the early 1270's.[4] The house of Rau was from Cascina, also in the Valdarno; by 1264 it had not yet broken completely with its rural home.[5] It is of significance that a partner of Albertus Sciorta, of whose origins nothing is otherwise known, was from Vinci, a little if famous town in the Florentine Valdarno.[6] In 1259 the notary Iacobus Tiniosi from Calci rented a fulling mill from the Pisan cathedral; in 1283 Baccione Tiniosi, almost certainly a relative, was leasing a ship to Venetians.[7] The house of Papa eludes us in its origins, but in 1263 a partner in the family's wool business was from Montemagno above Calci.[8] Of these men the career of Ranuccinus de Vico is typical.[9] When Ranuccinus moved to the city from the Valdarno about 1270, one son became a pannarius, probably his father's profession; the other followed the new trade to France and in 1283 died there. From what we know of the Delle Brache family, once later myths have been removed, we may con-

---

4. ASP Roncioni, 21 July 1284, Galganus Alliata condam Ruberti de Calcinaria. Cf. Volpe, "Pisa," p. 299.

5. 2543 70v, 17 Jan. 1264, Ventura Rau nuntius filius quondam Guidonis de Cascina. In 1263 Ventura Rau rented a city house from Matheus de Tegularia, 2543 49r, 24 Aug. 1263.

6. 2545 127v, 24 March 1284, Vollia filius Foresis de Vinci comitatus Florentie. Like so many other immigrants from the Valdarno, Vollia was professionally a merciadrius, 2545 37r, 21 March 1283. See above, p. 157, n. 88.

7. ASP San Lorenzo alle Rivolte, 9 Oct. 1259, and 2545 85r, 27 Sept. 1283.

8. 2543 36r, 5 June 1263. In 1285 an Albertus Papa owned land in the Serchio valley, "in loco dicto pratale," 2629 283v, 30 Oct. 1285.

9. 2545 65r, 27 July 1283.

clude that its patrimony stood at Vulmiano in the Valdiserchio, whence, again approximately during the early 1270's, they moved to the city.[10] Finally, the Breve antianorum, the correctors of Pisa's guild statutes in the democratic periods, help confirm this predominance of the Valdiserchio, Piemonte, and the Valdarno as an important cradle of Pisa's new families.[11]

And these areas we have seen before. They are Pisa's sheep centers, and the centers, too, in the period before the industry was urbanized, of wool manufacturing. We have already seen, in the careers of Iohannes Falcone and Terius Agnelli, how vigorously these men could pursue the way of sheep.[12] Still, we cannot presume that these figures were originally or ever exclusively sheep owners. This agricultural enterprise paralleled rather than anticipated an equally vigorous enterprise within the city. Professionally, these new men appear frequently as notaries, but that occupation, other than an interest in efficient business training, tells us nothing. More revealing is another profession frequently associated with their names. Iohannes Falcone as a pannarius or apothecarius, a cloth salesman, responsible for selling the countryside wool in the city. As lanarii, whose function was nearly identical, appear a Papa, Gatti, Aiutamicristo, and in the 14th century, Rau.[13] Lazarius Talliapanis in bringing wool to the city was ful-

10. See P. Pecchiai, "Una Famiglia di mercanti pisani nel trecento," SS, 15 (1906), 71, for the family's possessions in the Valdiserchio.

11. From the correctors of Pisa's statutes listed by Bonaini, Stat., 3, 152 ff., and the Breve antianorum (up to 1300), where I count upward of forty immigrants from these areas.

12. See above, pp. 119 ff.

13. Gerardus Gactus was one of the first consuls of the guild of which we have record, ASP Olivetani, 5 Sept. 1268. Iacobus Papa quondam Bonaventure was a partner in a wool company, 2543 36r, 5 June 1263. Iacobus dictus Puccius lanarius condam Bernardi Aiutamichristo, 2521 203v, 17 Oct. 1307. See also Stat., 3, 747, for a list of other consuls of the art of wool.

filling an identical function without assuming a title. And for many of these families, no great search is needed to find a relation, either through business partnerships or marriage, with lanarii or apothecarii.[14]

Let us risk a generalization. The center of Pisa's urbanization revolution was a petty merchant—pannarius, lanarius, apothecarius pannorum, merciadrius, or nothing —who originated in the contado and who lived by bringing to Pisa's urban market the wool products of her countryside. This man knew the situation, problems, and opportunities of both city and contado; he was able to promote the simultaneous revolution in both from which industrialization was achieved. His rural roots, his interest in wool, gave him a policy to pursue. His late arrival in the city, the social gap which separated him from the aristocracy gave him a kind of self-consciousness, a psychology, whose collective manifestation was the popolo and whose fruits were an unabashed ruthlessness and cruelty in the pursuit of ends which the Renaissance would see again. He was the man with a goal, with an enemy, and with a future.

Perhaps this scheme appears unduly to ignore overseas commerce and Pisa's great maritime tradition. And that tradition's importance let us not disparage. Commerce was, as we have seen, a foundation of the process of urbanization. Moreover, these new men turned to the sea almost as soon as they turned to the city. The office of consul of the sea by the late 13th century almost universally knots their careers.[15] Still, Pisa's overseas commerce, the servant of prior-existent markets, more nearly reflected than pro-

---

14. For Dell' Agnello, Falcone, and Ranuccius quondam Guidonis Rossi, see above, pp. 119 ff. An "apothecarius pannorum de lana" was related by marriage to the Murscii, 2545 102r (1302). The daughter of Gerardus Rau married a pannarius, 2545 38v, 9 May 1302. Pina filia Nerii Fecis married a Ticius lanarius condam Leopardi, 2545 40r, 13 June 1302.

15. See Schaube, *Konsulat,* pp. 52 ff., for list of consules maris.

voked this economic change. It stood apart from the inter-
locked conflict over enclosures and urbanization where the
issue was decided; it is not the field where roots must be
sought. Of this 13th-century conflict, commerce was the
spoils and not the battleground.

On both the old and the new in Pisan society, the later
13th century saw two developments of overriding significance: (1) the decline of the aristocratic trade through the
policies of the democratic regimes, the disaster at Meloria,
and the industrialization of wool; and (2) the rise of
Florence to unquestioned industrial, financial, and demographic supremacy in Tuscany.

Pisa's aristocratic families were confronted with the
choice of adapting themselves to the new economy, or of
retreating to the land. Into the psychology of those who
chose the land the contracts give a curious insight. After
Meloria, Salimbene in particular dwells on the despair of
Pisan women, the "noble, rich, and powerful," who in
groups of thirty or forty journeyed to Genoa on foot to
seek news of their loved ones.[16] When they learned many
had died, from "starvation and hunger and poverty and
misery and sadness," the women tore their faces.

In the chartularies of the early 14th century, some noble-
women of the generation of Meloria have left their wills.
One was Gerardesca, the widow of Guinithellus of the
Sismondi and apparently the mother of Rossus Buzzac-
carinus, an admiral in the Genoese war, whom we have met
paying the commune's debt to Anconese bankers so that
Pisan merchants there would not be penalized. In 1309
Gerardesca attached to her will the clause that her heir
could at no time in her life sell or alienate any of the
inheritance.[17] Another was Brida Del Bagno, a relative of

16. *Cronica,* p. 770.
17. 2523 233v, 29 May 1309, will of Gerardesca relicta Guinithelli de
domo Sesmundorum et filia condam Lamberti Masche.

Panuccio, a Pisan lyric poet. In making her will in 1313, she writes the following provision:

> My inheritance is given under these conditions . . .
> that my heirs the brothers Mascha and Bacciameus and
> Mascharinus my nephews cannot or should not or each
> or any of them cannot or should not sell or donate
> pledge or alienate to any person or institution any of
> my real property of this my inheritance at any time.
> And if they sell or donate, pledge or alienate . . . that
> sale or donation or pledge may neither be valid or
> binding.[18]

These provisions are not isolated ones. The psychology which would bind future generations to inalienable land is a psychology of crisis, which perhaps we can find too in the poetry of Brida's relative Panuccio Del Bagno, impressed as he was by the fickleness of fate and the downfall of the mighty.[19] Psychologists tell us that in periods of stress some men seek to retreat to that stage in their personal histories where security had once been found. For an important segment of Pisa's aristocracy, the troubled times of the late 13th century seem to have brought about a retreat to the land they had never renounced.

18. 2630 142r, 3 Oct. 1310.
19. On Panuccio, see *Rimatori siculo-toscani del dugento*. Ser. prima. *Pistoiesi—Lucchesi—Pisani*, ed. G. Zaccagni and A. Parducci (Bari, 1915), and E. Cristiani, "I Dati biografici ed i riferimenti politici dei rimatori pisani del dugento," *Studi Mediolatini e Volgari, 3* (1955), 7–26. See especially his poem beginning "Perchè di rota ha 'l mondo simiglianza" (*Rimatori*, p. 174). For examples of other similar restrictions placed in wills, 2525 24r, 28 Sept. 1309, will of Bettus Nichus de Lanfrancis. 2546 5r, 21 May 1312, will of Lippa uxor Simonis de Putingnano. 2546 27v, 15 Oct. 1313, will of Bona uxor olim Ugolini filii condam Bonaccursi de Ripafracta et filia condam Iacobi Ghalliani de Balneo. 2630 39r, 28 July(?) 1315, will of Teccia uxor olim Francisci Guidalocti et filia condam domini Iohannis Cavarghie de domo Gaitanorum.

But hardly had Pisa's new capitalist houses won at home, when the Florentine shadow fell upon them. Well has P. Silva interpreted Pisa's political disputes in the 14th century in terms of "Florinizing" and "anti-Florinizing" factions, although his further reduction of these parties into shippers and industrialists was premised on a priority in Pisa's industrial development which in wool she never enjoyed, and a dichotomy between commercial and industrial entrepreneurs which the industry, in its beginnings, never saw.[20] Pisa's dilemma vis-à-vis Florence was not so much whether she should favor her commerce or industry but whether she should surrender and adapt to the Florentine primacy, or, like a kind of robber baron, straddle Florence's trade routes, tap that trade by taxes, and be prepared to fight for the privilege.

Under Florence's shadow, Pisa's classes realigned. Turning their organization, their commerce, and their sheep, to the service of Florentine industry, the capitalists now wanted peace with the hinterland; they were the Florinizers. Their old allies the artisans and their old enemies the aristocrats fused in opposition. Out of the welter the aristocrats emerged once more Ghibelline, as of old, and the capitalists adopted the Guelf name they had formerly fought.[21] Out of the welter, too, comes this conclusion: Pisa, which by the urbanization of industry had reduced her contado to subservience and had urbanized wealth as well —which in the 1260's and 1270's lived through her golden age—found that the process had swirled upward beyond her control. By the early 1300's she found that she was coming to stand vis-à-vis Florence in the same way that,

20. The idea is expressed both in Silva, Gambacorta, and idem, "Intorno all' industria e al commercio della lana in Pisa," SS, new ser. 1 (1910), 329–400.

21. Discussed in Volpe, "Pisa," pp. 202 ff.

fifty years before, her own contado had stood *vis-à-vis* her. Urbanization and concentration continued, but Pisa was forced from the center. She abandoned forever her historic position as "head of the Tuscan province," and, a second-rate city surrounded by greater powers, waited on issues not hers to decide.

APPENDIXES

The notarial entries and parchments printed below are meant primarily to illustrate the material of this book. Toward that end and in the interest of space I have made liberal use of the ellipsis and paraphrase and have felt free to dispense with the critical apparatus that a complete and definitive edition of the chartularies or parchments would require. In Appendix VI, however, I have given full transcriptions of some typical contracts, which will serve to illustrate partially Pisa's commercial and agricultural institutions until a full edition is given us.

APPENDIX I

1. The population of the urban parish of San Cristofano in Kinsica, 1272–74, as reconstructed from the chartularies of Ugolinus quondam Iacobi, nos. 2515 and 2516. Names in italics are newcomers to the parish, as stated explicitly in the documents or revealed by the formula "qui moratur Pisis in cappella sancti Cristofani" rather than "de cappella sancti Cristofani." Names marked with an asterisk are of those who participated in the parish meeting regarding a new well as recorded in 2515 25v, 3 April 1273.

(1) Adornettus magister quondam Paganini, 2516 4r.
(2) *Albertus dictus Bettus quondam magistri Riccomi, 2515 140r.
(3) *Albinellus quondam Melsi, 2515 48v.
(4) *Andreas tabernarius quondam Ranuccini de Casciaula, 2515 74r.
(5) Bacciameus quondam magistri Bellomis, 2515 105r, 144r, 144v.
(6) Bacciameus quondam Guidonis Guercii, 2515 146r.
(7) Bectus lanarius quondam Granelli, 2516 31r.
(8) *Bella relicta Bergi notarii de Farneto, 2516 12r.
(9) *Bencivenne filius quondam Baruccii de Fasiano, 2515 83r, 95r.
(10) *Benvenutus tinctor quondam Orlandi, 2516 61v.
(11) *Bergus Menabovis.
(12) Berlingerius, 2515 115r.
(13) *Bindus quondam Rainerii et nepos Gerardi quondam Pandulfini Ciacii de Putignano, 2515 121v.
(14) *Bonacursus fornarius quondam Manini de Vicarello, 2516 30v.
(15) *Bonaiunta pelliparius quondam Salvi Buratti de Settimo, 2515 104v.
(16) *Bonaiuncta Viviani.

(17) *Bonaiunta de Cascina.

(18) Bonannus spetiarius quondam Iacoppi, 2516 6ov.

(19) Bononcontrus quondam Gerardini, 2515 141v.

(20) Bonsignore dictus Ciaffulus quondam Petri, 2515 54r, 115r.

(21) Bursa, Iacobus, 2515 57r, 122r, 145r.

(22) Castagneto, comites de, 2515 62v, 132v.

(23) Chituccius calthularius, 2515 67r.

(24) Cima quondam domini Iacobi Morandi de Florentia.

(25) Cima quondam Venture de Pistoria.

(26) Ciolus quondam Bandini de Putignano, 2515 48v.

(27) Ciolus quondam Iunte calthularius, 2515 87v.

(28) Daniel quondam Menobovis, 2515 112v.

(29) Federigus quondam Ildebrandini Nasi, 2515 126r.

(30) Fiorensius condam Schiarde florentini, 2516 15v.

(31) Fortinus ferrarius quondam Bonacursi, 2515 52r, 77r.

(32) Francus casearius et olearius quondam Albertini, 2515 92r.

(33) Gentile quondam Petri de Camerino, 2516 19v.

(34) *Gerardinus vinarius.

(35) Gerardus de Fasiano, 2515 139v. Pisan ambassador to
    Charles of Anjou in 1269. Relazioni, no. 140.

(36) *Gerardus Rigolecti de Florentia, 2515 123v.

(37) Giorgius quondam Mainecti de Florentia, 2515 65v, 122r.

(38) Gottifredus quondam Rainerii Armingossi, 2515 122r.

(39) Gregorius pelliparius et pissicarius, 2515 95v.

(40) Guardavilla barberius quondam Raffetti de Pontremuli,
    2515 22v, 76r.

(41) Guido quondam Porcellini de Florentia, 2515 62r, 2516 4r.

(42) Guido quondam Rodulfi, 2515 138v.

(43) Henrigus nuntius, 2516 37v.

(44) Henrigus tabernarius quondam Gerardi de Curtibus, 2515
    75r.

(45) Iacobus aurifex, 2515 40v.

(46) Iacobus dictus Puccius filius Bernardini, 2516 29r.

(47) [Iacobus dictus] Puccius tinctor quondam Bianci, 2516 4v.

(48) *Iacobus pelliparius quondam Bonacursi, 2515 124v.

(49) *Iacobus Iannibelli.

(50) *Iacobus calthularius quondam Iohannis, 2515 34v, 54r,
    75v.

(51) [Iacobus dictus] Puccius quondam Iunte cultellarius, 2515
    87v.

(52) Iacobus dictus Puccius quondam magistri Manni, 2515 74r.

(53) [Iacobus dictus] Puccius quondam Sardi.

(54) *Iacobus calthularius quondam Strenne de sancto Cassiano vallis Arni*, 2515 54r.

(55) *Iacobus dictus Puccius filius Tedicii quondam Lanfranci de Fasiano*, 2516 14v.

(56) Iacobus Vecchionis quondam Bonacursi, 2515 43v.

(57) *Ianne mariscalcus quondam Carenacci de sancto Miniato*, 2515 42r.

(58) Ildebrandinus dictus Bindus quondam domini Gerardi Raffaldi, 2515 12r.

(59) *Ildebrandinus quondam Guittonis de Settimo*, 2515 108r.

(60) *Iohannes de Crespina.

(61) *Iohannes dictus Vannes quondam Galgani nuntius de Pettori*, 2515 74r.

(62) *Iohannes dictus Vannes quondam Guidonis de Massa*, 2515 41v.

(63) *Iohannes dictus Vannes quondam Francardi*, 2516 31v.

(64) *Iohannes dictus Vannes Guercius quondam item Iohannis*, 2515 57r.

(65) Iohannes quondam Martini, 2516 19v.

(66) *Iohannes dictus Iohanninus quondam Rafforsati de sancto Geminiano*, 2515 72v.

(67) *Iohannes de Pergula vinarius quondam Thomazini*, 2515 140r.

(68) Iuncta relicta Prove, 2515 75v.

(69) *Lambertus vinarius quondam Aliotti de Marciana*, 2515 136v.

(70) Lapus quondam Niccoli, 2515 65r.

(71) *Lensus quondam Genarii*, 2515 132r, 150v.

(72) Lucrese relicta Niccoli pelliparii, 2515, 145r, 2516 18r.

(73) *Luctus Civerini quondam Brunecti de Fasiano*, 2516 34r.

(74) *Lunardus Talenti.

(75) Luparellus bastarius filius quondam Tabernarii, 2515 118v.

(76) Marcus quondam Gratie tabernarius 2515 7r, 95v.

(77) *Martius quondam Rainerii Martii de Septimo*, 2515, 76r.

(78) *Marzuccus filius Corbuli de Putignano*, 2516 15v.

(79) *Matthea filia quondam Bene fabri de Carmignano*, 2515 126r.

(80) *Matheus quondam Alfonsi de Casciaula*, 2515 74r.

(81) *Meus quondam Diedi de Xandra,* 2516 15v.

(82) *Michael Menobovis,* 2515 112v.

(83) *Monte filius Guidonis Rodulfi,* 2515 42r.

(84) *Nicolaus dictus Grosseta quondam Guittonis de Sassa,* 2516 10r.

(85) Nicolus quondam Bonaguide, 2516 39r.

(86) *Nuccius de Singna filius quondam Puliensis de sancto Miniato,* 2515 82r.

(87) Paganellus fornarius quondam Bonacursi, 2515 94r.

(88) Paganellus tabernarius, 2515 139r.

(89) Pelegrinus bastarius et sellarius quondam Salvii, 2515 23v, 78r.

(90) *Pelegrinus tabernarius.

(91) *Puliense quondam Puliensis calthularius de sancto Miniato,* 2515 82r.

(92) *Rainerius aurifex quondam Bonacursi de Fasiano,* 2515 108r.

(93) *Rainerius quondam Henrigetti de Putignano,* 2515 119r.

(94) *Rainerius dictus Nerius tabernarius quondam Lamberti de Cascina,* 2515 40r.

(95) Rainerius quondam Niccoli Carranti, 2515 64r.

(96) *Ranuccius de Putignano,* 2516 21v.

(97) Riccadonna quondam Guelfi, 2515 96r.

(98) *Ricovetus quondam Iacobi florentini,* 2515 117v.

(99) Scornigianus, Periciolus (2515 128v), Marzuccus (2516 33v) and * Gontulinus.

(100) *Taddeus de Putignano.*

(101) *Taddeus Massarghii.

(102) *Talentus corrigiarius quondam Bernardi de Rinonichi.*

(103) *Tedicius Sardus quondam Lanfranchi de Fasiano,* 2516 3v.

(104) *Thomazinus pelliparius quondam Marignani,* 2515 123v.

(105) Thomazinus Lamadina quondam Iohannis, 2515 48v, 36v.

(106) *Torscellus Maglavathi.

(107) Travus quondam Benis sensalis.

(108) Simon Manovelli lanarius, 2515 48v.

(109) *Simon molendarius quondam Guidonis,* 2515 44r.

(110) *Ugolinus calthularius.

(111) Ugolinus Marti, 2515 53r.

(112) Ugolinus sellarius, 2515 141r.

(113) *Ugolinus de Triana.*

(114) Ugolinus vinarius quondam Fornarii, 2515 131r.
(115) *Upethinus de Putignano.
(116) *Vincens vinarius.
(117) Ventura testor quondam Cisnellis, 2516 8v.

APPENDIX II

2. The debasement of the Pisan denarius. Pisan money first appears about 1150, as a close imitation of the Lucchese.[1] From surviving coins and contemporary records, we can pretty well reconstruct the standards according to which Pisan denarii were minted. From each ounce of alloy, forty coins were struck (or from each pound of alloy by weight, forty solidi). This remained the standard of weight for Pisan petty denarii throughout the 12th, 13th, and into the 14th century. The alloy of the earliest coins was half silver and half copper, or, in the language of the period, each ounce (twelve denarii) of alloy contained six denarii of silver and six of copper. One mark of pure silver was worth theoretically $2\frac{2}{3}$ pounds, in the sense that that many Pisan denarii could be struck from each mark of silver.[2]

The 1160's and 1170's were years of grave monetary disorders throughout the whole of Italy. After the Peace of Constance (1183), however, when peace was finally achieved between Emperor Frederick Barbarossa on the one hand and the papacy and the communes on the other, a general effort seems to have been made to restore order in the Italian monetary system. Apparently as part of this restoration, Pisan money was itself stabilized about 1190. Pisan denarii were struck at the same weight as before, but the silver content was cut in half. Each ounce of alloy now contained three denarii of silver and nine of copper. From a mark of silver could be struck, therefore, $5\frac{1}{3}$ pounds.[3]

1. See Herlihy, "Coinage."

2. Cf. *Codice diplomatico della Repubblica di Genova*, ed. C. Imperiale, 2 (Rome, 1938), no. 4, where in 1164 a mark of silver is worth "soldis xlviii lucensium de Pisa vel Lucca." It was usual for coined money to be worth slightly more than the actual value of the silver it contained.

3. According to Leonardo Fibonacci (writing in 1202), one pound of silver was worth seven pounds of Pisan denarii, which means one mark was about $5\frac{1}{4}$; in 1203 one mark was worth five pounds (see Davidsohn,

In terms of this money, the gold florin, first struck in 1252, was worth twenty solidi.

These standards of weight and purity for the Pisan denarius were maintained at least up to 1250, as we know Sienese money, virtually equivalent to the Pisan, was being struck according to those standards in that year.[4] After 1250 the denarius enters a new period of fluctuations and was not stabilized again until the middle 1270's, when the silver content was once more reduced by one half.[5] Each ounce of alloy contained one and one-half denarii of silver and ten and one-half of copper. From a mark of silver could now be struck 10⅔ pounds. The florin was worth theoretically forty solidi.

In the late 1290's, Pisan money enters another period of fluctuations, and when it was stabilized in the early 14th century, its alloy contained only one denarius of silver to eleven of copper. From one mark of silver could be struck sixteen pounds, and one florin was worth, theoretically, sixty solidi.[6]

The values here given are theoretical, in terms of the silver content the coins contained. In fact, however, the value of the denarii was determined too by the volume of coins that the mint issued, so that, if the volume was restricted, the value of the denarii in terms of un-minted silver or of larger coins (the silver grossi or the florin) tended to rise. As the following tables will illustrate, the petty denarii tended

Forsch., 4, 317). In terms of Sienese money, theoretically equivalent to the Pisan, one mark was almost six pounds in 1210, five pounds two solidi in 1227, later frequently five. Cf. Regestum senense, ed. F. Schneider, RCI, 8 (Rome, 1911), no. 478. As late as 1248 (Davidsohn, Forsch., 4, 316 ff.), the mark was worth five pounds of Pisan denarii.

4. Cf. D. Promis, Monete della Repubblica di Siena (Turin, 1868), p. 326, document I, extract from Breve dei iurati degli ufficiali del comune di Siena, 1250.

5. By 1258 the mark rose to 7½ pounds of Sienese money. Cf. Regestum volaterranum, ed. F. Schneider, RCI, 1 (Rome, 1907), no. 698, 23 March 1258; and for the equation of Sienese, Pisan, and Volterrese money, ibid., no. 746, 3 May 1263. Cf. also Promis, Monete di Siena, document II, Deliberazione del Consiglio della Campana.

6. Cf. C. Violante, "Per la storia economica e sociale di Pisa nel trecento. La riforma della zecca del 1318," Bullettino dell' Istituto Storico Italiano per il Medio Evo e Archivio Muratoriano, 66 (1954), 1283, document dated 25 Aug. 1317. "Et quod moneta parva sit de solidis quadraginta in libra et mictatur in qualibet libra uncia una argenti fini . . . et dictus florenus valeat solidos quinquaginta sex denariorum et non ultra."

usually to circulate at an exchange rate slightly above their actual value in terms of their silver content. In 1283–86, Pisan denarii reached a peak value for the period at about 12 per cent above par, undoubtedly reflecting the restriction on minting them that the statutes of 1286 contain.[7] Conversely, an increase in mint output tended to lower the exchange value of the petty denarii, and apparently it was possible for the coins to circulate even at a rate slightly below their actual value in terms of their silver content. This meant in turn that a mint, if it greatly increased its output of petty denarii, would possibly produce coins actually worth slightly less than the silver that they contained.[8] To avoid this penalty for turning out large volumes of petty denarii, the mint could either restrict its output or debase its coins. In periods of financial stress, when the commune had decided to mint a large volume of coin to help it in its financial difficulties, its only recourse was debasement. The periods of debasement in the early 1270's and late 1290's seem, therefore, to be introduced by periods in which Pisan denarii dropped in value below the worth of the silver they contained. We know that in 1271, Sienese merchants complained that "because of the falling exchange" (*pro defectu cambii*) of Pisan small denarii, they could get only 3,910 gold ounces for the money given them by the Pisan commune, when they had expected 4,000 ounces, and in another transaction, 3,912 instead of 4,000.[9] Conversely, about 1276, after they had been stabilized, Pisan denarii began to gain in value, reaching a peak in 1286, when, as we have mentioned, further minting of them had been forbidden.[10]

3. The Pisan denarius and the gold florin. Those values marked with an asterisk are taken from C. Cipolla, *Studi di storia della moneta* (Pavia, 1949), pp. 55–7.
One florin equals in Pisan denarii:

7. *Stat., 1,* 292.
8. As in the late 1250's when the value of a mark of silver had risen above seven pounds, or in 1296 and 1297, when the value of the florin had risen above forty solidi.
9. *Relazioni,* n. 273, 14 March 1271.
10. See above, n. 7.

Year	Source	Solidi	Denarii
1252	Pisan and Florentine denarii equal under Tuscan monetary league	20	
1277*		36	
1278*		36	
1278	ASP San Silvestro 19 June 1298	36	10
1283	2545 47v 5 April	34	4
1283	2545 56v 16 May	34	4
1286	ASP Roncioni 28 March	34	
1287*	ASP San Martino 13 September	38	4
1288	ASP Primaziale 3 January	36	10
1289*	ASP San Lorenzo alle Rivolte 17 January	36	10
1289*	ASP San Martino 11 February	36	10
1291	ACA 30 April	36	10
1291	ASP Cappelli 23 June	36	10
1291	ASP Olivetani 11 August	36	10
1291	ASP Primaziale 2 October	34	6
1292	ASP San Michele 2 January	34	6
1292	ASP Cappelli 23 January	36	10
1292	ASP Olivetani 7 February	34	6
1292	ASP Cappelli 16 February	36	10
1292	ACA 23 February	36	10
1293	ASP San Martino 3 September 1288	38	4
1294	ASP Roncioni 27 July	38	8
1295*	ASP San Martino 16 March	34	6
1295	ASP Primaziale 3 December	34	6
1296	ASP Pia Casa di Misericordia 23 July	40	
1296–97	*Tuscia*, 2, 249	40	2
1297	ASP Cappelli 20 May	41	
1297	ASP Roncioni December	43	3
1304	ASP Comune A 83, 14r	53	6
1306	2521 125r 21 January	53	10
1306	2521 175v 24 May	53	11
1308	2523 19v 28 June	54	
1311	ASP Comune A 84, 84	54	
1312	2546, 14r	58	
1317	ASP Comune A 86, 1v	55	9
1317	August 25, Violante, "Storia economica," p. 183	56	
1322	ASP Comune A 88, 26v	59	4

4. The Pisan denarius and the gold ounce of the Regno.
One gold ounce equals in terms of Pisan solidi:

Year	Source	Solidi
1203	ACC 27 August	100
1253	ACC 22 March	120
1263	2543, 32r	110
1268	Cf. Davidsohn, *Forsch.*, *4*, 321	120
1269	ASP Roncioni 5 June	125
1271	ASP Primaziale 24 April	160
1283	2545 83v 24 September	170
1283	2545 93v 3 November	150
1299	Zeno, *Documenti,* no. 44	210
1299	" no. 45	205
1299	" no. 46	206½
1299	" no. 110	205
1304	ASP Olivetani 26 January	205
1308	Zeno, *Documenti,* no. 133	205
1308	" no. 139	200

5. The Pisan denarius and the silver grosso.
One *grossus duorum solidorum* equals:

Year	Source	Denarii
1263	2543 57r 3 September	24
(One *aquilinus grossus argenti* equals:)		
1272	2515 146v 31 August	26
1279	ASP Alliata 22 April	33
1283	2545 34r 1 February	29
1283	2545 89r 1 August	31
1290	ASP Alliata 15 April	31
1290	ASP Alliata 26 October	29
1292	ASP Alliata 17 October	31
1294	ASP San Lorenzo 13 May	33
1296–97	*Tuscia, 2,* 249	33
(One *aquilinus novus grossus* equals:)		
1297	ACA 29 July	24
1298	ASP San Lorenzo 31 January	24
1298	ASP Roncioni 25 July	24
1301	2545 89v	24
1302	2545 16v	24
1305	ASP S. Anna 15 March	24

6. Rent for an artisan's shop. The rent is for one year.

		Pounds	Solidi
1264	2514 6v	3	10
1264	2514 11v	4	
1264	2514 13v	3	
1264	2514 42v	4	
1272	2515 93v	5	
1272	2515 115r	2	
1274	2516 13v	5	
1283	2545 93r	16	10
1301	2545 29v	5	
1301	2545 40r	5	
1301	2545 94v	4	

7. Price of a staio of grain. Our best indication of what grain actually cost is the assessment of an obligation in money or in grain as a substitute or its sale directly to a consumer for immediate payment. The sale of grain for future delivery was a common means of concealing a loan and the price received will be considerably below the grain's market value.

			Solidi
1208	ACC 30 August	Estimate	10
1233	ACA 30 August	"	9
1263	2543 14v 18 April	Purchase price of Sicilian grain	14
	2543 16r 23 April	Future delivery	7½
	2543 17r 30 April	Purchase price	16
	2543 20r 3 May	Future delivery	8
	2543 22v 11 May	Future delivery	8
1264	2543 96v 30 May	"	5⅓
	2514 45r	Purchase price	14
1272	2515 89v 7 November	"	16
	2515 132r 7 June	" of "granum maremanum"	20
1273	2515 34r 21 March	Purchase price	16
	2516 10r 13 December	Future delivery	10
	2516 25v 19 March	"	6
1277	ASP Cappelli 5 January	Estimate	20
	ASP Olivetani 1 February	"	20

			Solidi
1279	2545 9v 1 October	Unknown	14
	9v 23 November	"	16¾
1281	9r 15 August	"	34⅓
1283	9r 1 October	"	13⅓
1284	9r 9 September	"	33⅓
1284	ASP Olivetani 8 November	Estimate	40
1285	ACA 13 November	" of "granum nostras"	45
1286	ASP San Paolo 4 June	"	50
1286	ACA 12 November	" "	40
1287	ACA 20 February	" "	45
1290	ASP Alliata 30 June 1291	Price to consumers	29
1291	ACA 5 September	Estimate	29
1299	ASP Comune A 82 45r	Price to consumers	22
1299	2527 42v 25 August	Estimate	15⅔
1309	2525 24r 24 September	Price to consumers	22
1322	ASP Comune A 88 72r	"	⁊0

8. Price for a barrel of wine.

			Solidi
1263	2543 8v	Local wine	⅜
1264	2514 8r	"	5¼
	28r	"	⅓
	28v	"	3
	33v	"	4
1272	2515 91r	"	6⅔
1281	ASP San Michele 13 November	Corsican	24
1284	ASP Primaziale 10 February	Local wine	6
1285	2629 249r	"	9⅔
1304	ASP Trovatelli 13 January	Greek	70

9. The value of a cow.

		Pounds
1264	2514 8r	8
	50r	6
1272	2515 85v	6
1273	2515 56v	11¾
1274	2516 26r	8

			Pounds
1285	2629	279v	11
		28or	15
1301	2545	90r	13
		95r	13
1302	2545	69r	14
		72v	14½
		78r	18½
		89v	27
1305	2521	31v	23
1306		49v	18
1314	2630	31r	15½
		33v	13
		37r	26

APPENDIX III

THE SALE OF THE PISAN TARIFF, 1247

10. The auditing of the sale of the Pisan tariff, ASP Alliata 24 November 1248.

(a) The accountants: Nos Gaitanus iudex de Gaitanis et Bandinus Bonbaronis et Rubertinus de Navacchio publici modulatores officialium et non officialium pisani communis qui anno proximo preterito fuerunt officiales et etiam eorum omnium quos ex forma nostri brevis perquirere et investigare tenemur rationem siquidem actus gestionis vel administrationis . . . emptorum supraposite duarum navium et quatuor galearum empte tempore domini Marini de Ebulo [1247–48] pisani olim dei gratia potestatis perquisivimus et investigavimus diligenter invenimus namque dictos emptores emisse introitus et proventus dicte supraposite a communi pisano pro pretio librarum viginti duarum milium centum denariorum pisane monete sicut nobis constitit evidenter per privilegium sive instrumentum emptionis supraposite antedicte.

(b) The purchasers: Gerardus Provincialis, Pericciolus Antonii, Sigerius Antonii, Ugolinus Bonamici, Leolus quondam Rainerii, Sciancetus(?) Martus Guerrisii, Andreas filius Banducci Sciancati, Rainerius Canneti bancherius, Dodus bancherius, Bergus notarius, Ugolinus bancherius, Benecasa Gigor . . . (?), Guido Panca filius Petri Porcelli, Oradinus de Turchio, Dominicus Gostantini, Benenatus Belcani, Uguiccione Boctaccii, Pandulfinus bancherius, Petrus . . . Gerardus Bandi, Leopardus bancherius, Rubertinus Kalenda et Albertus.

(c) The *depositarii*. [Illegible] quondam Guidonis et Michaele quondam Burgensis fratres penitentie positi et constituti a communi pisano ad ipsam solutionem recipiendam recipientes pro communi pisano.

(d) The accounting. The purchasers of the tax had advanced the

commune, "ex forma consilii senatus inde data" 500 pounds, "que
deerant furnimento dicte armate."

	pounds	solidi	denarii
Advanced to commune	500	—	—
Paid to *depositarii,* 1247–48	11,050	—	—
Still to be paid	188	10	8
SUBTOTAL: MONEY GIVEN FOR TAX	11,738	10	8
Tax discounts to foreign merchants. From the			
Regno	680	8	10
Regno, Provence, Savona, and Aragon	2,431	8	8
Savona	670	13	
Tunis	67	2	4
Aragon	210	15	6
Regno	6,298	5	
SUBTOTAL: TAX DISCOUNTS	10,358	9	4
Salary of notary	3		
SUBTOTAL: SALARY	3		
TOTAL: THE PRICE OF THE TAX	22,100	—	—

APPENDIX IV

11. 2543 32r 31 May 1263. Dilecto nepoti suo Lamberto filio Lucterii de cappella sancti Laurentii de Kinthica Pisarum qui fuit de burgo sancti Genesii Lazarius quondam Talliapanis qui fuit de scripto burgo sancti Genesii et nunc moratur Pisis in cappella sancti Cristofori salutem cum vero amore. De prudentia et dilectione tua plene confidens te precepi et per hoc publicum instrumentum tibi mando et volo ut illa cappella noningenta octoginta una circa vel si plura aut pauciora sunt que Rainerius quondam Iohannis Longi de Pectori tibi pro me nomine accomandisie dedit ut dictus Rainerius mihi retulit et dicit vendas quam melius potes et quam melius deus tibi concesserit et eorum pretium suscipias et scribe in tuo ratiocinio uncias et tarenos auri quas et quos inde suscipies et habebis et pone in capitali singulam unciam auri quas inde habebis per solidos CX denariorum pisanorum parve monete et ex dictis unciis et tarenis auri eme res et merces prout tibi melius videatur et ipsas res vel merces mihi mittas vel deferas quam citius potes omni meo risco et fortuna maris et gentis. Sub hoc pacto quod tu possis et debeas inde consequi et habere quartam totius lucri quod inde habebitur per unciam auri omnium ipsarum unciarum et tarenorum ponendo singulam unciam per solidos CX denariorum sicut dictum est supra. Ad hec ego Rainerius scriptus modo scripto mitto tibique per hoc idem publicum instrumentum do et concedo parabolam et mandatum et ad tui cautelam hanc inde cartam Iacobum publicum notarium quondam Ildebrandini de Carraria Gonnelle nos scripti Lazarius et Rainerius taliter scribere rogavimus. Actum Pisis Kinthice in apotheca domus sancti Sepulcri scripta. Presentibus Ugolino notario filio meo scripti Iacobi notarii et Belloste calthulario quondam Bonristoris (?) testibus rogatis ad hec. Anno domini M CC LXIIII indictione VI pridie kal. Iunii.

Non dubitetur de datali quia verax est.

12. 2543 33v 1 June 1263. Iuncta cappellarius de cappella sancti Marti Vie Calcisane interrogatus a Lazario quondam Talliapanis qui moratur Kinthice in cappella sancti Cristofori fuit confessus se in veritate accepisse et apud se habere ab eo in una parte in lana agnina nigra pro faciendo ei cappella secundum formam carte rogate a Bonavite notario de Biuti libratas XLIII et in alia parte in denariis libras XXV et solidos X bonorum denariorum pisanorum parve monete. De quibus omnibus scriptis quantitatibus vocavit se bene quietum et pacatum ab eo et eum liberum et renunciavit exceptioni non habitarum et non acceptarum rerum et non numerate pecunie. E converso dictus Lazarius interrogatus a scripto Iuncta fuit confessus se in veritate iam accipere et apud se habere ab eo de ipsis cappellis que dictus Iuncta ei facere debet ex forma scripte carte rogate a scripto Bonavita notario cappella CLXXX. De quibus cappellis CLXXX vocavit se bene pacatum et eum liberum. Et taliter etc. Actum Pisis Kinthice in apotheca domus sancti Sepulcri scripta. Presentibus Treuguano quondam Bandini et Becto lanario quondam Granelli rogatis testibus ad hec. Anno domini M CC LXIIII indictione VI ipsa die kal. Iunii.

Postea vero eodem scripto anno et indictione scripta videlicet VIII idus Iunii in scripta apotheca scriptus Lazarius interrogatus a scripto Iuncta fuit confessus se accepisse et apud se habere ab eo de predictis cappellis ab eo sibi factis cappella CCCC . . . que capiunt in totum libratas XLII. De quibus cappellis CCCC et cet. Presentibus Bonnano quondam Iacoppi et Guido vinario quondam Uguccionis rogatis testibus ad hec.

13. 2543 47r 13 August 1263. Dilecto nipoti suo Lamberto filio Lucterii de cappella sancti Laurentii de Kinthica Pisarum qui fuit de burgo sancti Genesii Lazarius quondam Talliapanis qui fuit de burgo scripto et nunc moratur Pisis in cappella sancti Cristofori de Kinthica salutem et sinceram dilectionem. Per hoc publicum instrumentum tibi notifico quod Rainerius quondam Iohannis Longi de Pectori lator huius presentis instrumenti michi retulit et dixit se nomine accomandisie dedisse et recommendasse tibi pro me nomine meo cappella de lana noningenta octogincta unum circa vel si plura vel pauciora fuerunt. De quibus cappellis ego quidem misi tibi publicum instrumentum confectum a Iacobo notario subscripto quod ad tuas manus credo pervenisse quo continebatur ut tu deberes et posses ea vendere quam melius posses et pretium eorum suscipere et scribere

in ratiocinio tuo eorum pretium et ponere tibi in capitali singulam
unciam auri ipsius pretii quod inde haberes pro solidis CX denariorum pisanorum parve monete. Et deberes ex ipsis unciis et tarenis
seu ex ipso pretio emere res et merces prout tibi melius videatur et
ipsas res et merces deberes michi mittere vel deferre quam citius
posses omni meo risco et fortuna maris et gentis sub pacto quod tu
deberes et posses inde consequi et habere quartam partem totius
lucri quod inde haberetur per unciam auri omnium ipsarum unciarum et tarenorum ipsius pretii ponendo singulam unciam auri in
capitali pro solidis CX prout scriptum est et de hoc etiam parabolam
tibi dedit predictus Rainerius per predictum instrumentum. Hinc est
quod nunc per hoc presens publicum instrumentum tibi et tue di-
lectioni et probitati firmiter significo mando et volo et te rogo ut si
vendisti dicta cappella et pretium eorum suscepisti et ex eo res et
merces emisti secundum formam predicti primi mandati facias et
facere debeas in nomine domini. Si vero dicta cappella nondum sunt
vendita dicta cappella pro me sine mora viso hoc presenti publico
instrumento scripto Rainerio des et restituas et tribuas. Si autem
vendita sunt et ex eorum pretio res vel merces nondum empsisti volo
et placet ut ipsorum pretium eidem Rainerio pro me et nomine
meo des et tribuas sine mora. Si vero dictum pretium ei dare non
velles volo firmiter et tibi mando ut facias et facere debeas prout in
predicto primo mandato et instrumento continebatur. Et si sic feceris
mihi erit gratum et placidum. Et firmum et ratum habebo et tenebo.
Et ad plenam firmitatem habendam Iacobum publicum notarium
taliter scribere rogavi. Actum Pisis Kinthice in apotheca domus sancti
Sepulcri predicta. Presentibus Bonocurso Fagnolo quondam Bonavite
de cappella sancti Cosme et Matheo quondam Armingossi de Putignano rogatis ad hec. Anno domini M CC LXIIII indictione VI idus
Augusti.

14. 2543 55r 15 November 1263. Cambius cappellarius de cappella
sancti Sebastiani de Kinthica filius quondam Nerii interrogatus a Lazario de cappella sancti Cristofori de Kinthica filio quondam Talliapanis de burgo sancti Genesii fuit confessus dictum Lazarium in
veritate solvisse et redisse Orlando (*sic*) Finelli de Senis pro scripto
Cambio de suis Lazarii propriis denariis pro pretio lane as ipso Cambio
comperate et habite ab ipso Ildebrandino (*sic*) libras viginti et solidos
duos bonorum denariorum pisanorum parve monete renunciando
exceptioni non solute et non numerate pecunie et non comparate et

non habite lane. De qua lana ex pacto inter eos habito dictus Cambius debet facere et dare scripto Lazario cappella franceschina tot et tanta quot et quanta capient per infrascriptam rationem quorum quodlibet esse debet unciarum novem et bene factum et debet ponere et dare ei singulare centenarium scriptorum cappellorum pro libris decem et solidis octo denariorum compensando sibi in pretio dictorum cappellorum sicut capient pro rata per predictam rationem predictarum librarum XX et solidorum II denariorum. Que cappella tot et quantacumque capient numero per predictam rationem idem Cambius promisit eidem Lazario dare per se vel per alium et cet. A hinc ad kalendas Novembris proximas. Sinè briga et cet. Sub pena dupli scripti pretii per stipulationem et sub ypoteca et obligatione suorum heredum et omnium bonorum suorum. Et renunciavit et cet. Et promisit et convenit se et cet. Et statuit et cet. Et taliter et cet. Actum Pisis Kinthice in apotheca domus sancti Sepulcri scripta. Presentibus Bonacurso Fagnolo quondam Benediti spetiario et Bonagrasia calthulario filio quondam Bernardi de sancto Miniato testibus ad hec rogatis. Anno domini M CC LXIIII indictione VI XVII kal. Decembris.

15. 2543 101r 13 September 1263. Iuncta cappellarius quondam Rodulfi de cappella sancti Marti Vie Calcisane confesses that Lazarius paid with his own money to Orlandus Finelli of Siena for the price of wool sixteen pounds four solidi, from which wool Iuncta is to make for Lazarius "cappella franceschina" of which each is to weigh ten ounces, at a cost of ten pounds per hundred, less the money paid by Lazarius for the wool. The hats are to be delivered November 1. Contract canceled 5 January 1264.

16. 2543 101r 13 September 1263. Pandulfinus cappellarius quondam Bernardi cappellarii de capella sancti Barnabe confesses that Lazarius paid with his own money to Orlando Finelli of Siena for the price of wool fifteen pounds seventeen solidi, from which wool Pandulfinus is to make for Lazarius "cappella franceschina" of which each is to weigh ten ounces, at a cost of ten pounds per hundred, less the money paid by Lazarius for the wool. The hats are to be delivered November 1. Contract canceled 5 January 1264.

17. 2543 72r 19 January 1264. [From the will of Lazarius] . . . Et fuit confessus se in veritate accepisse et habere . . . ab Rainerio notario de sancto Stefano ad Barbiallam de curte sancti Miniatis pro

dote et nomine dotis Moltocare filie sue . . . et uxoris sue scripti
Lazarii . . . libras LXXXX . . . Item iudicavit scripte uxori sue
habitationem totius domus sue scripti Lazarii quam habet in burgo
sancti Floris videlicet quod donec ipsa custodiet castitatem et innupta
permanserit . . . Et dixit et voluit ut donec dicta uxor sua sic habi-
tare voluerit et habitaverit in predicta domo posita in burgo sancti
Floris ipsa debeat in ipsa domo habere et tenere de bonis suis predicti Lazarii saccones III et carpitas III et paria III linteaminum pro
pauperibus ibi hospitandis et pro eis emendis iudicavit . . . libras
VIII. Item dixit et voluit ut ipsa uxor sua possit et debeat dare de
suis Lazarii bonis libras X denariorum pauperibus consanguineis
scripti Lazarii quos videlicet ipsa congnoverit magne indigere et
quibus ei videbitur. Item iudicavit scriptis nepotibus suis . . . totam
terram et casamenta quam et que ipse Lazarius habet vel habere
videtur in burgis veteribus sancti Genesii et in burgo sancti Floris
. . . [Some legacies:] Item iudicavit Benvenuto germano scripte
Moltocare uxoris sue illas libras octo denariorum quas ipse Benvenutus dicto Lazario dare tenetur per cartam rogatam a Gualando
notario occasione pecudum ab eo emendarum . . . Et Baldinecto
lucchesi qui moratur Ianue vel eius heredi libras XV denariorum
quas ei deberat ex prestantia maris . . . Item reliquid et dari voluit
pro satisfactione decimarum et primitiarum quas ipso tempore suo
dare debuit et non dedit solidos XL denariorum dandos plebi sancti
Genesii . . . Et hospitali sancti Bartholomei de Alpibus solidos XX
denariorum pro dei amore et sancti Bartholomei alpini . . .

18. 2543 90r 30 March 1264. Rainerius dictus Cingelancea de cappella
sancti Petri ad vincula filius quondam Brunaccii [confesses to Lazarius
that he has received] ab eo in societate maris cappella DCCC siciliana
lane nigre in duobus saccis posita sibi in capitali pro libris LXXXIII
bonorum denariorum pisanorum parve monete portanda ad suam
Rainerii voluntatem . . . infra suam henticam ad riscum maris et
gentis in presenti viadio quod . . . faciet a Pisis Messanam et quocumque alio iverit vel miserit . . . ad quartum proficuum inde habendum [Rainerius promises to return capital and three-fourths of
the profits upon returning to Pisa].

19. 2543 90v 1 April 1264. Lambertus filius Lucterii . . . de burgo
sancti Genesii qui moratur Pisis in cappella sancti Laurentii [confesses
to Lazarius that he has received] in societate maris libras XX . . .

infra suam henticam . . . de Pisis Messanam . . . [Lambertus promises to return capital and three-fourths of the profits upon returning
to Pisa].

20. 2514 20r 13 October 1264. Iunctarellus de sancto Miniate filius
Bonacorsi quondam Bonaviti coram me Iacobo notario et cet. recepit
et habuit in societatem maris a Lazario quondam Talliapanis olim
de burgo sancti Genesii qui nunc moratur Pisis in cappella sancti
Cristofori libras decem bonorum denariorum pisanorum in denariis
grossis argenti de duobus solidis unus que capiunt et valunt libras
decem denariorum pisanorum parve monete portandas a se infra
suam henticam in presenti viadio quod deo dante facturus est Pisis in
Pulliam et de Pullia in Alexandriam vel alio quocumque iverit vel
miserit pro bono et utilitate sue hentice sine fraude ad riscum maris
et gentis in quacumque navi vel ligno iverit vel miserit ad quartum
proficuum inde habendum. Et ipse Lazarius sic eas ei portare et
tractare concessit in nomine domini. Qui vero Iunctarellus per
solempnem stipulationem convenit et promisit scripto Lazario se et
suos heredes et bona ei et cet. Obligando ad penam dupli et cet. Et
sub ypoteca suorum bonorum quod infra unum mensem proxime
postquam de scripto viadio ipse Iunctarellus cum hentica sua vel cum
maiori parte sue hentice Pisas erit reversus vel postquam ipsa hentica
sua vel maior pars Pisis erit relata vel postquam inde ipse Iunctarellus
inde erit inquisitus a scripto Lazario vel suo certo misso reddet et
solvet ei vel suo heredi aut suo certo misso ad eius voluntatem predictam summam cum tribus partibus totius lucri quod inde habebit vel
in totum quod inde ei eveniet. Sine briga et cet. Quartam partem
totius lucri sibi retinendo. Et renunciavit et cet. Actum Pisis Kinthice in scripta apotheca domus sancti Sepulcri. Presentibus Uguiccione quondam Bandini et Bonaiuncta quondam Uguiccionis Omicii
testibus rogatis scripta die.

Cassa est parabola scripti Lazarii data Pisis in scripta apoteca.
Presentibus Scolare filio Lucterii quondam domini Iacoppi de Monte
et Ugolino notario filio meo testibus ad hec rogatis M CC LXVIII indictione X VII kal. Aprilis.

APPENDIX V

21. The *societas maris*. See no. 20 above.

22. The *societas terre*. 2543 65r 29 November 1263. Bonaiuncta vinarius qui moratur in cappella sancti Martini de Guassalungo filius quondam Guidonis Iuncte de sancto Prospero de Viacava coram me scripto Iacobo notario et cet. recepit et habuit in societate terre in arte de vino libras quadraginta tres bonorum denariorum pisanorum parvorum a domina Bonaventura relicta Henrigetti de Favullia filia quondam Rainaldi et sorore quondam Gregorii notarii tractandas a se in societate in terra in civitate pisana in arte sua de vino bona fide sine fraude ab hodie ad unum annum proximum et tantum plus quantum inter eos concordia erit ad illam partem lucri que utitur Pisis in arte vinariorum habendam. Et ipsa Bonaventura sic eas ei in societate in dicta arte vini tractandas concessit in nomine domini. Qui vero Bonaiuncta per solempnem stipulationem convenit et promisit scripte Bonaventure se et suos heredes et omnia bona sua habita et habenda ei obligando ad penam dupli capitalis et lucri per solempnem stipulationem solempniter a se ei promissam quod ab hodie ad unum annum proximum faciet inde veram rationem et reddet et solvet per se vel per alium ei vel suo heredi aut suo certo misso cui preceperit predictas libras XLIII denariorum cum illa parte lucri que inde ei eveniet. Sine briga et cet. Quas expensas si que inde fierent reficere promisit. Et renunciavit et cet. Et dedit eidem plenam bailam parabolam et mandatum intrandi in tenere et possessionem omnium bonorum suorum presentium et futurorum superius obligatorum pro predictis omnibus sua auctoritate quandocumque voluerit. Et constituit se predicta bona pro ea precario de cetero tenere et possidere. Hoc actum inter eos quod satisfactio scripte societatis vel scripti debiti probari non possit per testes nec alio aliquo modo nisi per hanc cartam seu scedam cancellatam vel per publicum instrumentum inde

rogatum et confectum per publicum notarium. Actum Pisis Kinthice in coro ecclesie sancti Martini scripti. Presentibus presbitero Filipo scripte ecclesie et fratre Michaele custode scripte ecclesie testibus ad hec rogatis. Anno domini M CC LXIIII indictione VII III kal. Decembris.

23. The *societas terre et maris.* 2545 16v 16 February 1302. Mannus condam Galle de Casale Maritime qui nunc moratur Pisis in cappella sancti Cristofori Kinthice coram me Bartholomeo notario notario scripto et cet. recepit et habuit in societate terre et maris a Lemmo condam Galgani de cappella sancti Martini Kinthice libras centum sexaginta denariorum pisanorum minutorum in aquilinis grossis novis de argento conputato quolibet eorum solidos II denariorum pisanorum minutorum tractandas et portandas a se Manno infra henticam suam in presentibus viadiis que ipse Mannus paratus est presentialiter facere a civitate pisana Bibbonam Maritime et ad quascumque alias partes et loca de Maritima de quibus ipsi Manno videbitur et placuerit et inde ad civitatem pisanam redeundo pro grano et blada inde emendis et reducendis et vendendis eundo et redeundo et per mare et per terram una vice et pluribus vicibus sicut et eo modo ipsi Manno videbitur et placuerit ad riscum et fortunam maris et gentis. Quas scriptus Lemmus eidem Manno sic portare et tractare concessit in nomine domini dei nostri. Et solenni stipulatione scriptus Mannus convenit et promisit scripto Lemmo reddere dare et solvere vel reddi et dari et solvi facere ipsi Lemmo vel eius heredi aut eius certo misso pro eo vel cui ipse perceperit scriptas libras centum sexaginta denariorum pisanorum minutorum capitalis cum duabus partibus trium partium totius lucri inde et ex eis proventuri. In denariis auro vel argento et cet. Ab hodie ad kalendas Maii proxime venturas. Sine briga et cet. Alioquin penam dupli totius scripte pecunie capitalis et scripti lucri et omnes expensas que inde fierent . . . predicto Lemmo dare et solvere solenni stipulatione convenit et promisit. Obligans inde se et suos heredes et bona sua omnia scripto Lemmo et eius heredibus. Et sic scriptus Mannus dedit scripto Lemmo plenam bailiam et potestatem intrandi pro predictis omnibus in possessionem et tenere omnium bonorum suorum ipsius Manni a scripto termino in antea et cet. Renunciando omni auxilio exceptioni et defensioni et cet. Sibi et suis heredibus et cet. Hoc acto inter eos ex pacto quod huius debiti solutio et cet. Actum Pisis Kinthice in ecclesia sancti Sepulcri. Presentibus Iohanni notario filio Baldanse et

Iohanne filio Albertini calthulario qui sunt de cappella sancti Sepulcri et Berto condam Vitalis de Gello Putido testibus ad hec rogatis.
M CCC II indictione XV XIIII kal. Martii.

Cassata est in totum a me Bartholomeo notario scripto parabola
scripti Lemmi data ab eo michi Bartholomeo notario scripto Pisis
Kinthice in domo mea et mee habitationis posita in carraria gonnelle.
Presentibus Ansaldo textore qui moratur Pisis in scripta carraria in
domo mea et Pardo lanario condam Grani de Calcinaria qui moratur
Pisis in cappella sancti Martini Kinthice et aliis testibus ad hec rogatis.
Anno domini M CCC III indictione XV V kal. Aprilis.

24. The *soccita*. 2514 5or 7 January 1265. Ugolinus de Farneta quondam Rustichelli interrogatus ab Ugolino sellario de cappella sancti
Cristofori de Kinthica fuit confessus renuntiando exceptioni non
habite rei se in veritate accepisse et apud se habere ab eo in soccitam
et nomine soccite unum bovem pili rossi cum cornibus relevatis sursum qui constitit scripto Ugolino sellario libras sex bonorum denariorum pisanorum parve monete de quo pretio promisit dictus Ugolinus de Farneta scripto Ugolino sellario solvere quartam partem pro
quarto pede ad eius voluntatem ut moris est soccite. Quem bovem dictus Ugolinus de Farneta ex pacto inter eos habito debet tenere et
pascere et custodire seu teneri et custodiri et pasci facere bona fide
sine fraude in soccitam et nomine soccite ad riscum et fortunam
suam scripti Ugolini de Farneta quantum est pro quarto pede et ad
riscum et fortunam scripti Ugolini sellarii quantum est pro tribus
pedibus scripti bovis laborando cum eo moderate de hinc ad
festum sancte Marie mensis Agusti proxime. Et pro ipsa soccita debet
ipse idem Ugolinus de Farneta dare scripto Ugolino sellario de hinc ad
scriptum festum sancte Marie mensis Agusti proxime staria duo
boni grani nostratis ad iustum pisanum starium tractum et para-
tum Pisis ad domum habitationis sue. Et per dictum festum debet
dictum bovem sicut boni moris est soccite vendere et dare et
partem sibi inde contingentem sicut boni moris est soccite sibi
tenere. Hec omnia prout scripta sunt promisit per solempnem stipulationem et sub ypotheca et obligatione omnium suorum bonorum et
heredum. Et renunciavit et cet. Ad hec Gualandus quondam Salem-
bene de Farneta fideiubendo pro scripto Ugolino de Farneta eius
precibus et mandato et etiam suo nomine proprio principaliter idem
per omnia promisit scripto Ugolino sellario facere et observare vel
fieri et facere et sub ypotheca et obligatione omnium suorum bonorum

et heredum. Et renunciavit et cet. Et ipse Ugolinus sellarius scripto Ugolino de Farneta scriptum bovem in soccitam concessit tenere ut suprascriptum est. Actum Pisis Kinthice in scripta apotheca. Presentibus Lupardo Simonis de Caldaviccioli et Benegrande quondam Guidonis Baracte testibus ad hec rogatis. Scripto die et indictione.

Cassa est parabola scriptorum Ugolini sellarii et Ugolini de Farneta. Presentibus Bonafide vinario et Branuccio germanis filiis Fabri a me Ugolino notario M CC LXVI indictione VIIII VII idus Octobris.

25. The *custodia.* 2543 57r 3 September 1263. Bartholomeus dictus Bacivethus quondam Stefani de Valtriano coram me Iacobo notario scripto et cet. recepit et habuit a scripto Donusdeo in custodia sua et nomine custodie unum bovem pili rossi blancacci cum cornibus tesis. Quem bovem promisit ei per solempnem stipulationem se et suos heredes et omnia bona sua ei et cet. Obligando sub pena librarum decem denariorum pisanorum nove parve monete per solempnem stipulationem a se ei promissam tenere et custodire et pascere vel teneri et custodiri et pasci facere bona fide sine fraude ab hodie ad kalendas Madii proximas. Et eum nullatenus obligare vel aberare. Pro pretio solidorum sedecim bonorum denariorum pisanorum parve monete videlicet pro solidis duobus denariorum pro quolibet mense. Quod totum pretium recepit et habuit a dicto Donusdeo coram me et cet. Vocans inde se bene quietum et pacatum ab eo et eum liberavit. Et precepit et cet. Et constituit et cet. Et statuit et cet. Et taliter et cet. Actum Pisis Kinthice eodem scripto die et loco. Presentibus Iuncta Faferri de Valtriano et Ugolino notario filio meo rogatis testibus ad hec.

26. The *societas ad medium proficuum.* 2514 6r 23 August 1264. Ugolinus quondam Gerardi de Colle Salvetti interrogatus a Bergo furnario de cappella sancti Cristofori de Kinthica filio quondam Torscelli fuit confessus se in veritate accipere et apud se habere ab eo in societatem ad medium proficuum inde habendum unam genicem pili rossi cum cornibus clusis que constitit scripto Bergo libras IIII denariorum pisanorum. Renunciavit exceptioni genicis non accepte et non habite quam exceptionem promisit ei non opponere sub pena dupli scripti pretii et sub ypotheca et obligatione omnium suorum bonorum. Hoc acto et constituto inter eos quod dictus Ugolinus debet dictam genicem tenere et custodire pascere bona fide sine fraude sicut boni moris huiusmodi societatis vel teneri custodiri pasci facere ab hodie ad quinque annos proxime et medietatem totius fructus et pro-

ventus quem deus ei dederit et habuerit interim de scripta et pro
scripta genice ei Bergo vel suo heredi dabit et solvet. Aliam medietatem sibi tenendo et in fine termini debet dictam genicem vendere
quam melius potuerit sine fraude et solutis et restitutis scripto Bergo
scriptas libras IIII et medietatem totius eius quod ultra predictas
libras IIII quando vendetur debet dare scripto Bergo vel suo heredi et
cet. Sine briga et cet. Aliam medietatem sibi retinendo. Hec omnia
scripta et singula scriptorum dictus Ugolinus convenit et promisit
scripto Bergo se ei facere et observare vel fieri et observari facere sine
briga et cet. Sub pena dupli estimationis . . . per stipulationem. Sub
ypotheca et obligatione omnium bonorum suorum et heredum
quorum . . . Et renunciavit et cet. Et dictus Bergus sic dictam genicem ei in societate concessit. Actum Pisis Kinthice in apotheca domus
sancti Sepulcri scripta. Presentibus Ugolino notario filio meo et
Bonanno quondam Iacoppi rogatis testibus ad hec. Anno domini M
CC LXV indictione VII X kal. Septembris.

27. The *custodia* or *guardia ad melioramentum*. 2515 131r 8 August
1272. Petrus quondam Iunte de Lavaiano novo interrogatus a Bonanno spetiario quondam Iacoppi fuit confessus se accepisse et apud
se habere ab eo in guardia ad melioramentum sicut boni moris est
melioramenti vaccam unam pili bianchi cum cum (*sic*) cornibus relevatis exstimatam communi concordi concordia (*sic*) libras novem
denariorum pisanorum minutorum. Renunciando exceptioni et
querele non habite et non recepte vacce quam et cet. Ad tenendum
custodiendum et pascendum omnibus suis expensis scripti Iunte ab
hodie ad festum omnium sanctorum et tantum plus vel minus quantum ipsi Bonanno placuerit ad medium melioramentum inde habendum a dictis libris VIIII sursum. Qui vero Iunta per stipulationem
convenit et promisit scripto Bonanno dictam vaccam ut dictum est
tenere pascere et custodire bona fide sine fraude et si contingerit dictam vaccam mori perdi vel macaneari culpa vel malaguardia ipsius
Petri convenit ei emendare et resargire ad penam dupli et sub ypoteca
et obligatione omnium suorum bonorum. Et renuntiavit omni iuri et
cet. Actum Pisis in scripto portico. Presentibus Data de Liliano quondam Carbonis et Bonaiunta notario quondam Raffaldi testibus ad hec
rogatis. M CC LXX III indictione XV VI idus Augusti.

Cassa est parabola dicti Bonani (*sic*) data ab eo michi Bartholomeo
notario quondam Iacobi notarii data scripta Pisis Kinthice in apotheca
domus Paganelli comitis de Castagneto. Presentibus Gerardo quondam

Ciconie de cappella sancti Cristofori Kinthice et Paulo clerico quondam Iacobi de Lunigiana conmorante Putignano in ecclesia sancti
Bartholomei testibus ad hec rogatis. Anno domini M CC LXXIII
indictione VI pridie kal. Februarii.

NOTE ON THE SOURCES

Notarial chartularies from the 13th century in the Archivio di Stato di Pisa, Archivio degli Ospedali riuniti di Santa Chiara, upon which this study is principally based, are as follows:

Notary's Name	Number	Folios	Entries	Years
(1) Iacobus de Carraria Gonnelle	2543	103	ca. 280	1263–64
	2514	50	125	1264–65
(2) Ugolinus son of Iacobus	2515	155	400	1272–74
	2516	41	125	1273–74
(3) Bartholomeus the second son of Iacobus	2545 *	153	400	1282–84
	2544	28	55	1284
	2545 *	204	450	1301–02
	2546–2550	—	—	1310–21
(4) Cherlus	2629	53	150	1285
(5) Ruffulus	2563	47	125	1293–1301
(6) Romanus de Musiliano	2527	47	160	1299–1300
	2528–2530	—	—	to 1327
(7) Rustichellus of Fucecchio (in the Archivio Montarelli della Volta)	—	—	—	1298

* bound together

Microfilms of Pisan chartularies (to 1300) are available at Yale University Library, New Haven, Connecticut.

These chartularies have been used to some extent by a number of writers on Pisan history, but on the whole their content, particularly in regard to matters relating to social and economic history, has been but little explored, as noted by R. S. Lopez, "The Unexplored Wealth of the Notarial Archives in Pisa and Lucca," *Mélanges Louis Halphen* (Paris, 1951), pp. 417–32. Readers are referred to Chapter 1 of the present work for a discussion of the nature of the notarial chartulary and its value as a historical source.

As regards both chartularies and parchments, Pisa's archives are not notably wealthy; in comparison with the archives of Lucca (Tuscany's richest from the standpoint of age), of Siena (which possesses the earliest Tuscan chartularies), or of Florence, Pisa's diplomatic deposits betray the heavy losses of an unhappy history. In 1316 to erase the memory of a hated tyrant, Uguccione della Faggiola, the Pisan archives were burned, and apparently for this reason the material antedating the 14th century is especially poor. Moreover, the use of Pisa's diplomatic archives is handicapped by the lack of a published inventory of parchment deposits, such as exists for Lucca and Siena. For no period of Pisan history is there a complete *regestum* of diplomatic material. Dal Borgo, in his *Raccolta,* published many, though not all, of the treaties of the Pisan commune and other documents dealing with public affairs. The work, however, shows the errors to be expected of a book printed in 1765, and it reveals alterations of material and a forgery (the oath of 1188) made to establish the antiquity of certain Pisan families. For an evaluation of Dal Borgo's work, see Cristiani, "Osservazioni." Dal Borgo's book, however, has yet to be replaced. F. Bonaini, "I Diplomi pisani inediti col regesto di tutte le carte pisane che si trovano a stampa," *ASI, 6,* Pt. II, Sec. 1 (1845), 1–120, attempted to provide a *regestum,* but the work was left unfinished. The nearest approach to one is N. Caturegli, *Regestum pisanum* (up to 1200), but the work was intended to serve as material for a history of Pisa's archbishopric and it is not a complete survey of archival material. Published parchments may be found scattered throughout A. Matthaejus, *Ecclesiae pisanae historia* (Lucca, 1768), Bonaini's *Statuti,* as appendices to numerous articles in the *Studi Storici* of Crivellucci and the *Bollettino Storico Pisano,* in Amari, *Diplomi arabi* and Müller, *Documenti* (the latter two dealing with commercial history), in A. D'Amia, *Le Sentenze pisane dal 1139 al 1200* (Pisa, 1922), in the *Codex Diplomaticus Sardiniae,* ed. P. Tola, and in Davidsohn's *Forschungen.*

Important parchment deposits are also to be found at the Carthusian monastery, the Certosa, at Calci, a little town near Pisa. The monastery's archives are under the supervision of the Italian state, and can be readily consulted by scholars. The Archbishopric of Pisa likewise possesses important records, divided into the Archivio della Curia Arcivescovile, the Archivio della Mensa, and the Archivio Capitolare respectively. These collections, however, are open to scholars only a few hours each day. A valuable guide to the archives of both Pisa and other Tuscan towns is now available in "Notizie degli archivi toscani," *ASI, 114* (1956), 320–694.

Needless to say, the archives of all Italy's principal cities and especially those of Florence, Lucca, Genoa, and Venice contain material pertinent to Pisan history. Further, much valuable material from those archives has been published. Most important is the series "Documenti di Storia Italiana . . . per la Toscana" (including the *Relazioni* and Santini, *Documenti,* cited extensively in this study), in which are published fifteen folio volumes (to 1952) and a second series of smaller works has been initiated. The series "Regesta Chartarum Italiae," containing the *Regestum pisanum,* is important particularly for material before 1200. For commercial history, the "Documenti e Studi per la Storia del Commercio e del Diritto Commerciale Italiano" contains the editions of Giovanni Scriba, of the Sienese *Imbreviature notarili,* of Zeno, *Documenti* (a selection of documents from Sicily)— all of which we have had occasion to cite in this study. Besides these series, basic to the history of any Tuscan town are the *Caleffo vecchio* of Siena, the list of privileges or transactions involving the commune which the commune thought worthy of copying into a single volume and hence of preserving, the *Liber censuum,* a similar collection of documents made by Pistoia, the *Consulte* or deliberations of the commune of Florence from the late 13th century, and Piattoli, *Consigli,* similar deliberations of the commune of Prato from the middle 13th century.

Apart from chronicles, the richest literary source for Pisa's history are the sermons of Archbishop Federigo Visconti (1257–77), contained in a manuscript at the Biblioteca Medicea-Laurenziana at Florence, Cod. Laurent.–S. Crucis xxxiii, sin. 1. A description of the codex and a summary of Federigo's life may be found in D. Lucciardi, "Federigo Visconti archivescovo di Pisa," *BSP, 1* (1932), 7–48, and 2 (1933), 7–37. Matthaejus, *Historia,* published a list of titles of the sermons and a full text of the one describing Federigo's Sardinian visitation of 1263. Use of the sermons is handicapped, since most are undated and follow no chronological order. They were drawn up shortly before Federigo's death (1277) under his personal supervision. While Federigo had actually delivered the sermons, most of them originally in the vernacular, he intended that they should serve as examples for the use of his successors; he therefore had them translated into Latin and arranged them to follow roughly the course of the ecclesiastical year, with rubrics telling for what Pisan church they were suited and what changes would be necessary to make them suitable for another. An edition would face the difficult task of establishing the original chronology. However, as early examples of a type of literature not fully studied, an edition of the sermons would make a valuable contribution especially to ecclesiastical and literary history.

Of Tuscan cities, Pisa possesses the oldest and in many regards the richest series of statutes and legal codes, all edited by Bonaini in his *Statuti*. Her *Breve consulum* of 1162 and 1164 are the sole-surviving in Tuscany. Her *Constitutum Usus,* dating from the middle 12th century, is, for the period, Italy's most important codification of customs, but, as mentioned in Chapter 1, it badly needs a new edition. Pisa further has a fragmentary *Breve potestatis* of 1275, a full redaction of 1286, and a *Breve pisani populi* from the same year—in contradistinction to Florence, Lucca, and Genoa, none of which has complete statutes from the 13th century. Pisa's 13th-century statutes, however, are not so old as Pistoia's (*Statutum potestatis* from 1246 and *Breve ordinamenti populi* from 1283, the latter given a magnificent edition by L. Zdekauer), or Siena's (fragments from 1262 to 1270, many redactions from the years immediately following), or Volterra's, recently edited by E. Fiumi, *Statuti di Volterra (1210–1224)*.

For narrative accounts, Pisan historiography is heavily dependent on other cities' chroniclers—G. Villani, D. Compagni, Fra Salimbene (who lived at Pisa many years) the continuers of Caffaro, Tolomeo of Lucca, and so forth. Pisa herself is in chronicles the poorest of the major Tuscan cities. For our period, they are characterized by a late redaction, a lack of personality on the part of the authors, and consequent brevity; and many need new editions. Some editions E. Cristiani is planning to make, but just what chronicles are to be re-edited or where they are to appear has not yet been decided. For critical discussion of the problem, see most recently E. Cristiani, "Il Giudizio sui partiti nei cronisti pisani del trecento," *Il Mulino. Rivista mensile di attualità e cultura,* 25–26 (1953), 581–99. For our period the most important chronicles are as follows. The *Historiae pisanae fragmenta* of Guido de Corvaria, published in *RIS, 24,* 673–94, goes from 1271 to 1290 (Pisan style) and was written by a contemporary, but is sketchy. The *Breviarium pisanae civitatis* (*RIS, 6,* 163–98) is a compilation of older chronicles made in 1370 by Michael of Vico, and is in many respects the fullest account of the years 1250–1300. Ranieri Sardo, *Cronica pisana,* edited by Bonaini in the *ASI, 6,* Pt. II, Sec. 2

(1845), 73–244, and the "Anonymus Muratorianus," edited in *RIS, 15*, 969–1088, were both composed sometime from the second half of the 14th century to the first years of the 15th, and hence were dependent on earlier accounts. A number of short chronicles may be found in the appendix to M. Gentile's edition of Maragone, *Annales* (notably the *Chronicon aliud breve pisanum* published earlier by Muratori), and in *RIS, 6* and *24*. Those in the vernacular date from the second half of the 14th century. Of other late Pisan chronicles, the only one of major interest for our period is Simone della Tosa, *Annali,* ed. D. M. Manni, in *Chronichette antiche di varii scrittori del buon secolo della lingua toscana* (Florence, 1733), which was utilized by Schaube in reconstructing the list of the Pisan consuls of the sea.

For bibliography on secondary studies concerning Pisa, indispensable is the *Bollettino Storico Pisano,* which attempts to record all new works on Pisa. For narrative accounts of Pisan history, still useful is R. Roncioni, *Istorie,* in *ASI, 6,* Pt. I (1844), a work written in the 16th century. While uncritical, Roncioni still reveals a broad familiarity with narrative sources and even diplomatic. Easily available in its edition by Bonaini, the work can serve the important function of illustrating what facts can be known concerning any particular event and provides a valuable orientation for further research in the primary material.

Pisan historiography in the modern period is dominated by the name of Gioachino Volpe. His two works pertinent to Pisan history in our period are his *Istituzioni* (roughly to 1250) and "Pisa, Firenze, Impero al principio del 1300 . . .", *SS, 11* (1902), 177–203 and 293–337. Other studies on the formation and growth of the commune may be found in numerous articles and book reviews appearing especially in the *Studi Storici* and the *Archivio Storico Italiano,* or in books, as in his studies on Volterra and Lunigiana in the series "Biblioteca Storica Toscana." Many other articles in the *Studi Storici* (notably Pintor, "Elba"; Brugaro, "Artigianato"; and Silva's study of the Pisan wool industry) reflect Volpe's influence; they make that journal, which never survived the first World War, one of the richest for the institutional and social history of the Tuscan commune.

Volpe's studies on Pisa are now old and easily criticized. His acceptance of the spurious oath of 1188 was a mistake not easily pardonable for a man as familiar as he with the sources. It is easy, too, to point out a misread parchment, or the undue influence of the politics of his day, as when he would have the Guelf and Ghibelline movements presage the 19th-century movements for Italian unification. As reference works, his books are extremely difficult to use; needed dates or discussions of institutions are to be found everywhere and nowhere. His weakness and his strength was his ability to bring a large mass of facts to bear on minute points, which perhaps might explain his predilection for the study of third-rate towns (Massa Marittima, Volterra, Lunigiana), concerning which his best work was done. Still, it would not be too much to say that Volpe marked an epoch in the study of the Italian commune. If we may speak of a "present state" in research on the commune, Volpe did most to establish it. It has been over thirty years since Volpe, becoming converted in the early 1920's to a "nationalist point of view" in history and to fascism in politics, virtually abandoned medieval history, and his interpretation of the commune has seen no profound revision. Volpe's approach was a reaction against an excessively nationalistic theory of the commune that in many ways partook of the spirit of the Risorgimento. This theory made the commune a peculiarly Italian revolt against the German feudal lords of the contado; it therefore distinguished the commune sharply from its feudal milieu, saw in it an organ primarily of merchants, and its history an effort on the part of those merchants to conquer their feudal surroundings. In attacking this theory, Volpe drew much inspiration from Marxism, but, in the words of Nicholas Ottokar, he took the best of Marxism. His formula that "the commune was the work of a restricted aristocracy, partly landed and partly commercial, at the beginning more landed than commercial," a formula illustrated brilliantly in his works, is the soundest characterization of the commune that can be found. It is unfortunate that because his works have not been translated, Volpe is little known outside of Italy. It is perhaps more unfortunate that Italian scholars themselves have not fully maintained that keen interest in the history of the commune manifested at the turn of the last century. But under fascism, with the accent on a "nationalist point of view," young historians tended to abandon research on the commune, as had Volpe himself, in favor of the modern period and especially the Risorgimento. The unfortunate result would seem to be that Italy, which possesses the richest field of study for medieval urbanism, has not contributed to the history of the medieval town to the extent that its importance merits.

On the institutions of the Pisan commune, A. Schaube's *Konsulat* stands next to Volpe's *Istituzioni* in importance. The work is a first-rate piece of scholarship; the author, however, was unable to use unpublished material and parts of the book, as might be expected after seventy years, need revision. On institutions, too, U. Congedo, *Il Capitano del popolo in Pisa* (Pisa, 1908), is undistinguished. Much of the large gap in Pisan history after 1250 will be filled by a history soon to be published by E. Cristiani, which will deal with the century 1250–1350 and will be in some respects a continuation of Volpe's *Istituzioni*.

For economic history, Pisan commerce figures importantly, of course, in the standard works of Schaube, *Handelsg.*, and Heyd, *Commerce*. Specifically for Pisan commercial history, the student may consult Rossi-Sabatini, *L'Espansione di Pisa nel Mediterraneo fino alla Meloria*. A short book, it makes some use of unpublished material but not much; within its narrower limits as a summary of Pisa's commercial history, it is an excellent work. For Pisan industries, Brugaro's study on artisans and Silva's on wool are both good, if in some ways incomplete, studies.

We might conclude with the remark that Tuscany's rich archives —with the possible exception of the Florentine, still to a surprising degree unexplored and unutilized—offer practically unlimited potentialities for research in almost every field of social and economic history that might interest the student.

INDEX

Acqui, 4
Acre, 29, 162
Addobbator, 141
Adriatic, 30
Africa, trade with, 30, 32, 153, 163–70, 174
Agliata (Pisan family), 171, 176, 180
Agnelli. *See* Dell'Agnello
Agriculture, 109, 160, 178 f., 181. *See also* Animal husbandry, Grain, Sheep, Wine
Aiutamicristo (Pisan family), 124, 176, 181
Albertus (son of Uguiccione Pandulfi), 118
Alexandria, 11, 30, 146, 162, 169
Alma, 129
Alpi Apuane, 21, 23
Alsalagamba. *See* Periciolus Alsalagamba
Altopascio, 99, 178
Alum, trade in, 26, 31, 156, 168
Ancona, 183
Angelus Spina (grain importer), 85
Animal husbandry, 26, 48, 116. *See also* Agriculture
Anziani (Pisan officials), 41, 49, 56, 59, 122, 124, 133
Apennines, 23
Apulia, 108
Arabs, 23, 33; at Pisa, 164
Arbavola, 100
Architecture, 25, 33, 39
Aristocratic faction at Pisa, xi, 19, 55, 60 f., 63–5, 67, 79, 112, 160, 172, 176, 178, 183; as tax collectors, 81–5, 88; tax exemptions of, 72, 74, 76
Armenia, 29, 108, 162

Armor, production of, 143 f.; trade in, 167. *See also* Iron
Arno, viii, 22–4, 28, 35–9, 42, 45, 81, 90–5, 97–9, 101–5, 129, 141, 178
Asciano, 91
Asia, trade with, 29, 126
Assopardi (Pisan family), 64
Auser, 45, 91 f.
Avena, 91
Azov, sea of, 29

Baccione Tiniosi (Pisan merchant), 172 f., 180
Balearic Islands, 23
Barbaricina, 93
Bardi (Florentine banking house), 115
Bartholomeus de Carraria Gonnelle (Pisan notary), 11, 109 f., 215
Beccune, 168
Benevento, battle of, 58
Bibbona, 109
Bientina, 81, 92, 95, 102
Black Death, 53
Boccaccio, 52
Bologna, 28, 54, 56, 76 f.
Bona (African city), 30
Bona (Pisan saint), 44, 49, 95, 98 f., 101, 103
Bonaini, F., 13, 136, 152
Bonifacio, 7, 30; notaries at, 7 n.
Breve antianorum of Pisa, 41, 117, 134, 181
Breve collegii notariorum, 9 n.
Breve consulum, 14, 73 n., 218
Breve curiae maris, 15, 30 n.
Breve pisani communis, 14, 19
Breve potestatis, 14, 218

223

England, 165
Era, 82, 92
Erovarii, 136, 138
Etruscans, 97
Extimum, 70, 73, 76

Fabri. See Iron workers
Fabricae, 129 f.
Faenza, 56, 73 n., 74 n.
Fagiano, 123
Falcone (Pisan family), 66, 119, 176;
 Iohannes, 119, 121–3, 181
Ferrara. *See* Ricabaldo
Fish, trade in, 27, 110
Flanders, 166; cloth of, 31, 150, 158,
 165
Florence, viii f., xii, 22, 24 f., 32,
 56–8, 60, 63, 77, 79, 92–4, 96, 98,
 101–3, 112, 127 f., 134, 144, 150,
 155, 160, 183, 185, 217; account
 books at, 20 n.; coinage of, 63;
 merchants of, at Pisa, 12, 28 n.,
 95, 102, 110, 132 n.; notaries of,
 6 n., 8 n.; Pisan trade with, 27 n.,
 134; population of, 43; walls of,
 viii, 35 n., 41, 43, 45; wool indus-
 try at, 134
Formica, 92
Fourth Crusade, 29, 162
France, 11, 30, 99, 108, 158, 165,
 169, 170 f., 173, 177, 179 f.
Francesco da Buti, 176
Francis of Assisi, St., 54
Frederick II Hohenstaufen, 56–8,
 133
Frederick of Austria, 100
Frediano (bishop of Lucca), 91
Fucecchio, 99; peace of, 60
Fuoriporta (Pisan quarter), 139 f.
Furriers, 37 f., 61, 148, 169
Furs, 145–52, 154; trade in, 26, 102,
 103 n., 149, 168 f. *See also*
 Leather

Gaitani (Pisan family), 62, 64, 81,
 126
Gambacorta (Pisan family), 169,
 171, 176 f.
Garfagnana, 21, 26, 90, 117–19, 178

Genoa, viii f., xii, 4, 23, 28, 30 f.,
 36 n., 44 f., 54, 56, 61, 82 n., 87,
 99, 106, 108, 122, 131 ff., 163 ff.,
 168, 171 f., 183; notaries at, viii,
 6 n., 7 n., 11
Germans at Pisa, 32
Germany, 23
Ghezzano, 101
Ghibellines, 55–7; trade with, 31,
 94, 122, 185
Giglio, 129
Giovanni Scriba, 147
Gonnella, 145–6
Grain, xi, 109 f., 115, 129; price of,
 112–13, 198–9
Greece, 32 f.
Gregory I the Great (pope), 91
Grosseto, 22, 83, 118
Gualandi (Pisan family), 58, 64, 66
Guardia, 120
Guardia ad melioramentum, 15, 213
Guarnacca, 146, 149
Guathalungo (ford of Arno), 95, 98,
 102
Guelfs, 55–9, 94, 185
Guido da Montefeltro, 60, 87, 122
Guido of Corvaria, 100, 103, 106
Guilds. *See* Pisa, guilds of

Hafsids, 165
Hatters at Pisa, 178
Henry VII (emperor), 122
Hohenstaufen, 55–8
Holy Land, 29, 39, 167
Homines vie Arni, 62, 126
Humiliati at Pisa, 154
Hungary, 32

Iacobus de Carraria Gonnelle (Pisan
 notary), 10–11, 215
Iacobus Tiniosi, 180
Immigration to Pisa, x–xi, 40–2,
 109
Iohannes the Paduan, 172–3
Iron, 128 f., 167; trade in, 26, 80,
 86 f., 110. *See also* Arms
Iron mines, 50, 129
Iron workers at Pisa, 38, 60 f., 85,
 129–34
Ischia, 26